Secret Destinations
Writers on Travel

Edited by Mark Rudman

Acknowledgements

"The Dangerous Thread of Things," "The Silence," "Who Is the Third," "In the Cup of a Lily," "Out of Desperation," "The First Days of Spring" and "Three Days" are from THAT BOWLING ALLEY ON THE TIBER by Michelangelo Antonioni, to be published this year by Oxford University Press, New York. Translated by William Arrowsmith and copyright © 1985 by Oxford University Press, New York.

"The Rains of New York" is from the book LYRICAL AND CRITICAL ESSAYS by Albert Camus. Copyright © 1968 by Alfred A. Knopf, Inc., copyright © 1967 by Hamish Hamilton, Ltd., and Alfred A. Knopf, Inc. Reprinted with the permission of Alfred A. Knopf, Inc.

"Streams" copyright © 1985 by Derek Walcott.

The cover art, "Day Fishing At Antibes," is by Malcolm Morley compliments of the Xavier Fourcade Gallery.

We would like to thank the National Endowment of the Arts for its support in the production of this volume. Thanks are also due to Michael and Karen Braziller, Lydia Davis, Peter Ginna, and Deborah Thomas.

This volume of *Pequod* is distributed by Persea Books, 225 Lafayette Street, New York, New York 10012: ISBN 0-89255-100-3.

PEQUOD 19/20/21

New York University   Washington Square   New York   10003

ISSN 0149-0516

We would like to thank the National Endowment of the Arts for its support.

Pequod 22, guest edited by Howard Norman, is editorially complete. Unsolicited manuscripts for *23* will be read between January and May.

Business Office and Subscriptions: The National Poetry Foundation, 305 Neville Hall, University of Maine at Orono, Orono, ME 04469-0122. Editorial Offices: Department of English, Room 200, New York University, 19 University Place, New York City, NY 10003. No manuscripts will be returned unless an SASE is enclosed. International copyright © 1985 by The National Poetry Foundation; permissions for reuse are reserved to Mark Rudman.

A Journal of
Contemporary Literature
and Literary Criticism

Numbers Nineteen/Twenty

SECRET DESTINATIONS WRITERS ON TRAVEL

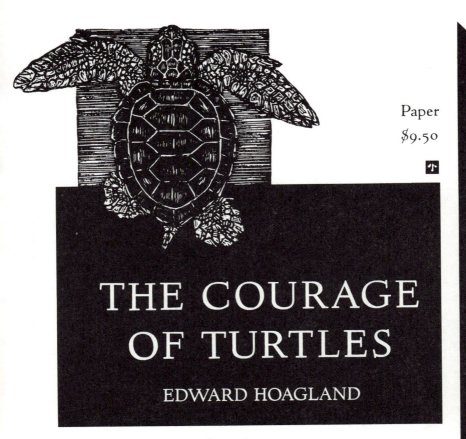

Paper
$9.50

THE COURAGE OF TURTLES

EDWARD HOAGLAND

Now in Paperback

"This is a book of essays. . . . It is also a work of art."   THE CHRISTIAN SCIENCE MONITOR

"He is a marvelous writer . . . generous, full of odd detail, very moving. . . ."   NEWSWEEK

NORTH POINT PRESS, 850 Talbot Avenue, Berkeley, CA 94706

 A Journal of
Contemporary Literature
and Literary Criticism

Pequod is one of the freshest and more approachable examples of
the little magazine whose object is to provide (in critic Robert
Boyer's words) "a living model of the literary mind struggling to
nurture and preserve . . . the best that has been thought and said."
Its editors . . . display an unpretentious literary intelligence. There
is neither underground bravado nor silliness, nor academic austerity,
nor any anxious grasping after status. Its stance is mature and its
progress as a contemporary anthology brings the excitement of new
writing alive for all readers.
DeWitt Henry, *Wilson Library Bulletin*

Work by the following writers, artists and translators has appeared in *Pequod* (over the past
10 years).

Yehuda Amichai * Michelangelo Antonionio * William Arrowsmith * Paul Auster * Russell
Banks * Roland Barthes * Georges Bataille * Robert Bechtle * Mei Mei Bersenbrugge *
Maurice Blanchot * Johannes Bobrowski * Yves Bonnefoy * Philip Booth * Bohdan Boy-
chuk * Harold Brodkey * William Bronk * Michael Burkard * Dino Buzzati * Hayden
Carruth * Raymond Carver * Lydia Davis * Carlos Drummond De Andrade * Stephen Dixon
* Stephen Dobyns * Sergei Dovlatov * Clayton Eshleman * Richard Estes * David Evanier *
Ross Feld * Audrey Flack * Jean Follain * Carolyn Forché * Jonathan Galassi * Amir
Gilboa * Louise Glück * Jorie Graham * Linda Gregg * Michael Hamburger * Robert Hass *
Seamus Heaney * Michael Heller * Edward Hoagland * Daniel Hoffman * Richard Howard *
Richard Hugo * David Ignatow * Yvonne Jacquette * Shirley Kaufman * Ann Lauterbach *
Sol Lewitt * Clarice Lispecter * Philip Lopate * William Matthews * Czeslaw Milosz * John
Montague * Eugenio Montale * Alberto Moravia * Kita Morio * Robert Musil * Carol Muske
* Sharon Olds * Gregory Orr * Boris Pasternak * Molly Peacock * Philip Pearlstein * Rich-
ard Pevear * Jayne Anne Phillips * Paul Pines * Katha Pollitt * Peter Redgrave * Mark Rud-
man * Bruno Schultz * Philip Schultz * Hugh Seidman * Harvey Shapiro * Louis Simpson *
William Stafford * Michael Stephens * Gerald Stern * Mark Strand * Mary Swander * Wislaw
Szymborska * John Taggart * Kotara Takamura * Tomas Tranströmer * Jean Valentine *
Ellen Bryant Voight * Charles Wright * Fay Zwicky

Pequod 305 Neville Hall, University of Maine, Orono, Maine 04469

Please enter a subscription to *Pequod* for:

Individuals: ☐ $16.00—2 years (4 issues)   ☐ $ 9.00—1 year (2 issues)
Libraries: ☐ $20.00—2 years (4 issues)   ☐ $10.00—1 year (2 issues)
Foreign orders, please ADD $2.00 per year for postage.

Name _____

Address _____

City _____ State _____ Zip _____

TRAVEL: A (RANDOM) SAMPLER

When he was at Croisset, he dreamed of the hot sand at the shimmering Nile; when he was on the Nile, he dreamed of damp fogs and shimmering Croisset. He didn't really like travel, of course. He liked the idea of travel, and the memory of travel, but not travel itself. For once I agree with Du Camp, who used to say that Gustave's preferred form of travel was to lie on a divan and have the scenery carried past him.

—Julian Barnes

All journeys have secret destinations of which the traveler is unaware.

—Martin Buber

Without cafés and newspapers, it would be difficult to travel. A paper printed in our own language, a place to rub shoulders with others in the evenings enable us to imitate the familiar gestures of the man we were at home, who, seen from a distance, seems so much a stranger. For what gives value to travel is fear. It breaks down a kind of inner structure we have. One can no longer cheat—hide behind the hours spent at the office or at the plant (those hours we protest so loudly, which protect us so well from the pain of being alone). I have always wanted to write novels in which my heroes would say: "What would I do without the office?" or again: "My wife has died, but fortunately I have all these orders to fill for tomorrow." Travel robs us of such refuge. Far from our own people, our own language, stripped of all our props, deprived of our masks (one doesn't know the fare of the streetcars, or anything else), we are completely on the surface of ourselves. But also, soul-sick, we restore to every being and every object its miraculous value.

—Albert Camus

I stood a long time in Mack's talking
New York with the gobs, Guantanamo, Norfolk,—
Drinking Bacardi and talking U.S.A.

—Hart Crane

And makes me end, where I begunne.

—John Donne

May those who are born after me
Never travel such roads of love.

—Hitomaro

Wild goose, wild goose,
At what age
Did you make your first journey?

—Issa

In this excess that's Rome I'll not mope long, . . .

—Stanley Kunitz

What about travel? Wouldn't you like to visit, say, China?

I wouldn't mind seeing China if I could come back the same day.
I hate being abroad. Generally speaking, the further one gets from
home the greater the misery. I'm not proud of this, but I'm singu-
larly incurious about other places. I think travelling is very much
a novelist's thing . . . travelling is necessary for them. I don't think
it is for poets. . . .

—Philip Larkin

In Death Valley salt gleams from a dried-up lake bed.
Defend, defend, defend yourself says the tick-tock of the blood.
From the futility of solid rock, no wisdom.

—Czeslaw Milosz

I have always known
That at last I would
Take this road, but yesterday
I did not know that it would be today.

—Narihari

16

And the child
We took on a trip
Said

'We're having the life of our times'

—George Oppen

Yet, if you remember, it is this that I felt (and you, too, I believe) when we were in Petersburg. As we rode along in the cab, the city seemed to be endless content without a plot, without material attributes—an overflow of the most fantastic content, dark, throbbing, feverish, in frantic search of a plot, a lyrical motif, a lyrical theme it could attach to you and me. If you are prepared to recognize the uniqueness and exceptionality of such a concept of the city and all objective things, and if you keenly feel this uniqueness, then you will understand my saying that the poet, when in such a mood, does not remark that which is characteristic and does not make observations, but merely confirms facts; the verbs and nouns of the world you are experiencing, finite nouns and verbs, are transformed into adjectives, into a whirlpool of *qualities*, which must be ascribed to concepts of the very highest order—to things, a reality, inaccessible to us. Not to concepts of the religious experience but rather to concepts of the poetical, of creative joy or sorrow (the two are identical in their pre-eminent sense: the poetical).

—Boris Pasternak

But the caverns are less enchanting to the unskilled explorer.

—Ezra Pound

It was not a night blown at a glassworks in Vienna
Or Venice, motionless, gathering time and dust.

—Wallace Stevens

And I will never come back.

—Mark Strand

The frontier pass is ungarded.
It is dangerous to travel.
Ten years wandering, sick at heart.
I perch here like a bird on a
Twig, thankful for a moment's peace.

—Tu Fu

It is necessary to uproot oneself. To cut down the tree and make
of it a cross, and then to carry it every day.
It is necessary not to be "myself," still less to be "ourselves."
The city gives one the feeling of being at home.
We must take the feeling of being at home into exile.
We must be rooted in the absence of a place.
To uproot oneself socially and vegetatively.
To exile oneself from every earthly country.
To do all that to others, from the outside is a substitute
(*ersatz*) for decreation. It results in unreality.
But by uprooting oneself one seeks greater reality.

—Simone Weil

And yet, always, there is this city:
you arrive near evening, . . .

and walk downstairs to survey the hotel bar. . .

in a city that's foreign and lovely
and yes, night falls
and it's yours.

—Natan Zach

The birds of
        Perigueux
sing back Gaul
        Roman and Jew

—Louis Zukofsky

Selected by The Editor

From TRAVELS

Oh Montessori, Montessori, white-haired woman,
the first of the dead I loved, "Child, child!" Still
I turn in the street when I hear that called out
behind me.

Slowly and in great pain "I" turns into "he" after
resting a little in "you." You into them.
The operation is performed under a local. Open-eyed.
Only the place anaesthetised with ice, or the drug of love.
They will call after you too "Dreamer! Dreamer?"
You won't be able to, you can't. What is your name now?
I took no name in vain. Names are for children.
Adults vanish from their names. Only their surnames remain.
Afterwards, Father, Sir, Uncle, Mister. Hey Mister,
You there! (Do you love me? That's different,
that's more than a name.) Afterwards numbers and
perhaps: He. He went out. They will return, they—hey there, hey.
The forest of names is withered, and the kindergarten
has shed the leaves of its trees, is black and will die.

On Fridays they stitched my handkerchief
to the corner of my pocket, to prevent me from carrying,
a sin on the Holy Sabbath. On festivals priests blessed me
from the white caves of their shawls, blessed me
with cramped epileptic fingers. I looked at them
and God didn't thunder. Since then his thunder
has retreated and become a great silence.
I looked and my eyes were not blinded.
Since then my eyes have opened wider and wider
from year to year, beyond sleep,
to the rim of pain, beyond eyelids, beyond clouds, beyond years.
Death is not sleep but open eyes, the whole body
gaping with eyes, pressed in the narrow space of the world.

Angels like sacred scrolls in velvet robes
and white silk petticoats, with crowns and silver bells. Angels
flew about me and sniffed at my heart and cried to each other,
Ah, Ah, with adult smiles. "I will tell your father."
And even now, after thirty-three years my father's blessing
remains in my hair, though it grew wild in the desert,
sticky with blood and Negev dust, though I cropped
and chopped it. Crew-cut war brush, and later
stylish French fashion stuck sadly to my forehead.
Still the blessing remains in the hair of my blessed head.

You come via Haifa. The harbor was new. The child was new.
You lay on your belly, not to kiss the Holy Land
but because of the riots of 1936.
British soldiers, wearing the cork helmets of a crumbling empire
threw open to you your life's new kingdom. What's your name?
Threw open to you with their tattooed arms: dragons,
women's breasts, thighs; a dagger, the coiled serpent, a rose,
girls: buttocks. Since then this script has sunk deep within you
not to be seen from outside; painfully engraved and as deep
as your soul, itself an inscribed parchment scroll, a mezuzah
lying aslant the length of your inner body.
You became a collector of pain in the tradition of this country.
My God, my God, why? Have you forsaken me?
My God, my God. Even then one had to call him twice.
The second time already a question, a first doubt: my God?

I haven't said the last word yet. I haven't
eaten yet, and I am already full. My cough is not
from smoking or illness. It is a compact
and economical form of inquiry.
Whatever has been is as if it never was.
And the rest I do not know. Perhaps
it is written in the difficult books on the shelf,
in the concordances of pain and the dictionaries of joy,
in the encyclopedias with stuck pages, like eyes
not wanting to let their dream go at dawn,
in the terrible correspondence
of Marx and Engels, you and I, he and God,

in the book of Job, in the hard words, lines
deep cuts in my flesh. Long wounds
red from whips, wounds full of white salt, like meat
that my mother salted and koshered, so that there would be no
  blood
only pink salt soaked in blood, only the pain
of searing knowledge, the sacred, the pure.
The rest—unknown, alien in darkness.
We will wait, bow down on our knees like the brothers in Egypt
  in the dark,
hiding servile faces, till the world can no longer
resist and will weep and cry out: I am Joseph
your brother! I am the world!

As at night with me the year the war broke out
I passed your mother's belly in which you crouched.
Our rhythm was the rhythm of the orchard pumps and the
  rhythm of shots.
It's started! Light and pain, iron and earth and stones.
Srones and flesh and iron in changing combinations
of matter. Render unto matter that which is matter's. Dust, dust,
from man thou cam'st and unto man thou shalt return.
It's started! My blood flows in many colors and puts on
red when it bursts out. My love's navel is an eye
to see the end. Beginning and end in her body.
Two creases in the right buttock, one in the left,
glasses glitter against white skin of belly, eyebrow
arches to the eye's cry. Silk, soft and black on tense
skin of thick thighs. Shoulder distinct and prominent,
halved by a cloth strap, black, precise.
Shoulder to shoulder, flesh to flesh, dust to dust.

A story and a child, love and again, world and ear,
time in a curled smile, loving and opening
the house to the night, the earth to the dead and the rain
after the gift of sun. Spring sprouted green words
in us, and the summer gambled on our arriving first,
and love burst out of us, all at once,
all over, like sweat, in the fear,

in the race of our lives, the game.
And children grew and ripened, for the water level
rises all the time with the terrible flood, and all their growth
is because of the rising flood, so as not to drown.
And still, his finger-tips dusted with moon,
like a schoolmaster's with chalk,
God strokes our head, his wrists already
song and angels! And what elbows! And what a face—
of a woman already turned to other matters. A profile
in a window.

The veins in my legs begin to protrude, because
my legs think a lot, their pace is thoughts. Into the desolate space
of my feelings wild beasts return, that left
when I tilled and drained, and made my life
a settled civilisation. Long rows of books,
restful rooms and corridors. My body
built for good resonance like a concert hall,
cries and shouts don't get through. The walls
absorbent and impenetrable. Waves of memory
rebound. And up above, in the ceiling,
childish possessions, soft words, women's dresses,
my father's prayer shawl,
half bodies, big furry toys, clouds,
lumps of good night, heavy hair:
to heighten the resonance.

Dust, dust, my body, the frame of half my life. Still
bold scaffolding of hope, shaky ladders
against the unfinished outside. Even the head
is no more than the lowest
of the extra floors that were planned. My eyes,
one alert and interested, the other
distant and indifferent, as if receiving all from within,
and my hands drawing sheets
over the faces of the dead and the living. It is done.
Shaving, my face is a clown's, foamy white,
the only froth that isn't anger's. My face
is something between mad bull

22

and migratory bird that has lost its way
and lags behind the flock, but sees
slow, good things before its death in the sea.
Even then, and ever since, I met
the stagehands of my life, the shifters of walls,
and furniture and people, putting up and taking down,
new illusions of new houses,
new scenes, vistas
in perspective, not real. Resemblance
not truly close. Everyone, all,
all my lovers and haters are directors and stagehands,
electricians for rigging up a strange light which
dims and brings near, changes and alters,
hanging up and hanging about.

All his life my father tried to make a man of me,
so that I'd have a hard face like Kosygin and Brezhnev,
like generals and admirals and stockbrokers and administrators:
imaginary fathers I made to replace
my father.
I have to screw into my face the expression of a hero
like a bulb screwed into its hard threaded socket
screwed in and lit up.
All my life my father tried to make
a man of me, but I always slip back
into the softness of thighs and the longing to bless:
"Who hast made me according to his will." And his will is woman.
My father feared a useless blessing.
To bless the Creator of fruit trees and not to eat the apple.
To bless without loving. To love without fullness.
I ate and was not full and did not bless.
My life spreads out and separates:
in my childhood there were still tales of kings and ghosts
and blacksmiths, now glass houses and shining space ships,
radiant silences without hope.
My hands are stretched out to a past not mine
and to a future not mine: it is hard to love,
hard to embrace, with hands like that,
a butcher sharpening knife on knife

23

I sharpen heart on heart. The hearts
get sharper and thinner and disappear. But my soul
still grinds, and my voice gets lost in the sound of metal.

On Yom Kippur, in tennis shoes, you ran.
And with Holy Holy Holy, you jumped up high
higher than any one, nearly up to the angels on the ceiling.
And in the circlings of Simchat Torah
you circled seven times and seven
and arrived breathless.
Pushing iron you thrust up
the Scrolls of the Law, in the Raising Up
with both trembling arms
so that all could see what was written, and the strength of your
  arms.

YEHUDA AMICHAI
Translated
by Ruth Nevo

THE DANGEROUS THREAD OF THINGS

What I don't know when I'm asked how a film is born is precisely how the birth itself—the delivery, the "big bang," the first three minutes,—takes place. And whether the images of those first three minutes have an inner life of their own. In other words, whether a film originates as a response to an inner need of its author or whether the question asked by those images is destined to be nothing more than a question, to have value—ontologically—for what it is.

Let me give you an example.

I wake up one morning with some images in my head. I don't know where they come from, how, or why. In succeeding days and months they recur, and I can't keep them from coming, I can't even get rid of them. I go on looking at them, and I make mental notes which I later jot down in a notebook.

I transcribe them here, with indications of the different places and moments in which this took place.

Rome. May 22, 1977, 5:30 P.M.

A woman with a stalk of cane in her hand, on a beach in the south. I have no reason for saying it's a southern beach, but this is something I know. With the cane the woman traces a line as yellow as the cane itself. The woman's wearing a white blouse and a brownish skirt, black shoes with high heels, a very long white scarf at her neck, her dark hair tied at the nape. I don't succeed in defining the color of the scarf, but I note that it's transparent like her blouse. I infer that the woman has no inhibitions and she's very beautiful.

A colorless day is in the making. The sea is calm, glassy.

Paris. The same day, 9:25.

The woman turns repeatedly backwards, to right, to left, without the slightest curiosity.

The beach ends at a promontory covered with shrubs and wild plants, extremely steep. Only when she looks in that direction does the woman show a certain apprehensiveness. The reason for this apprehensiveness is a violet stain there in front of me that slips away whenever I think I've caught it.

25

Paris. May 27th, 6:00.
A pathway covered with sand or dust leading to the beach. It's very steep. Two horses come down the path, slipping down side by side, digging in their hooves and raising a huge cloud of dust.

Out of the dust appears a girl.

The girl goes up the path and meets the horses coming down. She passes between the two animals as though she hadn't seen them. She gazes intensely ahead of herself, at something or someone.

But there's no one up there, there's nothing there. Only the wind. It's the wind, not the horses, raising the dust. The horses have disappeared.

Khiva (Uzbekistan). June 26th, 6:45.
The sky is transparent and gives the feeling that from one moment to the next you can see beyond, see the infinite. The sky is one color. The infinite is another color that we don't know.

One fact suddenly becomes clear to me: the two horses belong to the girl's father. They're two old horses. They were colts when she was a little girl. Now they're twelve, she's eighteen. Her father was sixty-nine, her mother fifty, when she was conceived.

She feels she's a monster.

Kokand (Tagikistan). May 28th, 4:30.
I don't know what the connection is between the girl and the woman. They reappeared to me side by side, the girl's pink darkened by the woman's brown. They move slowly forward, the woman one step ahead of the girl. Always together. Close but not touching. An important fact. They're two individual people, not to be confounded, and the little space always between them suggests the amorous space in which they move, extremely narrow.

Maybe they love each other. Or maybe they think they love each other but it's not true. But for whom isn't it true if there are no witnesses of their feelings?

Melbourne. July 9th, 2:45.
Again, the woman's on the beach with the girl. Both of them look

26

as though they were at home in this place. They spend a large part of the day here.

I seem to recall (it's a piece of information with the savor of a memory) that the girl had a sister a few years older than she and that, given the very advanced age of her parents, this sister was her whole domestic world. When she died, the girl was overcome by such a great feeling of loneliness, inward emptiness, and even loss—as though a part of her had been taken away—that she set about finding somebody who could take her place, on whom she could discharge the burden of her affections.

Now she thinks she's met her, this person. She likes the bond, clean and clear, that's developed between them.

Sidney. July 13th, 10:00 P.M.
It's not true that the relationship is clean and clear. The girl has the revelation one evening when she sees the woman at the foot of her bed gazing intently at her with heavy eyes.

Nothing indicates whether the house is hers or the woman's. No furniture but a bed. A window opens in front of the bed. Outside the window can be seen a fire on the beach and the horses come and go, shining with reflections from the fire.

Once when they were colts they used to gallop, running wild, over this sand.

The woman says something to the girl, I hear the voice, not the words. But there's nothing incomprehensible in that sound. This is the idea, and it was suggested to me by a remark in Faulkner's *Sartoris*:—"If you have the bad luck to fall in love, I'll kill the man."

Paris. October 18th, 5:30 A.M.
The girl's with a man. I don't know how much time has passed, but it's not important. The man's talking, he gestures with both hands and little movements of his head. From the way the girl waits to hear, it's clear she's greatly interested in his words, she's greatly interested in him. She looks at him the way she looks at the sea, with the same enchanted gaze.

Paris. Same day. 9:00 A.M.
It's morning and I'm thinking of this glimmer of a story while

27

outside it's snowing. I say I'm thinking because this time it wasn't spontaneous images that took me back to the plot. I willed it myself. I suddenly noticed that the unconsciousness with which the film was coming into being would never amount to anything unless I impose limits. In other words the moment's come to organize the ideas and only the ideas. To transform all this instinctive material into reflective substance. To think of the subject in terms of articulating the scenes, of beginning, development, and end, in short, of structure. It's necessary for the image-making to become intelligible (I was about to say "edible"); you have to help it provide itself with a meaning. Roland Barthes says that a work's meaning can't be created on its own, that the author can produce only conjectures of meaning, of forms if you like, and it's the world that fills them.

But how can Barthes rely on so uncertain an entity as the world?

With these thoughts in my head I look at the snow coming down on the roofs and I'm tempted (more than a temptation, it's a curiosity to verify what happens visually) to make it fall on the beach and the horses also, and to put the two female characters together at the window to look at the sight, in an atmosphere of easy surrender, or uneasiness, or anguish.

The man's appearance could take place in a second reel. I'm dealing probably with a mature man, a man who no longer has the patience and unconsciousness that love requires, who no longer has the language of love.

The woman's position is different. She expects nothing where the girl's concerned. She observes in her a resistance not so much physiological as psychological and then resolves to assist her, to do her pleasure, and if this pleasure is one with the man's, so much the worse. Or so much the better. So long as they don't exclude her. She'd threatened to kill him, but it's too obvious that at the point they've reached it would be a sure way of putting an end to the affair. And although she has a mature capacity for endurance, she couldn't endure that.

And the girl? The girl is freer of preconceptions but it's also she who least perceives the dangerous thread of the affair in which they're getting entangled. For her the woman and the man are only places, like that house and the beach with its horses symbolic of her childhood, in which to live, fulfill herself emotionally and sexually.

Paris. Same day, 1:00 P.M.
I go again to the window. The piercing cold makes the wholly white landscape more vivid. And it's from this whiteness that I get the feeling of finding myself looking at a blank page on which to begin writing again, or rather of a huge screen to be filled.

Whiteness is a color-shadow, it's been said. And while I pass hurriedly over this consideration (which is Rudolf Steiner's), suddenly a thick shadow settles down on the events imagined up to this point. Its entanglements, its twistings, its forcings fuse and fuse again, then dissolve. What remains is a flat, linear story, the story of two women who at different times have loved the same man. Chance makes them meet and talk of this man, who in this way becomes the cause of their bond, no less profound than that which they had with him. No retrospective jealousy. Only friendship. The most limpid and most problematic of all sentiments.

This is the subject I wrote. Jotted down in a notebook a few months later, on my return from Khiva, it remained there, forgotten in a little hotel of which I remember the wide corridors and the filthy toilets.

The odd thing is that this subject, born years ago, is ideally situated after another written later and that it's imbedded in the film I'm about to start shooting. In fact, it's the sequel to it. All of which implies that, if it's only cause and effect that set this event after the other in my mind, then it's necessary to acknowledge in mental events the same movements and mechanisms that coordinate (or disconnect) the real events of our lives.

THE SILENCE

At the beginning a dialogue, a brief one, which will clarify a breakdown in relations concealed for years by both husband and wife. The usual habits, the usual hurt. But now that—by chance—they've at least begun to open up, the woman wants to have it all out.

—It's over, admit it. That way everything will be out in the open and we'll know what to do. It's enough to know what we want. Isn't that so? Answer me. Isn't that right?

The husband nods without saying a word. She's silent too. Now that everything's out in the open, now that they're being honest, they have nothing more to say to each other.

A story of husband and wife who have nothing more to say to each other. To shoot just once not their conversation but their silences, their silent words. Silence as a negative dimension of speech.

WHO IS THE THIRD? . . .

When I've completed a film, it's always with great effort that I start thinking of another. But it's the only thing left for me to do, and that I know how to do. Sometimes I linger over a verse I've read, the poem is for me extremely moving:

> *Who is the third who walks always beside you?*

When a line of poetry becomes a feeling, it's not difficult to put it into a film. This line of Eliot has frequently tempted me. He gives me no peace, that third who walks always beside you.

THE FIRST DAYS OF SPRING

The sensation I have when I feel it is that the shrilling of the telephone wires in the country makes the landscape impatient. Especially in the first days of Spring, when one hears more.

I think of this impatience transferred to people, peasant families for instance. It's not true that the peasants are patient. And I think of the crisscrossing of the telegrams in those lines, with all their stories. And of a soundtrack based on that shrilling. . .

THREE DAYS

I remember the green meadow, the reddish house, the paving of sun-baked bricks in the midst of the grass. The girl too was full of sun. A sun as Nordic as she. I'd never seen her before, she smiled at me with great naturalness and I smiled too but suddenly stopped to ask her if she'd like to come live with me. A profound amazement shone on her face. But not so profound as the point-blank question justified.

She then came to live with me. It lasted three days. And they were three days of profound amazement.

IN THE CUP OF A LILY

To breathe in the cup of a lily. . .

I don't recall who wrote this other line of verse, but the first time I read it, it found its way into a letter written many years back, a letter which could be part of an epistolary film.

I should say what I mean by epistolary film, but that would be a technical discussion and inappropriate. I allude merely to the potentiality which cinema has for sharpening our sense of the absent interlocutor, i.e. the recipient of the letter, by showing him or listening to him.

With an air of total self-confession, the woman who writes what follows is thinking of the man, of his possible reactions, of his eventual response. She is provoking them. Behind her words there is more of him than her. I mean that, for the length of the letter, I'd hold my camera fixed on the recipient at least as much as the writer. To feel the collision of their voices.

Dearest,

You come to see me on Sundays and that's where my week ends. Now I tell you that we can't go on like this, painfully ending the week this way and then starting all over on Monday. I feel I'm falling to pieces, and I no longer believe in it. What's to be done? Do you think there's anything to be done? Yesterday I went to bed early. I wanted to weep over myself, to think, to free myself. I didn't sleep a wink. I've never seen how a room spends the night. There was a lily on the table and the room was bathed in its perfume. In the cup of the lily there's a shadow that makes the flower more white. I put my mouth into that shadow and breathed until I almost fainted. I went to sleep this morning, which is Monday.

OUT OF DESPERATION

Without a word a girl sits down at my table in a bar in a cafe in Piazza Bologna in Rome. She's extremely excited. She tells me she's just witnessed a kidnapping. Two young men in plain view grab a man and shove him into a car which drives off at great speed. They're armed and nobody can do a thing.

The girl has beautiful dark eyes and a strange way of looking. Looks that are like rustlings. She says she's a maid in the house of an old lady, a former history teacher. Her life is lived in the same way as that seventy-year old woman. Her world is there in the windowpanes and every afternoon the girl goes out and wanders through her world, which is the neighborhood where she lives. When she comes back home, her mistress is sleeping and out of desperation she starts reading the history of Italy.

On the street one day she stops to talk with a boy of her own age. He's not a talker. She likes him. Shyly the boy tells her of his interest in her. And there she is. And she falls into the net of her destiny—terrorism, underground existence, prison, escape. . .

Out of desperation.

MICHELANGELO ANTONIONI
Translated
by William Arrowsmith

WATCHING A FILM WATCH US:
ANTONIONI'S *THE PASSENGER*

> "If the doors of perception were cleansed every thing would appear to man as it is, infinite."
> For man has closed himself up, till he sees things thro' narrow chinks of his cavern."
> —Blake, *The Marriage of Heaven and Hell*

"This is a film," Antonioni commented,[1] "about someone who is following his destiny, a man watching reality as reported, in the same way that I am watching him, and"—this to the interviewer—"in the same way that you are pursuing me. You could go back and find another camera watching me and another one watching the other camera. It's surrealistic, isn't it?"

The surrealistic quality is of course deliberate, sustained with fastidious technical control throughout, in narrative, theme, dialogue, composition. Realities fold into one another; disparate geographies suddenly intersect, revealing the emergent "character" as the personal continuity, even the consciousness, linking these otherwise disconnected landscapes. People fade, disappear or melt into each other, then re-emerge, come into focus. Past and present overlap, as in the flashback via the tape voiceover in the opening scenes in the desert hotel, or in the flashback crosscutting between Locke's London house and the wedding in the rococo church in Munich.

The shaping is schematic; the effect often ironic. Locke, following a white horse-drawn bridal cab—which might be a funeral cab—the wrong way down a one-way street, enters a cemetery to come upon a wedding, which in turn intersects with the death (fallen petals, burning boughs) of his own London marriage. The past lives the characters, the future keeps opening into the past. The destiny Locke is following is another man's, yet he can make it his own only because he is finally *not* the other man, but himself—a new man emerging from the old. But his destiny lies *through* that borrowed identity. *Lui, c'est moi.*

Locke must lose himself before finally coming on a self that is, however inchoate and brief, finally *his*. Locke is a self dissolving, then forming. The others, it is suggested, are also partly interchangeable identities. "Are you still looking for Locke?" Rachel's lover asks her. In the dim corridors of Gaudi's neo-Gothic Palacio Guell, the girl, disappearing, says: "People disappear every day." "Yes," Locke replies, "every time they leave the room." On the moviola Rachel and Knight watch the shots of an African witch-doctor, filmed by Locke, turn the tables on his interviewer by reversing the camera, turning it on Locke. Whereupon Locke makes the witch-doctor's (and the director's) point by abruptly moving from between the curtains, *off* the frame, literally dissolving from view. Knight at the moviola, telling Rachel of *his* vain search for Locke in Barcelona, scores the point, saying: "He disappeared."

Or the same events are reported by different media, different observers, for different audiences. The camera itself makes autonomous assertions, from the point of view of no identifiable observer, as though to declare the presence of an unseen watcher, a camera eye/"I"—that sees what those it observes do not and so provides us with another perspective. It is this unknown observer that shows us Locke in medium shot by his sand-buried Land-rover, then on his knees in frustration, and finally, as though to give that medium shot the wide-angled perspective of the desert, follows the direction toward which Locke kneels, panning on and on over the salmon-pink desert. The same camera follows the black insects crawling up the lightcord in Locke's bedroom, or, the picture hanging over the bed in the Hotel de la Gloria. Nothing is quite what it seems to be; nothing is ever *all* it might be. The director gives us the process of Becoming itself: an iridescent, intermittent reality that defines itself by dissolving and then reforming, acquiring shape, texture, and solidity, according to a complex cinematic poetry of the unfolding world of the "given." Closely observed, with growing detachment, the sensuous solidities of routinely coded vision dissolve to reveal themselves in new and unsuspected ways, as though we had never seen them before. We see the object, but as through a looking-glass: existing according to a different logic, in a surreal dimension. Beneath the hatched outlines, as the perspective changes, on detaching itself from the clichés of narrative and character, the real object begins to emerge. In the individual and idiosyncratic, we begin to glimpse the generic; the infinite in the finite. The aim is that of any classically ambitious art—the disclosure of the full reality of things by fusion of "foreground" and "background," "here" and "there," time and the timeless. We see "with parted eyes,/When everything seems double." Past and present fuse; place and space coalesce into an all-inclusive "space"; the limited individual reveals the species' passion for transcendence; the bounds between life and death, body and soul, dissolve before us.

I

The source of this scrupulous doubling by the dislocated eye lies, not in Antonioni's penchant for surrealism or Pirandellian "metaphysics," but in his own lifelong meditation on transcendence. Not transcendence in the philosophical sense, but rather as the ego's passage beyond the limits of the self, its merging with, or dying into, the larger world, the "otherers" that lies beyond the ego.

In *The Passenger*, above all in the miraculous final "take," the director's persistent efforts to give *visual* expression to the idea of transcendence culminates. But with a striking difference from the earlier films—a difference defined by the prodigious technical skill brought to bear upon its visual articulation.[2] Here, for the first time in Antonioni's *oeuvre*, the theme of transcendence takes on an overt, though typically understated, religious dimension. The point is crucial, though it will doubtless be resisted by those viewers who have, quite properly, stressed the essentially secular outlook of the earlier films. But with *The Passenger* the religious theme is, however tentative, tangibly, powerfully present; the film will inevitably be under-read or misread if the viewer imposes his own expectations or fails to confront the *fact* of the visual text. The religious theme is, in point of fact, an emerging theme of his work, as the director has himself stated. Four years after *The Passenger*, Antonioni began work on a film entitled *Patire or morire (Suffer or Die)*; production was cancelled at the last moment for financial reasons. The film, the director said, would have been a "transcendental story," which would "fundamentally express the groping of the protagonist toward God—a protagonist who does not believe in

God but is moving in that direction."[3] We should not, of course, confuse the director with his protagonist; the film is the work of a firmly secular director characteristically curious about all human behavior, and above all the passion for transcendence, whether its expression is religious, quasi-religious, erotic or technological.

The transcendence expressed by the earlier films is patently secular, and, for the most part, negative in its aspect as a metaphor or symptom of modern malaise, above all that of Eros. Insofar as it is positive, it produces that sense of tragic loneliness (sometimes mistakenly called "alienation") felt by the individual who refuses to surrender his fragile, emerging "self" to the warm oblivion of Eros or the embrace of the collective "One." But whether secular or religious, negative or positive, the idea is rooted in what might be called "the pathos of the self"—that pathos that hungers to escape the limits of the body and "burns a whole in our being without ever achieving its real end—true otherness."[4] An example would be *La notte*, where it is expressed by the desperate yearning of the party "sleepwalkers" to escape, through compulsive eroticism, the pain of individuality. The shimmering blank void of the black swimming-pool lures them toward it, *into* it, just as the bubble of Roberto's car, sliding slowly through the rain, its occupants oblivious of everything else, sealed in each other, expresses its brief, doomed bliss. And in *Blow-Up*, it is the collective effort of the Carnaby Street crowd of "swinging London" to make Thomas forget what he has seen in the park—that individuating discovery of death; in *Eclipse*, the struggle of Vittoria's "imprisoned feelings" to escape the bars of their cell. Without exception every film repeatedly reports this yearning for transcendence, for escape from the pervasive solipsism of the modern self, estranged from all forms of traditional community, and to that degree its hunger for otherness intensified and exacerbated.

But there is another form of transcendence, which is a crucial theme in almost every film. If men transcend themselves by "dying into" others, a larger identity that promises to annul the pathos of self, there is also a Faustian form of transcendence—the yearning to sprout wings, or fins, to transcend mortality by *technological escape* into another world, even beyond this world; to experience the divinity of technical power. In the photographer's studio in *Blow-Up* are two centrally placed photographs of a parachutist and a frogman—men changing, adapting, transcending themselves. The amateur rocketeers in *La notte* express the exhilaration of reaching out "for the moon"; in *Eclipse* it is the relief of escape as the plane lifts off from the troubled ground of Rome, making for Verona. But nowhere is it more perfectly portrayed than in *The Passenger* itself, in the image of Locke, liberated, he supposes, from the prison of his old self, leaning out of the cage of the cable-car moving over the deep blue of Barcelona harbor, waggling his wings like a gull. The same idea of technological power as quasi-divine release from the earth underlies the film's concerns with cars and the theme of escape from "reality" symbolized by these prosthetic machines whose breakdowns at key points in the film trigger Locke's essential "decisions." Relentlessly, the director chops away at Locke's machines, his cameras and tape-recorders, even his dark glasses, leaving him at last alone with himself to meet his death.

Technological escape is in turn linked to Antonioni's primitivist themes. Painfully conscious of his weakness and sterility, "civilized" Western man tries to revive himself by returning to his origins, to the primitive or past creature in himself, even the animal. Hence the African sequence in *Eclipse*; the girl in *La notte* embracing the flanks of a stone satyr; in the obsession with aphrodisiacs in *Red Desert*; the pterodactyl-airplane in *Zabriskie Point*; the nostalgia for the sea and the past in *L'avventura*. In *The Passenger* Locke's very presence in Africa—his personal need to make contact with the rebels fighting in the desert—tells us indirectly, as does the witch-doctor directly, more about Locke—the hunger for a vitality he does not have—than about the elusive rebels. But Locke's *means* of making contact—that blue Landrover with its invasive roar in the desert silence—the tape-recorder and camera; the media protocol of "factual" questions that prohibit meaningful response—these are the instruments of the transcendental Faustian. We know him by his instruments and his reliance upon them. Locke is like Thomas in *Blow-Up*; only when he abandons, or is abandoned by, his prosthetic devices, is he capable of a different way of viewing and a different kind of transcendence. Hence the pointed failure of the Faustian devices at both beginning and end of the film—the stalled Landrover repeated in the useless Avis car with its punctured oilpan. The Faustian equipment fails in order to provide Locke with an unmediated encounter with a very different reality—one from which every shred of social and cultural privilege has been stripped away. Just as Thomas in *Blow-Up* learns at last to see, to use his human eyes, so Locke can confront death as a contemporary "unaccomodated man." You can learn most about a man, the film suggests, by looking at his luggage, not his personal history; so the film chops away at Locke's luggage, leaving him finally nothing but himself, the traveler divested of everything, and finally, even his passenger. In the final scene he is nothing but that self which, because he feared it didn't exist, made it possible for him to usurp another man's identity, which he then feels compelled to live, even at the risk of death, and so dies into himself.

Compelled to live, that is, all the way, "for better or worse." So, at first, it seems: for "better" with the money that liberates him in the cable-car over the blue Barcelona water; for "worse" as he moves down his road, back toward Africa, to his fateful erotic encounters with the mysteriously coded ladies—Daisy, Marina, Lucy—of Robertson's appointment book. He watches his own borrowed identity unfold, and then, at the film's end, by active possession, become his own. Clearly, there has to be a self before it can be transcended. But the transcendence depends upon its being *seen*, upon our involvement in this unfolding destiny which is vicariously the viewer's also. We see different events, as through different cameras at different angles, all watching each other. First, a man living on borrowed papers—an existential Mattia Pascal[5]—becomes himself; then the same man, fulfilling the identity he has borrowed, transcends himself. *Lui, c'est moi*: we *see* it.

Here in *The Passenger*, for the first time, the director confronts the religious matrix of his various transcendental themes. In earlier films religion is merely a significant absence—e.g. shots of empty churches whose emptiness is offered as a tacit, at times ironic, gloss upon the rituals of Eros that have replaced institutional religion. Eros is ill because it must perform the tasks of all the dead or dying institutions of traditional culture—family, *paese*, and religion. This is more than Eros can do, a fact which deforms it into a compulsive malaise. Emptied of its original religious and metaphysical source—escape from the self and selfishness into a larger community, a higher fulfillment—its energies are diverted into mere serial eroticism, the desperate attempt to drown "oneself" in another's being, in the narcosis of pleasure, irresponsibility, oblivion. Being metaphysical or religious in origin, this Eros cannot be satisfied by surrogates. Locke wants to die as "Locke," to become Robertson; but gun-running isn't enough; there is a subliminal spiritual purpose behind gun-running—a mission, a "vocation" even.

Whatever one's personal text for this theme, it cannot be evaded in dealing with a body of work like Antonioni's, whose master-theme is "the fantasy of freedom," the radical need of the imprisoned self to escape its prison, to move beyond the "frame" that confines it, to *become* whatever in it is struggling to emerge. The classical text for this theme is the famous passage in Plato's *Symposium* where Aristophanes explains why lovers crave each other so desperately. Men were originally, he says, united creatures, bisexual wholes; then, because of our arrogance, we were divided, like the halves of a tally:

> So when any lover is fortunate enough to meet his other half, they are both intoxicated with affection, friendship, and love; so intoxicated that they cannot let each other out of sight for a single instant. . . . The fact is that both their souls are longing for a *something else* [ti allo]—a something to which they can neither of them give a name, and of which they can only give an inkling in cryptic sayings and prophetic riddles.

Ti allo. Something else—an X, some condition to which neither lover can give a name. It is the discontented Eros craving this *ti allo* that Locke's search for a new self, a *vita nuova*, reveals, and that achieves such astonishing visual expression in the final "take." Where the poetry is, there one finds the poet. Whether *The Passenger* is ultimately a religious film is not the real question; but Locke's "passion" must be understood in terms no less "spiritual" than those *imposed* by the script and the visuals. That "passion" is visually expressed in the film's last seven minutes as a literal passage of the soul or psyche through the bars of its cell

39

in "language" of such intense, wordless, kinetic purity that it is impossible to suppose that the director is merely esthetically involved. The whole film seems in fact to have been made for this finale, for this visualization, *vision* even, of what Dante called *trasumanar*—the process whereby the human transcends itself and which, as Dante himself declared, it is beyond the powers of words to express:

> *Trasumanar significar per verba*
> *non si poria; pero, l'esemplo basti*
> *a cui esperienza grazie serba.*[6]

[That *passing beyond humanity* may not be put into words; therefore, let the example suffice anyone for whom grace reserves that experience.]

II

In images but also in the narrative of a journey as an unfolding destiny, the film shows Locke to be, in some unconsciously groping way, a transcendental man. In the life he borrows from Robertson, he discovers the secular residue of what would once have been a religious vocation. The point will no doubt be vigorously resisted; yet the religious account of Locke's odyssey is suggested with an insistence that, for the elliptical Antonioni, suggests thematic urgency. This is not to say that *The Passenger* is an overtly religious film or that the director has renounced his earlier secular viewpoint. For whatever reason the film is so constructed that the attentive viewer is required to come to terms with an account of human destiny that is both contemporary and secular, but also in some clear sense spiritual. It would be critically mistaken to insist on the primacy of either of these two accounts; the religious must not be reduced to the secular, nor the secular treated as though it were a mere gloss on the "deeper" spiritual account. At stake is the *continuity* of the transcendental impulse in *both* accounts; the way in which foreground and background, apparently discontinuous, intersect at a deeper level, and finally dissolve into each other.

At least twice the script alludes to the difficulty of shaking old habits—habits that persist beneath all efforts to adopt a new identity, to remake oneself. Smoking, for instance, at the most trivial level. At a deeper level, the whole world of genetic and cultural inheritance, including the human disposition to violence and aggression. As the old man in the Umbraculo says to Locke: "Other people look at children and they imagine a new world. . . . But me . . . when I watch them, I just see the same old tragedies about to begin all over again. . . . They can't escape from us." The children are biologically *bound*; in the genes they inherit, the whole human past shapes them, *lives* them. The world of the foreground—*now*, the present and contemporary—has the appeal of boundless freedom, even infinity, about it. But the body that hungers for that freedom is a finite thing, limited by its past, by constraints of nature and culture, by its specific and generic habits, by its instincts. But also by its cultural conditioning—the social habits created by physical environment and habitat—the world of objects and products, of buildings, roads, language, gardens, billboards, customs, even articles of personal use, everything that is "luggage." Locke's deepest desire is to dissolve; he does so by doing away with everything that has hitherto defined him—all those objects, relations, and habits that compose the artifact called "Locke." Inwardly he feels hollow, filled with an emptiness like the desert to which he feels drawn, emptiness to emptiness. There in the desert he dissolves, becomes Robertson. Stripped of the accidental, he can discover the necessary and essential—the life stirring like the breath of wind in the dead Robertson's room in the expectant void of the desert. Locke is a dissolving man disappearing into the desert horizon; like Antonioni's characters generally, he declares his psychic reality by inserting himself into the apposite geography, a landscape and an emptiness like his own. He reveals his interior state by his journey. Destiny is destination. A man moves toward what he is becoming, as Locke moves persistently, even while wavering and retreating, toward the desert, just as Aldo in *Il grido* moves towards the great waste expanse of the Po Delta whose receding horizon expresses that *ti allo* concealed in his obsessive love for Irma. The journey is thus potentially dramatic, not narrative, expressing both what the disappearing traveller now is, but also the man he is becoming—the man "appearing." The "passenger" (Ital. *passagero*, a way-farer, a transient-in-passage) declares his immediate psychic

41

state by the landscape he seeks, but also the fact that *something* is changing: he is drawn to a place which is himself but also "other" and more than himself—the tally of his own incomplete nature. The emptiness in him is pregnant with new life.

Locke in the desert of Chad is a man in transit, defined by a borrowed mission that partly expresses himself. He is a man in crisis, trapped in a dying marriage and a professional "success" that prevent him from changing or growing. The professional but also personal mission of this caged man is an encounter with unknown and elusive rebels struggling, like his feelings, for freedom against what oppresses him. This mission, he believes, will give him, as a professional observer, a first-hand relation to reality. The rebels in this sense *are* Locke, what he wants to be—a man struggling for freedom. To Robertson he says that it is men, not landscapes, that interest him but his actions belie his words. Locke's Landrover roars into the frame—the desert we see before and after the transient intruder, so sharply contrasted with the image of the majestic Bedouin floating silently by on his camel, at home in the desert—and, there where the road gives out, digs in. Then we see Locke enraged and frustrated—frustration in every gesture, the whole impasse of his life declared as he throws up his arms and shouts, "I don't care!" Then a medium shot, and we see him sink to his knees, arms stretched out before him, forehead touching the ground and body extended *away* from the Landrover toward the desert stretching on into the infinity lying beyond the frame. It is this reaching out which is now revealed— Locke reaching out towards the desert, and then the desert reaching out beyond itself, as the camera pans slowly, steadily, right. But it is in fact helplessness and resignation, even despair—the "death-wish" one might say of the "old" Locke—expressed by a ritualized gesture, an unmistakable salaam.[7] Slowly, tremblingly, following Locke's extended arms, the camera pans on and on over the infinity of apricot colored dunes, forcing the viewer to see and feel this wide-angled immensity as a vast *otherness*. Later, back in Locke's hotel bedroom, the camera makes the same point in a tiny detail: an image of black beetles or termites crawling slowly up the electric cord on the wide expanse of white-washed wall. As the wall diminishes the beetles, so the desert's infinity dwarfs the human being prostrate before it, in human scale, expressing for us if not for him, a sense of his finitude and insignificance, even humiliation. His Faustian machine bogged down, Locke is suddenly humanly humbled, helpless, though perhaps not yet fully aware of the fact or the meaning of his own gesture.

Later on, toward the close of the film Locke will half-consciously recognize his limitations and insignificance. His Avis car broken down, he sits on the curb; behind him a white wall broken by a green-blinded window. We see him grope in the street, pick something up, place it against the white wall and squash it: a cochineal bug (no flower), a tiny red bloodstain on the white desert of the wall. The abrupt violence with which Locke squashes the insect shows that he *sees*, resents, but also tentatively accepts his own analogous fate, his transience and insignificance, even the extinction irritably enacted by his own hand. All this without a word. But it is this non-verbal acceptance, this acquiescing "decision," that gives the suggestion of a latent sacrifice; of Locke as a knowing, even willing (or perhaps will-less) sacrificial victim. His life may be irritably given, but it is, for the moment, given. Obedient to his unfolding fate—for his acceptance of it means that it is *his*, not Robertson's—Locke freely chooses to risk his life, even to sacrifice himself. Later, outside his window on the bullring-oval of the plaza of Osuna, we hear, among other sounds, a muted bull-ring trumpet saluting the death of the sacrificial victim.

The film is so constructed as to reveal, step by step—now advancing, hesitating or retreating—Locke's groping aspiration—to make or, more precisely, let the "new Locke" supersede the "old Locke," caged in his coded world. Everything converges in the last shot. Like the exploding house in *Zabriskie Point*, or the fable-like coda of *Red Desert*, or the great montage of *Eclipse*, the final shot of *The Passenger* is an epiphany that binds the various themes in a single comprehensive kinetic "image," itself a wholly new statement of those themes at a higher level. Viewed from the finale, the film's structure is immediately apparent. A formal prologue states the main themes in their visual and chromatic terms: internal and external geographies, the narrative "quest," dissolving identity, the desert (like Eliot's in *The Waste Land*) as the condition of a spiritual death and rebirth. The

43

narrative proper—Locke's discovery of himself in Robertson's identity—ends with the breakdown of the Avis car, corresponding to the stalled Landrover with which the narrative begins. As so often in Antonioni, that narrative is essentially internal. The external world with its landscapes and stopovers, the events of its "story line," express the psychological stages of Locke's journey as the making of an identity, an identity, according to the director's effort to create here and elsewhere, a visual poetics of destiny. Beneath the intricately detailed *poetry* of the narrative, Locke's secular pilgrimage gathers momentum as it moves slowly towards its destination—that destiny revealed in the transcendence of the finale. Guided by no conventionally accepted sense of "vocation," Locke vacillates, feeling his way according to the nudgings of genetic memory and purpose, the voice of some hidden but insistent *daimon*. That voice is hard to hear, overwhelmed as it is by the coded noises and roles of the public world. Hence Locke's constant progression but equally persistent regression as he struggles to heed religious feelings that have no normalized place in a secular age. Hence too the director's efforts to avoid overtly conscious striving; the dissolving Locke simply doesn't know, at least until the close, where he is going. Words don't matter; what counts is the visuals, which express the inarticulateness of gathering consciousness. Locke dissolves, dying as Locke in order to come upon a prior, deeper "self"— that tougher self, "Who," in Eliot's words, "never talks, who cannot argue."[8]

Only by dissolving can Locke discover this new self and appear at last in his own right—only to disappear again, but at a higher level. Robertson in this sense is Locke's *alter ego*. If Locke *initially* feels the exhilaration of a new identity, of *being* Robertson, he later comes, first by necessity and then by some velleity of choice, to accept the responsibility imposed by that new identity. Through responsible possession of his own emerging fate, shadow Locke finally becomes true Locke—no longer Robertson but the person potentially present, buried beneath the old Locke and Robertson's borrowed *persona*. "I never knew him," says Rachel when the police ask her to identify Locke's body; and she is right. The Girl, asked if she knows him, answers, "Yes"; and she too is right. The new Locke has emerged from the old.

That emergence of the "new" from the "old" is made explicit in two crucial scenes, both of which were—inexplicably, infuriatingly—excised by M. G. M. editors from the American print. (European viewers can see the integral version, as the director shot it.) In the first of these scenes, Locke, newly returned from Africa, enters his house in Lansdowne Crescent. Upstairs he finds, pinned to the door, a note from his wife to her lover. In the study, as he removes money and papers from the desk drawer, we see a book on the desk—Alberto Moravia's *What Tribe Do You Belong To?*—which Locke had presumably been reading in preparation for his African trip. But the unanswered question echoing in that title is clearly addressed to Locke as a man. What tribe does *he* belong to? The tribe of mindlessly opining or "objectively" reporting media role-players, or that of free autonomous, individual human beings? The second, and much more important, of the excised sequences comes near the end of the film, just after the visit to Plaza de la Iglesia. Locke and the girl enter a beautifully green, almost paradisal, lemon grove. Lying on the lush grass, looking up at the green leaves overhead, Locke talks of giving up his effort to keep Robertson's appointments. "The old me," he says, pointedly rising, "is getting hungry." Disgusted by his rejection of Robertson's itinerary, the Girl leaves the frame; as she leaves, the frame divides. On one side is the Girl, walking up the dry bed of a sand-colored arroyo; on the other, the "old" Locke, sheltered in the green of the lemon trees. He leaps after her, out of the grove and into the arroyo. Overtaking her, he persuades her to continue on his journey toward the desert landscape to which the "new" Locke is now committed.

His attenuated sense of identity makes it initially possible for Locke to melt easily into Robertson. But even in this negative form, however faintly at first, his hunger for transcendence can be discerned. It is this yearning that draws him toward the desert, itself defined as a waiting, breathing expectancy; it is the desert, or *something* in the desert, if only a void waiting to be filled, that triggers his adoption of Robertson's identity. When he finds Robertson, face down on the bed, the clothes on the wall rustle ever so slightly. But the rustling is apparent only because the camera shows us Locke leaving the frame; in the abandoned vacancy, which his departure forces the viewer to inspect, the clothes on the wall begin to stir. *Something* is there—a barely perceptible breath. What? Locke goes to the window, opens the shutter, looks out. At what? Desert immensity, and now on the sound-track the sound of a flute; then, in the foreground, a herd of goats scattering, defining the expense of desert reaching to the horizon, and revealing the source of the flute—a goatherd. Locke returns to the room, looks up: a fan slowly revolving—time passing. The camera pans down the electric cord, and suddenly there is Locke in Robertson's shirt, transformed to Robertson. Clearly Locke goes to the window and looks out because he intuitively links the stirring of the clothes on the wall with a breath of air coming from that desert world outside the shuttered window. The room itself is a cell, *locking* him (the wordplay is persistent) into the stale air of his old self, cutting him off from whatever it is that lies—a living, breathing presence—beyond the confines of cell and frame. Only later does the slowly revolving fan reveal itself as the "cause" that lures Locke to the window.

In one masterly summary the director gives us a wordless visual account of Locke's first decisive transformation and its personal motives (the sense of imprisonment, of being trapped in old habits and encoded clichés), and the metaphysical quality of his decision to move "off the frame" by disappearing into the desert, that destination now gathering direction within him. In his conversation with Robertson, Locke declares that he prefers people to landscapes; this is the "old" Locke speaking. The emerging Locke, whose motives we see gestating in this shot, unconsciously shares the attitude expressed by Robertson in the later flashback glossing this scene: "The desert is beautiful. . . . It's the immobility—a kind of waiting, an eternal suspension." The language is reminiscent of Pavese: the notion of a place, in which the absent god lives on; a living suspension. As the narrator of Pavese's *Dialogues with Leucò* says of the wild country around him: "What else could people have looked for in a place like this, if not an encounter with the gods? But in every deserted place, an emptiness, an expectation remains."

III

But the most telling visual statement of Locke's emerging "vocation" is the secular sacrament performed with the agents of the Chadian rebels in front of the high altar of the rococo church in Munich. Locke reaches this church by a kind of self-revealing serendipity, aimlessly following a bridal coach. Passing through a graveyard embowered in leaves and flowers, he enters the church, as the old secular Locke would presumably have done, through a side-door. He is, knowingly or unknowingly, retracing his past, above all his own dead marriage. But that past and its memories are cultural as well as personal. He stands quietly in the church, by his chosen position excluded from the wedding ceremony by an iron grille. The wedding itself is intricately cross-cut with scenes of Locke's London home and marriage, past and present combining as though simultaneous or were taking place in some timeless present. The ceremony over, Locke, presumably immersed in memories, sits in a pew, meditating. There he is interrupted by the Chadian agents. The contractual "sacrament," enacted before the altar, compels the viewer to see the ritual exchange of money as somehow related to the altar, as an ironic sacrament of its own. Repeatedly the camera picks up the gleaming gold of the altar cross, and the gilded frames of the Stations of the Cross flanking the altarpiece. After the exchange of money, the camera pans slowly *down* the whole altar, revealing a formal Gloria, the *ascent* of a saint in ecstasy, surrounded by clouds and angels, all enclosed in the intricate scrollwork, the leaf-and-shell-forms of Bavarian Rococo. Then, as though to make clear the context of this Gloria, the director shows us the whole church—a continuous tissue of sculptured and painted architecture. It is at *this* point that Locke opens the envelope the Chadians gave him and says in quiet astonishment, "Christ." Then, as though suddenly aware of his surroundings, he exclaims, in embarassed apology: "Christ!"

Locke is semi-consciously participating in a shadow sacrament. From this point on his progress is portrayed as a groping passage through the Stations of the Cross, a religious "mission" implicit in his later conscious "decision" to complete Robertson's itinerary. If his mission never becomes overtly religious, it

47

nonetheless tangibly informs the rest of the film, making the viewer aware of an older ghostly meaning surviving in the secular Gloria of the finale, which corresponds to the formal Gloria in the Munich church. The Girl has her own personal reasons—she believes in Locke, she loves him—for urging him to keep Robertson's appointment in Osuna: "He believed in something. That's what you wanted, isn't it?" But her personal reasons are wholly compatible with the secular Gloria of the finale, which corresponds to the quasi-sacramental analogy. The "something" in which Robertson, and later Locke, believed, is Antonioni's equivalent of Plato's *ti allo*, the transcendent object of that hunger for meaning and a redeeming purpose which Locke cannot renounce. Antonioni's purposes may be to offer a covertly religious account of human aspiration, or at least of Locke's behavior here; but more probably the purpose is to suggest the persistence of the passion for transcendence in an age when creeds no longer enlist that passion. It survives, not as formal religious behavior like the traditional saint's ecstasy, but as the impulse that once found adequate expression in that ecstasy and persists even now as existential or cultural "vocation." The one habit men cannot, without ceasing to be men, "kick," is the habit of meaning; they can no more rid themselves of that habit than they can "kick" the habit of evolving, adapting. Divest a man of everything; let him arrive at his destination without luggage, either religious or physical, and he will inevitably display the quality that makes him human—above all, his passion for transcending himself, for evolving. The book Locke was evidently reading when Robertson died, the book he picks up on leaving his room, and which we see among his possessions when they are opened by Rachel is entitled: *The Soul of the Ape*.[9]

IV

Prehistoric man evolved as man when his arboreal ape-ancestors descended from the trees and adapted themselves to the vast treeless savannahs of central Africa. Caged and sheltered by his green Edenic habitat, the pre-human forest apes had no need to evolve. But when the Miocene forests shrank in the great Pleistocene drought, they had to adapt or die. It was the adaptive, evolving ape who left his native trees and made himself human in the empty grasslands of the central African plateau and the South African veldt. It is this tale of adaptation—how the ape acquired a human "soul," i.e. a new consciousness of himself—that Locke has been reading. Beneath the narrative of the evolving Locke, there is a running analogy with the evolution of the species. Locke's emerging *persona* is in fact a complex of three discrete but cohering strands—personal, religious, and anthropological. Their common denominator is change. Personally, Locke is a man in crisis, at a point of "passage," in mid-life and career-frustration; a man changing. Religiously, he is the secular pilgrim passing through the upward stations of his cross, toward a new vocation and an unknown fate. Anthropologically, he is emerging and "ascending" man, leaving the shelter of his treed life, at once paradise and prison, for the exposure of open country and the dangers of the void. The anthropological metaphor is more glancingly stated than the religious, but is no less urgent and pervasive. Its first overt articulation is that book—*The Soul of the Ape*—which we see lying in Locke's suitcase. There is of course no literary allusion intended here. We are not expected to be familiar with the book; the title serves simply as a visual introduction to the images which will sustain the governing idea. The *idea* of *a transcendental* ape—not easily conveyed visually—is the immediate point (just as later, in the final "take," it will be the idea of the *soul* or psyche itself). In the sequence at Barcelona, for instance, we see Knight pursuing Locke. Locke disappears behind a group of birdcages stacked on the sidewalk; the last shot is of a caged monkey being lifted across the frame and disappearing in the same direction as Locke. The metaphor is more actively present in the studied portrayal of Europe (London, Munich, and Barcelona) as an arboreal habitat which Locke leaves for that treeless expanse of Africa or African Spain where, by transcendence or mutation, he at last becomes himself.

The film everywhere presents an elaborate image of modern Europe as a green bower—a bower constantly contrasted with Locke's ascetic desert geography. Hence the severely inflected polarities, so typical of Antonioni: Europe and Africa; city and country; present and past; man-made colors contrasted with quieter earth-colors; etc. In human terms, it is predictably the woman—the Girl, played by Maria Schneider—who, as "a finer filter of reality," embodies the sense of the world-as-arbor. When we first see the Girl—Schneider's pleasantly simian features nicely adjusted to the arbor imagery of her habitat—she is sitting in the court of the Bloomsbury Centre, reading. She leans back, her head framed by the green leaves of the plants behind her, and the motif stressed by the floral tracery of her blouse. Visually, she is in "her element." But she is also adaptable. Like Vittoria in *Eclipse*, she has the natural knack of mobility, *balance*; unlike the maladaptive Locke, she constantly corrects for excessive light or shade, for too many trees or too much open space. If boskiness is her natural element, she is also visibly at home in open country, as in the large open court of the Centre, where she still can touch the leaves. When she and Locke veer off the road in the desert broom and mesquite of southern Spain, she looks at the huge expanse of scorched mountains and blue sky and says simply, "It's beautiful." In one of the film's most striking shots, the Girl is contrasted and then paired with Locke as his *natural* complement. She asks him, "What are you running away from?" Locke replies, "Turn your back to the front seat." We see her standing in the car, looking back, her arms outspread among the branches and leaves of the trees overhead, at home now in her element as he was at home in free flight over the deep blue water of Barcelona harbor. Then we see her from the front of the car, and the road and the trees, but above all the trees, converging and disappearing behind the car—the silent visual answer to Locke's question. Her world is Nature; the attenuating vital and emotional energies of Locke (superbly portrayed by Nicholson's low-keyed, dead-pan manner) stand for that extinction of animal spirits, the death-wish of the body required by the Spirit.

For Locke is literally running toward the desert and his own death, homing toward the parched, almost African world of southern Spain. He moves *away* from the leaves, leaving the green, bowered world behind him. In one of the more violent cuts in the film, through the blazing gasoline crackle of *green* leaves burning (no autumn leaves, these), we glimpse the figure of Locke. He has deliberately pruned away every green leaf and bough he can reach, arousing protests from his neighbor and, more important, from Rachel who comes rushing out in her nightgown, shouting, "Are you *crazy?*" He is symbolically destroying the protective screen of his English arbor; the leaves are burnt with a violent glee that reveals his detestation of the green cage in which he perceives himself as imprisoned. Hence the almost obsessive boskiness of Locke's house in Lansdowne Crescent, with its hedge of encircling green and blossoming flowers, placed so carefully beside the steps where he mounts, and the glimpse of greenery into which he disappears. The excessive vegetation of Lansdowne Crescent is then repeated in the florid rococo Munich church with its bridal flowers and leafy scrolls and fern-like iron grille. Depending on where one stands, these bowered worlds are variously paradise—the security of the protecting leafiness against the glaring light of an intolerable reality—or prison, where the feelings are penned in and change is impossible. The Munich wedding itself suggests a stifling vernal imprisonment: the green *Gemütlichkeit* of German and Western middle-class life, designed to screen out reality, to protect its inhabitants from the spectacle of change and immensity that might otherwise open up around them. Even death—those prettified grave stones with their floral carvings and symbols of easy resurrection—is adapted to the uses of snuggery, the sense of the world as man's natural nest.

In sum, an image of the modern world self-protectively still embowered in the Ptolemaic universe, still in the grip of its old heady Renaissance illusion of Central Man and Central Man's self-centered certainties. The idea is not a new one for Antonioni, who persistently employs cosmological perspectives in his films. In the famous Cannes interview after *L'avventura*, he remarked that modern man "no longer possesses the exuberant confidence of Renaissance man who, unlike us, inhabited a Ptolemaic universe." Modern man lives scientifically and technologically in the present, but morally in the past, burdened by the "baggage of old habits." "Man, who has today no fear of the scientific unknown, is afraid of the moral unknown." In *The Passenger* the Ptolemaic universe is depicted as a huge bower, excluding the reality that lies "beyond the frame"—the new, exploding, isotropically receding, perhaps infinite post-Copernican universe, with its incalculable violence, its incomprehensible event horizons. Toward that unknown world beyond the Western frame, toward the blinding white light of a new reality, Locke is drawn—a man in adaptation, a man evolving—out of his cozy green shelter.

Europe in this perspective is metaphorically both bower and birdcage—continent of birdcage-cities represented in miniature by the birdcages stacked on the sidewalk of Barcelona, itself a beautiful birdcage-city. But these paradisal cages can never quite exclude the threatening reality outside. The desert keeps intruding: that desert violence that suddenly erupts at a sidewalk cafe in Barcelona, masked by playing fountains; or the secret violence contained in the "black hole" of the locker in the Munich airport—a violence which Europe exports to Africa as marketable Faustian technology, and which returns to Europe as political violence and terrorism. In Munich Antonioni juxtaposes two incongruous architectures—the functional modern geometry of the Munich airport, its blazing primary chromatics contrasted with the green pretence of the rococo church on the dead suburban street. In London too, Lansdowne Crescent—the fashionable, mindless pretence of English middle-class life—is contrasted with the square of the Bloomsbury Centre, all birdcage cubicles and concrete where Locke first sees the Girl, reading no doubt a book on architecture. She has presumably been drawn there by the architect's (unsuccessful) effort to create an apartment complex which is not, like Lansdowne Crescent, a regression into the past, nor, at the opposite extreme, a purely functional and geometrically dead modernity. In both complexes the purpose is contrast and incongruity: an architectural commentary designed to elucidate the tension between past and present, natural and man-made, organic and functional. In Barcelona the commentary is also architectural, both glancing and comprehensive. Thus the two Gaudi buildings shown generalize the image first presented by the Umbraculo: latticed light; a slatted roof curving upwards like the top of an ornate birdcage, but a birdcage open to the world, where Locke waits for his mysterious appointment. There, for the first time in his career, Locke really interviews an old man— without camera, without recorder—who begins his life story, with its vista of time and space, "Once a long ways from here . . ." and its children, repeating the old human tragedy: "They can't escape from us."

That birdcage image is more strongly emphasized in the first Gaudi building, the Palacio Guell. That this structure is a cage—superbly habitable no doubt, but still a cage—is indicated by the birdcage hanging over the head of the appropriately drowsing custodian. The interior is dark, "good for hiding in," the Girl observes, and we see what she means. At the top of the domed room star-like holes admit a Ptolemaic illumination. The camera pans down the wall, where the slotted lateral windows admit "a dim religious light." On every side, with each shift of camera angle, a richly embowered texture: vine-leaves, tendrils of stone and wood; ornamental brickwork; lacy designs of Moorish inspiration. But most noteworthy is the neo-Gothic quality of the ensemble—the religious gloom, the sense of the medieval past in those dark enclosing textures, in the organ and paintings, the dozing custodian. An image of a drowsing world, almost a dead one. It is the sense of claustrophobic enclosure that triggers Locke's departure for another Gaudi building, one more suited to his psychic needs. We are not told why he leaves; the motivation is stated elliptically by the fact of departure and the stark contrast between the two buildings. Just as Locke keeps moving steadily toward the desert, so in Barcelona he moves from building to building in the self-defining mode of Antonioni's characters, who constantly tend to insert themselves in an external world which matches and thereby reveals their internal reality. In Gaudi's famous Casa Mila, where Locke and the Girl now go, the sense of the architectural birdcage abruptly vanishes. It is open space, not enclosing interiors and cubicles, that Locke wants, and, when we first see him and the Girl in Casa Mila, they are already on the roof, somehow at home in that fantasy landscape whose monochrome tiles and sculptured abstractions recall the expanse of the desert, its wind-eroded shapes, even its termitaries. Compare, for instance, Gaudi's fantastically sculptured chimneys and ventilators with the photographs of the desert—odd buttes, stony outcroppings—hanging over the reception-desk of Locke's hotel in Chad, and the affinity is apparent; indeed, it is generally held that Gaudi's structures were inspired by the landscape of Chad during the architect's visits to Africa. Even in the monochrome tiles Antonioni subtly evokes the desert; those same triangles of tile, white or ochre like those glimpsed earlier on the reception-desk of the Chad hotel.

But unlike the Bloomsbury Centre in London, Casa Mila is an attempt, in an apartment complex, to relocate man *in* nature. Not man *over* nature, center stage, as in the Ptolemaic conception, but a great architect's attempt to restore the balance between organic and functional, public and personal, free space and privacy. Hence the shot of the whole facade of Casa Mila—a lingering shot, permitting us to recognize the serpentine movement of the chamfered floorslabs, and the intricate iron scrollwork—tendrils of seaweed, it seems, woven about the cavelike openings of balconies and windows. Man and god; light and dark; natural forms merging with functional purpose; curve and line, creating the sense of privacy and peace; a world designed to permit shelter and security—the bower-feelings—but also open to the larger world, the "other" world of nature and society. Everywhere the design insists upon forms derived from desert and sea, and all that they imply of vistas of time and space. Foreground and background in formal balance; the transient confronted by the permanent in a way that does not mock the transient or deny permanence by prettifying it or screening it out. The building is one of Gaudi's most striking secular designs; but there is evidence that the structure was originally to have been surmounted by a colossal statue of the Virgin, who would thus preside over the foreground wilderness of sculptured abstractions that house ventilators and chimneys. Here, combining desert abstractions with the clotheslines of everyday life (emphasized in the film by a domestic argument taking place on a balcony below), Gaudi intended to place the divinity to whom the whole building was to be dedicated and in whose absence we see an image of the desert as glimpsed by Robertson: beautiful, immobile, waiting.

As Locke and the Girl move southwards down the Costa del Sol, the desert and sea loom larger. The trees thin out, the parched horizon opens up. We don't see the sea, but we hear its movement, always louder. But the more the landscape opens out, the more compulsive become the human efforts to contrive a screen against it. At a sidewalk cafe, Locke and the Girl are seated at a table. An iron grille separates *them* from *us*; interwoven with the straight bars of the grillwork are beautiful volutes of iron, crescents, tendrils. One tendril curls down around Locke's head from the right; another loops the Girl's head on the left, holding them briefly bonded in the tension of line and curve. Behind Locke, stacked cases of empty bottles, their emptiness reflecting his.[10] Beyond them a man sits staring at the white light pouring in at the fringe of the frame; on the soundtrack, the sea beating on the shore. Their privacy, the image suggests, is relative to the world lying beyond them; it looks *outward* toward what it excludes—us, the seated man. The seated man also looks outward toward the world beyond the frame—toward the white light and the sound of the sea. In earlier films the malaise of Eros is rooted in the compulsive privacy with which the lovers seal themselves off; Eros blots out the environing world in the obsessive intimacy of the "closeup." Here, on the contrary, Eros is depicted as healthy; its necessary inwardness is, like the privacy of Casa Mila, intensified through its relation to a larger environing world. The world beyond the frame is *seen*, heeded.

Locke and the Girl press on. The next sequence is set in a compulsively overdone Moorish restaurant, all flowers and filigree, where the police locate Locke's rented car. The pretty coziness of the restaurant stands in direct intentional contrast to the bleakness of the world it attempts to exclude. From behind still another grille we see Locke and the Girl embowered in almost aggressive floweriness. Locke gazes out towards the blue of the sea in the distance; we hear its beating on the shore as he gazes. But is he perhaps looking at the attractive woman in the red bathing-suit in the foreground? When the Girl asks him what he's thinking about, he smiles and says, "Nothing." And we know he has been looking at the sea, at that expectant blue nothingness. The restaurant with its obsessively decorative embowering, is architecturally designed to occlude the sea, just as on the street-side, it purposively screens out the man-made desert of the tourist "strip," jangling and intrusive. When Locke and the Girl go outside to meet the policeman, the restaurant's exterior is revealed for the first time: fake Moorish crenelations, a long row of thickly intergrown arborvitae planted as a screen. Against what? Against what we next see and what there is no artistic need to reveal unless the purpose is to indicate just what that cozy arbor of the restaurant excludes: the coastal highway, a broad band of ugly cement, parched yellow mountains to the left, streetlights overhead, a clutter of dreary apartment buildings, two motorcycles roaring away. The dirt and ugliness, in short, of the "real" world expressed verbally in Locke's parable of the blind man at the close.

Steadily South. The sound of the sea grows louder. When Locke reaches Plaza de la Iglesia, the camera shows part of the buildings before he and the Girl enter the frame. Our attention is being directed to the site and the architecture: functional modern buildings, geometrical and soulless, apparently abandoned, grass prinking up between the cement slabs, the church itself nothing but a godbox. Of trees and shrubbery hardly a sign; only the glaring sun, a white light beating down on white buildings; one or two people. In the siesta stillness can be heard, just off the frame as it were, the sound of the sea. "No one here," says Locke to the Girl, (echoing Claudia's "Non c'è nessuno" in the uninhabited development town of *L'avventura*).

The sea remains out of sight. The director is saving that image—the sea as visible nothingness or otherness, an infinite blue void associated with death—for the final "take." We *hear* it, an absent presence coming ominously closer, as the surf-sound increases. Linked to that sound is the indelible image of a rebel Chadian being executed by government soldiers (according to Antonioni, an actual, not a simulated, execution). Shocking but also strangely, even beautifully moving, it is as disturbing to Rachel and Knight watching it on the moviola as it must have been to Locke (and the director) when it was shot. The condemned man, in a pinkish shirt, hands bound across his chest, stands before a group of stacked barrels, striped light blue at top and bottom; in the middle a band of pink matching the condemned man's shirt and the desert. The execution is pointedly set on the shore, the blue of Lake Chad beyond it. A shot of the firing squad; then, immediately after, a shot of an expanse of blue water and surf, nothing else. The shots ring out, the victim sags and shudders under the impact of the bullets, then convulsively lifts his bound hands—a wing motion, the trembling flutter of escape—and then a shot of the sea. Blue water, nothing else. The sequence of execution and blue water—foreground and background constantly related—declares the connection between death and the blue void of sea and sky. An execution, a death, violence, light pink and blue, pink desert, blue sea, the sound of the surf—images of death and transcendence, of death *as* transcendence. An image too of a sacrifice—the prisoner's bound hands lifting, as though in prayer—a passion. And the sound linked to this kinesthetic cluster is heard now in the distant beating of the surf which we hear later, linked again to a shot of sea and sky, in the coda at Osuna.

A related point. It is the emphasis upon transcendence—on Locke's desire to supersede himself, to become his own internal void at a redeeming level—that makes the love-story here so simple and natural. Because his real aspirations lie elsewhere, "beyond," Locke is not tempted—like Sandro or Anna in *L'avventura*, or the erotic sleepwalkers of *La notte*, or Aldo in *Il grido*—to make of Eros a consuming all. Moved by other purposes, something beyond sex, Locke and the Girl are not subject to the obsessive eroticism of the "human zoo." Locke and the Girl *like* each other. They are lovers and, by conventional standards, strangers—though the banality of the conversation between them is offset by the deeper *visual* intimacy, far deeper than the old bond between Locke and Rachel (or between Rachel and her coarse lover). We discern their intimacy visually, by means of the grilles and enclosures looping and linking them, excluding us. We see them in their hotel room from outside: two small figures on a balcony, their intimacy intensified by the dwarfing expanse of the wall. Only once, presumably to resolve doubts, the narrative camera intervenes to show them, at a tactfully discrete distance, down the corridor, lying on a bed, comfortably naked, side by side. Because they accept transience—the passing moment and what it brings—they have no designs on eternity, no need of that compulsive Eros that elsewhere in Antonioni's work obliterates the background and feeds compulsively on its dread of what has been excluded. Their love is fragile, casual, provisional, affectionate, natural, uncaged. They recognize each other as transients, as peregrine; as much at home in reality, both foreground and background, as it is possible to be. Their paradise is a provisional bower, daily built to suit the needs of the site, the time, and themselves. They hear the sea, they see the sky. If Locke emerges as something more than a passenger on Robertson's identity, it is in large part because of what has happened between him and the Girl. Not because love makes the world less ugly, but because it makes the void habitable and the ugliness endurable. As Robertson observes, men *do* live—with manifest dignity, as that Bedouin passing by on his camel so expressively shows us—in the desert.

In the final shot, as I said, everything converges. It is quite impossible to do this sequence, as brilliant artistically as it is technically, critical justice. Stripped of all his luggage, shielded from the blinding white light only by his green-tinted glasses—all that's left him of the green scrim of his European past—Locke checks into the modest Hotel de la Gloria. The Girl has preceded him. As though blind already, or acting out the blindness of his own fable, he asks her, now physically half removed from him (they share adjoining rooms), what she can see from the window. Framed in the glass of the wardrobe, she tells him: details of ordinary life. "And dust. It's very dusty." His eyes are shut as she sits down, touching his face, and caressing his closed eyes as though to screen them from the savage light outside. Locke tells her his parable of the blind man who recovered his sight. At first elated, like Locke in the fresh elation of Robertson's identity and the disavowal of his own, he was gradually overwhelmed by the ugliness around him, then locked himself into the darkness. Three years later he killed himself. Locke's story is clearly about himself, but also about the embowered world he has left behind. In that world too the curtains are drawn against the naked white light of an intolerable reality. Its denizens are those who have, by long habit, blinded themselves, instinctively screening out the light, accustoming themselves to "living" in darkness. Unlike the Girl, herself a native of that world, *they* never leave it, fearing everything that would suddenly be revealed—the dirt, the ugliness, the boredom—if they left the organized pretense of their boxes. Humankind, as Antonioni's favorite poet wrote, "cannot bear very much reality."

Blindness and sight. One need not be a classicist to see here at least a casual resemblance to that Oedipus who, when he had eyes, could not see; and came to see, like Tiresias, only when his blindness made it possible to see with visionary eyes. And there are the Tiresias-like figures of the film's two old men—the old man with the cane in the Umbraculo, who reminds Locke of the recurrently enacted human tragedy; the old man with the dog in the plaza at Osuna, watching the recurrent tragedy. Or the figure of blind man guided by a girl who acts as his eyes. And the whole controlling metaphorical structure of sight and blindness in both the Greek play and the film.

However that may be, it is clearly optics and perception which Antonioni has in mind throughout, but above all at the close, just before the final encounter with death. "Now at last I see things with a certain lucidity," said the dying Tommaso in *La notte*; sedated with morphine, only when dying does he at last see with waking vision what, as a sleepwalker drugged with work and career, he could not. Again, in *Blow-Up*, the photographer at the film's close at last sees with human eyes that reality to which his optics and professionalized routine perception have blinded him—a breakthrough that occurs only after his encounter in the park with death and transience. So with Locke here.

At dusk the sky reddens; the sun is setting. Locke tells the Girl to leave. We see her dress blowing in the gentle breeze, like the clothes on the wall in Robertson's room: something is stirring, something outside, out *there*, moving in the air. As she leaves, Locke opens the windows onto the plaza, repeating his own action in Robertson's room after discovering the dead body. We look out on the plaza: a man passing. Then we are shown Locke, the bed, the small picture hanging over the bed. The camera pans up the picture: water, a stream, vegetation, trees rising on the left, a hill or cliff, and at the top a building—a monastery it seems—and then, higher still, clouds and sky. An *ascent* from stream and trees to buildings, and then the bare hill; beyond the hill, blue sky. Locke takes a cigarette and lies down on the bed, eyes open, looking out the window. On the bed lie his discarded dark glasses. Off now, off for good. In the adjoining room the Girl, seated on a chair, huddles into herself. All we can see now is Locke's feet and legs and trunk lying right side up on the bed. Then feet and legs turn over, the body face down, in the same position as Robertson's dead body on the salmon-pink blanket of the bed where Locke found him.

Then, from outside, the slow, patient detailing of the life of the plaza. An old man, appearing with something—what?—from a door. The learner-driver car. The Girl looking back apprehensively at the barred window. The plaza itself, with its looping

Moorish wall and, through an open arch, an ogive of blue, the blue sky beyond the walled enclosure. Then the boy in the red shirt—the old violence beginning all over ("They can't get away from us")—as the murderers' Citroen drives up. Two men moving toward the camera; a girl running. Time is narrated in discrete, apparently unconnected events. Only the vantage-point seems fixed, unchanging, the camera behind the barred window looking steadily, taking in everything that unfolds before it. Slowly we become aware that even this fixed point is also moving, the eye slowly advancing while the right and left hand sides of the frame shrink, and then there is nothing but the bars and the world beyond it, and the spaces between the bars gradually widening. But at this point a motorcycle sputters, then the dull *pom* of a pistol—or is it a motor backfiring?—followed by a trumpet phrase—a bullring fanfare—in the distance, and a car driving off. And now the camera begins its long, slow glide toward freedom, floating out, ever so gently rocking, like a disembodied thing, toward the unimpeded world of the plaza. Only two bars remain in the window; a siren sounds, and, with something like a shudder, the camera—the eye, the "I," or it, whatever "it" might be that acts like this, the psyche, the soul, could it be?—squeezes through the bars. There it hesitates briefly, as though looking for a way out—what way? where?—loops in a long double curve around the plaza, feeling out this new enclosure, the larger social space of the plaza. But now we see that the plaza itself is only a larger cell, a new cage with its own barrier encircling it—that Moorish wall through which, as once through the bars of Locke's room, we glimpse the larger world beyond in the ogive of blue sky, the aperture of the wall. And now, above the wall, that larger space defines itself as a horizontal band of blue sky. The camera—a disembodied, floating X—still groping, but more purposively now, suddenly reaches the end of the wall—where sea and sky open out toward infinity and final freedom. A blue world now suddenly revealed—no bars, no impediment—in which all the blues of sea and sky in the film converge in an image of absolute transcendence. Then, finally completing its circle, the camera comes to rest on the immediate foreground, on Rachel's car, and the small bulk of the Hotel de la Gloria profiled against a blue-white sky.

Now, from outside, excluded by the grilled window from which it has just escaped, the camera looks into the room, disclosing Locke's body. But the body is no longer in the same position in which we last saw it, face downward on the bed, back turned to the light. Now feet and legs lie right side up. The body is *face-up*, as it must have been when Locke faced his murderer, looking his own death in the face. It is astonishingly elliptic, but an ellipsis wholly characteristic of a director who fastidiously disdains traditional narrative realism, insistently demanding that the visuals, not the script, carry the essentials of the story. As in poetry, whose meaning often lies in the density of the unspoken thing, so here the crucial fact of Locke's possession of his own identity is wholly contained in a single visual sequence. In all of Antonioni's work, there is no more extreme ellipsis than this. To fulfill Robertson's fate, Locke has only to die. This he can do as we see him preparing to do, turning over on his stomach like the blind man in his own parable, passively waiting for death. Up to this point, Locke's fate is parallel to, superimposed upon, Robertson's. Until now the narrative question has been: Will Locke have the courage to fulfill the identity he has usurped? He is a passenger on Robertson's passport, as the Girl is a passenger on his destiny, "along for the ride." Locke became a passenger in part because he was sick of being an observer. Robertson and Locke both die as strangers and transients in another country to which they come as nomads. They both die, like strangers, in rented rooms. Locke, in short, fulfills Robertson's destiny, keeps Robertson's appointments. But, much more important, he also dies *his own*—Locke's own—death. In dying, he comes upon himself, becomes himself. In Antonioni's ellipsis—the turning-over, face upward, to the light, confronting death—lies the essential, self-defining individual act: a decision to face death, life, reality with seeing eyes, unshielded, without spectacles, just as in a parallel death and passion, the Chadian victim faces the firing-squad. This body in the bed is not that of "Robertson" played by an actor simulating him in life and death; nor is it any longer the body of Locke, the old Locke, as Rachel and the Girl make clear in their identification of the body.

I spoke of a "passion." However secular or elliptical, Locke's death is also a passion—lower-case, to be sure—and part of a lower-case secular gloria. That passion and gloria mark the attainment of an unfolding destiny. Locke's fate is one in which his own self-awareness and emergent "decision" are implied. He chooses to risk death and thereby freely participates in his own unfolding fate. At the outset it was *something* in Locke—that generic human quest for *ti allo*, for meaning and a redeeming purpose—that drew him to the desert. There is in Locke, we come to see, an interior void. He *is* the desert to which he is drawn. But the film steadily inflects the idea of the desert. Like death in Bakhtin's famous phrase, the desert is pregnant. This void world, image by image, is refined as a void in which there is a mysterious tremor, a strange expectancy. A *living* void: we think the air is dead, but the clothes on the wall begin to stir; the black dots in the foreground reveal themselves as running goats; the silence seems absolute until broken by the sound of an insect buzzing. And, scene by scene, image by image, Locke's emptiness is shown to be *like* this desert. His hollowness begins to stir as, one by one, the collection of useless habits that once defined him, and the defences he still carries with him, fall away. His silence increases; the prepared script of past life and professional "viewpoint" are discarded for a kind of rudimentary and daily improvised "action." He is the hollow man who, precisely because he is hollow, is capable of being filled, of becoming more than himself; whose emptiness is the condition of his transcendence. Negative transcendence, as in Eliot's poem:

> In order to arrive there,
> To arrive where you are, to get from where you are not,
> You must go by a way in which there is no ecstasy. . .
> In order to possess what you do not possess
> You must go by the way of dispossession,
> In order to arrive at what you are not
> You must go through the way in which you are not.[11]

Again it is the hollow man who, because he is hollow, can reveal the generic beneath the individual, the genotype that precedes the phenotype. Locke transcendent reveals, as his individual habits and old identity dissolve, the generic human hunger for transcendence and meaning. *We* are Locke. Hence the informing parallel with the pilgrim or saint, whose assumption is a literal elevation *out of* and *beyond* himself in an ecstasy which means not joy but loss of self, passage into a larger life. Hence also the parallel with evolving Pleistocene man who dies as the forest creature he used to be in order to adapt to the dangerous void in which a changing environment, a changed world, require him—and us—to live. For that void is ours, the viewers'; now that our world has changed, we too must strip away the habits that bind us to the Eden we have lost. We must adapt or die, even when adaptation means dying out of oneself, dying into change.

This *trasumar—transhumanization—*is the meaning of the final shot. We see first the "soul" separating from the body, body and soul "riving," just as the camera "awareness" squeezes with a final shudder through the bars of its cell, out into the larger world of others, the great social "arena" of the plaza—another form of the void that lures Locke from the beginning: the world of the collective life, participation in the endlessly repeated human tragedy, acceptance of life and death. And, finally, a third transcendence as "it" gropes its way along the wall of the plaza, seeking the blue it can see through the wall and above it, and finally breaks through into the freedom of blue sea, blue sky.

Down below the lights at dusk come on, and over the door of the Hotel de la Gloria the stained-glass panel lights up—red, green, blue—in sign of a secular glory attained. The lights burn more brightly now, the rightly modest image of the building outlined against the sky; from within, a din of voices—men, women, children. An affirming image of the ordinary world at its ancient business of figuring, and transfiguring, itself. A real, an ordinary world. Profiled against a larger evening sky of darkening milky blue, the doorway grows slowly, gradually luminous. But the light is immanent radiating from within, not without. And this ordinary white light generates a small panel of warm colors glowing above the door, as a kind of supervening chromatic Gloria, white becoming color just as the ordinary generates the extraordinary, or as body, by virtue of some evolving aspiration, out of its own discontent, its feeling of being void and incomplete, creates a spirit of its own, a soul.

The gloria born of this conviction of inward discontent—the feeling of incompleteness, of a needy inner void which produces

63

the hunger for *ti allo*—is nowhere better expressed than by Leopardi, in many ways so like Antonioni, above all in his anguish of solitude and his obsession with transience and mortality, and his lifetime preoccupation with that metaphysical tedium which Italians call *noia*:

> *Noia* is in some sense the most sublime of human emotions. Not that I believe the examination of this emotion yields the consequences which many philosophers have sought to derive from it. And yet our inability to be satisfied by any earthly thing or even by the entire earth. . . . To imagine the infinite number of worlds and the infinite universe and feel that our minds and desires would still be greater than such a universe; *always to accuse things of insufficiency and nothingness, and to suffer the want and the void: this seems to me the best proof of the grandeur and nobility of human nature.*[12]

WILLIAM ARROWSMITH

NOTES

1. In "Antonioni Speaks—and Listens." An interview by Renée Epstein. *Film Comment*, iii, 4 (July/August, 1975), p. 7.

2. See Antonioni's own account of the filming of the final seven-minute shot in the plaza of Osuna in "Michelangelo Antonioni discusses 'The Passenger,'" *Filmmakers Newsletter*, viii, 9 (July 1975), p. 25.

3. See "Antonioni Returns in a Film Reflecting a Religioso Turn" in *Variety*, Oct. 4, 1978, p. 6. The title *Patire o morire* is the motto of the Carmelite Order founded by St. Theresa. Antonioni's narrative nucleus for the script of this uncompleted film is "Quel corpo di fango" in the director's collection entitled *Quel Bowling sul Tevere* (Turin, 1983), to be published in English translation by Oxford University Press in early 1986. Production on the film was actually begun in 1979; the cast included Francesco De Sapio, Giancarlo Giannini, Mick Jagger, Amy Irving, and Romolo Valli. The film was abandoned for financial reasons.

4. Roger Shattuck, *Marcel Proust* (N.Y. 1976), pp. 103 ff.

5. The disappearing "hero" of Pirandello's novel, *Il fu Mattia Pascal* (*The Late Mattia Pascal*), who takes advantage, unsuccessfully, of his own reported death to make a new life for himself.

6. *Paradiso*, i, 70-2.

7. Only the perceptive Penelope Gilliatt has noticed the religious nature of Locke's gesture and posture—in "a position like a Muslim praying." *The New Yorker* (April 14, 1975), 112.

8. Edward's words in *The Cocktail Party*, Act I, Scene 2.

9. By Eugene Marais. Published, with introduction by Robert Ardrey, in New York and London in 1969. Marais was a South African zoologist, the author of *My Friends the Baboons, The Soul of the Ape*, and *The Soul of the White Ant* (a study of South African termitaries, plagiarized by the Nobel laureate Maurice Maeterlink).

10. For the same visual idea-image, compare the scene in *Red Desert* in which Corrado discusses his Argentinian expedition with the workers he hopes to recruit. The empty blue demijohns—designed for oil or wine—are an image of those workers over whose faces the camera pans, suggestive of their condition: human beings stacked for export, but also men anxious, empty, drained, their own internal void corresponding to the unknown world to which they are being expelled.

11. From "East Coker" in *The Four Quartets*.

12. *Pensieri*, 68. Roughly the same idea is expressed in Eliot's famous dictum: "We mean all sorts of things, I know, by Beauty. But the essential advantage for a poet is not, to have a beautiful world with which to deal: it is to be able to see beneath both beauty and ugliness; to see the boredom, and the horror, and the glory."

THE YOUNG WIDOW STUDIES THE SKY

1

The sky looked just like this the day
He taught me how to step off cliffs backwards.
What did I trust that afternoon? I leaned
Backwards over the Palisades Kepler ledge.
Did he trust the webbed nylon strap he'd wrapped
Around my hips? Or my boots with their gussetted
Tongues? Or the three-strand, five-thousand-pound
Tested rope that belted him to the basswood
And me to him? Below, the stones on the shore
Looked like pebbles. What good would the spun-glass
Helmet have done? I stepped into the air.
For a moment my feet found nothing to kick
Against. Then all I could do was lean back
Against the rope. He lowered me past the wasp
Nests, past the crumbling ledges, past the juniper
Seedlings rooted in handfuls of dirt, past the smooth
Face of rock studded with steel pitons, slowly
Past the tops of the willows and cottonwoods.
I landed beside the river. When I looked
Up, there was just a limestone cliff between us.

2

We were painting the back porch. We looked up
And saw a small cloud descending on our aluminum
Ladder. We backed down and stood in the driveway.
We even forgot to argue. We just stood there,
His arm touching mine, waiting to get stung.
We could have gone inside. But we just stood
There, with our eyes closed. The swarm surrounded
Us, soft pellets striking our feet, necks, legs,
And faces, whirring like hundreds of metal-edged
Pinwheels. They turned the air into something viscous,
Until it seemed we stood underwater, and then
We were the water, our skins the top of a lake
Pockmarked in a storm. Did I think we were two

Trees whose roots crossed each other so often they'd never
Be hacked apart? We just stood there, watching
Them ripple on the porch roof. They wove themselves
Into a blanket of gray-gold mohair, tailored
Themselves to fit the dovetail joints, the dogwood trees,
And then the sumac. We laughed at the stripes of barn red
House paint smeared on the outsides of our thighs.

ELEGY

In Wainwright they say the plane went down in the Brooks Range,
    perhaps near Porcupine River, or perhaps in the Arctic Ocean;
It was spring, the rivers were breaking up, and the mist settled in
    for weeks.
The plane went down in March, when it rains one day and snows
    the next;
When the ice fields split into islands big enough to crush ships.
The plane went down in the early spring, when the snow still
    drifts in the wind, snow so fine it works into the tightest
    weave of a man's coat;
In the north, where the snow is hardened and serrated by winter
    winds, where metal sled runners wear out in days, and where
    men do not leave heel marks;
In the spring, when the winds begin to drop, when the snow turns
    soft and honeycombed, and cannot support a man's weight;
In the spring, when the winds leave, and the insects come, swarms
    of insects that can weaken a man until he cannot walk;
In the far north, where magnetic compasses are useless.
Snowshoe frames can be made of metal from plane keels, sleds
    built from wings, harnesses woven from shroud lines;
Cloudy streams of fresh water can be found; and salmon, tomcod,
    needlefish, and pike caught;
But the Brooks Range stretches from Cape Lisburne to
    Demarcation Point, and few of its mountains are mapped.
The plane went down in the north, where valley glaciers crack
    into crevasses above deep, granite beds;
In the spring, when rivers swell with melt water, when
    snowbridges are swept away, and debris dams up the streams;
In the north, where the overflow fills the flatland with shallow,
    swampy lakes.
Beaver, marmot, and ground squirrel can be trapped; and molting
    spruce grouse, arctic loon, and ptarmigan can be snared.
Bushes can be dug for the starchy roots; cup-fungus, bracken,
    and the inner white bark of willow, poplar, and birch can be
    eaten;

But the north is filled with rose-capped mushroom, water
hemlock, baneberry, and amanita.

A plane crashed six years ago in the Bering Sea, in water so cold
it paralyzed the pilot's hands, but he used his teeth to lash
himself to a raft with ripcord.

A man went under for forty minutes in the Yukon River, but was
pulled up breathing because the water had been just cold
enough.

But masses of sea-ice crowd into the bays in the spring, colliding
with each other and the coast, and the booming can be heard
for miles.

A woman lifted an ice-wall in Kotzebue, fracturing her spine, but
she held the ice up so her husband could crawl out.

A plane crashed near Eagle, and a woman dragged her husband
from the fuselage, and she melted snow in her mouth, and
brought it to him, until help came.

A Galena trapper was lost two years ago, but his wife waited, and
pounded beef suet, berries, and bacon with a wooden mallet
into pemmican, for his next trip out, and he was found;

But tundra streams wander aimlessly in the spring, and often lead
to marshes filled with mosquitoes, midges, and blackflies.

CHRISTIANNE BALK

THE GULLY

1

The man called Freckle Face, whose true name was Naldo de Araujo, was a busdriver with a dangerous route—through the Gully and along the waterfront to the airport and back, turning around at Central Square, where all the buses turn around, and doing it again, four times a day. He was only twenty years old, unmarried and making good money as a driver, and despite his many freckles and reddish hair, he was attractive to the women, possibly because he had lots of money to spend on taking them dancing, buying them Johnny Walker Red and giving them little presents, such as nylons and stuffed animals. He lived for the women, as he himself often said, and when he was robbed in his bus in the Gully in the middle of the day twice in one week, he was angry enough to kill someone for it, especially after the cops laughed at him and the dispatcher at the bus depot told him that if he got robbed one more time this month he would be fired.

"It's company policy, Freckle Face," he said. "Three times in a month, and you're gone, man." The dispatcher stood in the garage holding his clipboard, waiting for the keys to the bus.

"Why?" Freckle Face asked. "What the hell good does it do to fire the driver?"

"Sometimes the drivers are in cahoots with the thieves. Not that you'd do such a thing, but even so, the company's got to have a policy."

Freckle Face handed over the keys, stalked out of the garage and went straight to a gambler he knew in the Gully two blocks from where he lived and bought a dark blue .45 and box of bullets. He put the loaded gun inside his lunch bag, and when a few days later he stopped at the corner of Angelina and Fourteenth and picked up two men wearing rumpled tan safari jackets to cover the pistols stuck in their belts, Freckle Face simply waited until they had paid and sat down, one of them way in the rear and the other directly behind him, as usual with thieves, and he reached down to his lunch bag on the floor, drew out the .45, spun around and shot the man behind him in the eye.

The other man leapt out the back door to the street and started running. Freckle Face grabbed the first one's pistol from where it had fallen to the floor, stepped over the man's body and jumped to the street, like Gary Cooper or Clint Eastwood, a gun in each hand. People in the bus and on the sidewalks, mostly women and children at this time of day, were terrified, a few were screaming, but when Freckle Face took off down the street after the second thief, everyone stepped back for him and cheered.

He caught the guy in a dead-end alley behind a Pakistani restaurant, and he shot him twice, first in the chest and then, up close, in the head. He took his gun, too, and walked quickly back to the bus, which was still sitting at the corner of Angelina and Fourteenth with the doors open and the motor running. He climbed into the bus, dragged the body of the first thief out to the street, put all three guns into his lunch bag and continued down Angelina and on out to the airport.

He himself never mentioned the event to anyone, but in a short time everyone knew about it—the dispatcher, the other drivers, the people and merchants in the Gully and the thieves. People started waiting especially for Freckle Face's bus, letting earlier buses go past. He was extremely popular with the women on his route, who smiled and hitched their dresses up their thighs a little as they climbed the steps of his bus and dropped their coins into his hand. No one, of course, mentioned to Freckle Face that they knew what he was carrying inside his lunch bag, and no one said anything to the police about it. When the police had driven into the Gully in a van to pick up the bodies of the two thieves, everyone on the street denied knowing how the men had died. "Who knows?" they shrugged. "Somebody just dumped the bodies there sometime during the night or maybe this morning when no one was looking. It happens all the time around here. You know that."

2

Over on the north side of the Gully, not far from the bus depot, a young man called Chink, whose real name was Felipe da Silva, worked in his parents' bakery with his mother, father and two younger sisters. One morning when he came into work late and hungover and expecting the usual harangue from his father, he met instead with the aftermath of a massacre. Apparently, moments before, robbers had walked into the shop and killed with guns and machetes all four members of Chink's family plus two customers, elderly ladies from the neighborhood. The white walls, floors, even the ceiling, were splattered with blood, grisly maps showing where the people had met their deaths and how. Chink's sisters had been shot in the front room of the shop, where they worked behind the counter, and the two old neighborhood ladies had been killed, each of them shot once behind the ear, just inside the door. They had probably walked in on the robbery. Chink's father had been cut down by a machete at the doorway leading from the back room, where the ovens were located, and his mother, also chopped practically in half by the machete, had been slain near the back door, evidently fleeing from the carnage.

Chink paused before each body, examined it for a second, stepped over it to the next, careful not to step into the huge spreading smears of thickening blood and flour, until he had worked his way to the back, where he found his mother's body. Opening the door to the alley in back, he stepped outside, and when he looked down to the ground, as if to pray or vomit, he saw several pairs of white footprints that led down the alley toward the rear of the building.

Instantly, Chink set off in pursuit of whomever had laid down the tracks. He jogged the length of the alley, turned left behind the building and climbed over a ramshackle wood fence to another alley, passed through to a packed dirt yard shared by the backsides of a half dozen tin-roof shanties, where he followed the white footprints across the yard to the rear of an old dark green panel truck sitting wheel-less up on cinderblocks. He tiptoed to the rear door of the truck and listened and heard the men inside counting the few miserable dollars they had taken from the bakery. Then he walked out to the street to a filling station, boldly stole a five gallon can of gasoline and brought it back to the panel truck, where he splashed the gasoline onto the packed dirt ground all around the truck, especially at the rear door, and poured more gas over the top and along the sides. Lastly, he dropped an old piece of iron pipe into the latch, jamming it, and lit a match, tossed it at the truck and ran.

Many people had watched the entire process from the beginning, and no one said or did a thing to stop Chink, and when the truck exploded in flames, the folks in the shanties, many of them mothers with babies on their hips, shouted with obvious pleasure. Later, when the firemen had put out the flames and had opened the rear door, three charred, utterly unrecognizeable bodies were discovered huddled inside. No one from the shanties knew who they were, how they got locked inside the truck or who doused the truck with gasoline and set it on fire. "We were inside cooking," they said. And no one—that is, no one from the police and fire departments—connected the bizarre incineration of the three young men in the panel truck to the massacre of the six people in the bakery two blocks away. In the neighborhood, however, everyone knew of the connection and spoke of Chink with sympathy and admiration, even those who used to think of him as a lazy, drunken playboy supported by his industrious family in a manner he did not deserve.

3

Then there was Saverio Gomes Macedo, called Tarzan, because of his great size and overdeveloped physique and the special way he cupped his hands around his mouth and yelled, which he liked to do at the start of every day. He would untangle himself from his hammock on the porch of his grandmother's shanty, step to the standpipe by the alley where the people were already lining up to fill their pans and jars with water for cooking, and he'd give his yell and beat good-naturedly on his enormous chest.

In exchange for caring for his aged grandmother, who was crippled with arthritis, Tarzan was allowed to sleep on the porch of her one-room cabin. Now and then he got himself hired for daywork, hauling bricks or laying sewerpipe down by the waterfront where the government was building hotels for foreigners, but most of the time he had no money and depended on his grandmother for everything. She, in turn, depended on her children, Tarzan's aunts and uncles, several of whom now lived in Florida and sometimes sent money.

The daughter who was Tarzan's mother had died of cancer many years ago, and no one knew who his father was. Thus Tarzan and his grandmother were extremely close, as close as mother and son. They spent most of their days and evenings sitting out on the shaded, tilted porch of the tiny cabin, where they watched the people pass on the street and chatted and gossiped about the old days and people they used to know. Despite his great size and obvious high spirits, Tarzan was in many ways like a little old man, which, of course, delighted his grandmother and amused everyone in the neighborhood who knew them.

For that reason most people were amazed by the transformation that Tarzan went through when his grandmother was killed. Her death was an unfortunate accident, and perhaps they expected him simply to accept it, as they would have, but he treated it as if it were a cold-blooded murder. Two drug dealers in the neighborhood got into a scuffle over money, not an unusual event, and while chasing each other down the alleys and across the yards of the neighborhood, shooting at each other whenever they caught sight of each other, one of them (it was never determined which one) shot Tarzan's grandmother, who was sitting on the porch waiting for Tarzan to come home from the store. She died instantly, shot in the throat, just as Tarzan rounded the corner and saw the pair of drug dealers dart between cars on the street, still shooting at one another, heading out of the neighborhood into an other. He roared, pounded his chest in rage, frightening those who heard him, and took off after the drug dealers.

He caught up with them late that night in the back room of a bar out near the airport. Apparently they had settled their differences and were once again doing business with one another, when Tarzan, huge with his anger and his fearlessness, walked into the dingy room, grabbed the two scrawny punks and dragged them out to the street. It was raining, and the street was quiet and almost empty, as Tarzan broke the pair's heads against each other, smashing them like cantalopes, again and again.

The bartender and the few customers who were there at the time later described with a kind of horror, a horror oddly mixed with pride, the sound of the skulls cracking as the enormous young man slammed the two men's heads against one another. Then, when clearly they were dead in his hands, Tarzan tossed the pair like sacks of garbage into the gutter and walked off in the rain. After that, because for a while the drug dealers stayed away, but also because of his pain, Tarzan was a hero in the neighborhood.

74

4

In the Gully, true heroes were almost nonexistent. Politicians and soldiers had lived off the people for generations, and athletes, singers, actors, figures whose faces were used to sell things people either did not otherwise want or could not afford, were, because of that, no longer trusted or admired or even envied. In the Gully, people had grown cynical. It was their only defense against being used over and over to fatten the already fat. They had learned long ago that it's the poor who feed the rich, not vice versa. And finally, when it was almost too late and they had almost nothing left to give to the rich, to the politicians, to the businessmen, to the foreigners, finally, the people of the Gully had turned away from all projects and enterprises, all plans, all endeavors that depended for their completion on hope. And when you give up hope and do it on principle, when you do it because you have learned that hope is *bad* for you, then you give up on heroes as well.

That is why, when Freckle Face heard people praise Chink and then Tarzan and saw how people admired them for their pain and rage, when, in short, he realized that he and the other two had become heroes, where before there were none, he determined to capitalize on it as swiftly as possible, before people settled back into their old and extremely useful way of dismissing heroism as a ruse.

He organized a meeting of the three in the back room of a café close to his rooming house, and when they had shaken hands, each of them slightly in awe of the other two, for they were as unused to genuine heroes as everyone else in the Gully, Freckle Face got quickly down to business. His plan was to build a watch-tower in the center of the Gully and for one of them to be posted there at all times, and when he saw a robbery going on, to give the signal, and the others would chase down the robbers and kill them.

"What for?" Chink asked.

"For money," Freckle Face said.

"Who'd pay us?" Tarzan wanted to know. "The police don't care."

"The robbers' victims," Freckle Face said. "We just return what was stolen and ask for a percentage for our troubles."

"It's wrong to kill for money," Tarzan said.

"God kills. You just pull the trigger," Chink observed. He was definitely interested. Since the death of his parents and sisters, the bakery had been closed, and Chink was down to panhandling on Central Square with a sign hanging from around his neck saying, "Help the Avenger of the Bakery Massacre!"

Tarzan needed money, too. With his grandmother's death, his uncles and aunts had sold her shanty to a man on the Heights who rented out hundreds of shanties in the Gully. Consequently, Tarzan had lately been sleeping under two sheets of corrugated iron in back of a warehouse where he hoped to find work as a warehouseman, as soon as his aunt in Florida sent him the money he needed to bribe the foreman to hire him.

Freckle Face was not much better off. His popularity as a bus driver had cut into the income of the other drivers, and in recent weeks Freckle Face had come into work and found water in his gas tank one day, his tires slashed the next, or a radiator hose cut, a distributor cap missing, every day another lengthy repair job that kept him in the garage, until he was taking home less than half of what he had been earning before the robberies. He'd stopped buying presents for his girlfriends, and they in turn had stopped turning down other guys. He used to be able to get several women to share him; now, despite being a hero, he could barely get one woman to wait for him to get off work and take her out dancing. A hero without money is just another man.

5

In short order, Freckle Face, Chink and Tarzan were making more money than they had ever imagined possible. Quickly, they had specialized, Tarzan as lookout, because of his ability to call out the location and escape route of a thief spotted from the watchtower. He owned a voice so loud and clear that every time he gave the alarm, the entire neighborhood became instantly involved in the pursuit and capture of the thief. Often, all Chink and Freckle Face had to do was follow along the pathway in the street that the crowd opened up for them and run directly down the alley people pointed at, enter the basement door indicated by an old woman with her chin, cross into the corner of the basement that stood exposed by a watchman with a flashlight, where

Chink would take out the .45 Freckle Face had given him and fire two bullets neatly into the man's head. That was Chink's specialty, shooting, and he did seem to believe that God did the killing, he only did the shooting.

Freckle Face's specialty might be called public relations. It was he who unclamped the dead thief's fingers from the stolen money and delivered it back to the shopowner or pedestrian who'd been robbed, and he, therefore, who negotiated the price of the return, he who divided the fee three ways. Also, when it became clear that, if they wished, they could expand their business to other neighborhoods in the Gully, it was Freckle Face who arranged to have the new lookout towers build, he who hired new lookouts, shooters and collectors, and he who knew to put Tarzan in charge of all the lookouts and train them to cup their hands just so and call out exactly, clearly, where the thieves were running to. It was Freckle Face who put Chink in charge of procuring weapons for the shooters and training them to use their guns efficiently and responsibly, and of course it was he who trained the collectors, implemented the commission system based on the system used by the bus company and kept track of all the accounts.

6

By now, Tarzan owned his own house on the Heights, where he liked to throw wild, lavish parties by the pool, and Chink lived in a condominium on the waterfront, where he kept a forty-foot cabin cruiser anchored year round, and Freckle Face was rumored to be sleeping with the daughter of the Prime Minister. They had come a long ways from the Gully and did not believe they would ever have to return, especially Freckle Face, who had made a whole new set of friends who called him Naldo and barely knew where in the city the Gully was located.

Sometimes, though, late at night, Freckle Face would get up from the bed he shared with the daughter of the Prime Minister, and he'd cross the parquet floor to the louvered doors that led to the terrace, and out on the terrace in the silvery moonlight he'd lean over the balustrade, light a cigarette and look down and across the sleeping city all the way to the Gully. He'd stand there till dawn, smoking and waiting for the sun to come up and for the people down in the Gully to come out of their shanties and go for water, start up their cookfires, head down to the waterfront looking for work or out to the airport to panhandle tourists or over to Central Square just to hang out. Freckle Face, miles away, up on his terrace, wearing a blue silk robe and smoking French cigarettes, would say over and over to himself, as if it were an incantation, I don't live there anymore, and no one I know lives there. The people who go on living there must want to live there, or they'd leave. Look at Tarzan, look at Chink, look at me!

Then, reassured, he'd go inside, shower, shave and dress and walk downstairs for breakfast, where the first thing he'd do is read the morning newspaper for the names and addresses of thieves shot last night in the Gully. After breakfast, he'd drive out in his brown Mercedes and call on the families of the dead thieves, offering first his condolences and then his card and a special cut-rate coffin and burial service from his Our Lady of the Gully Funeral Parlor chain. Later, he'd drop by the office and go over the figures. After that, lunch. Then a workout and massage. Then—who knows? Real estate, maybe. Import-export. Hotels. Life is surprising.

RUSSELL BANKS

ON MANDELSTAM'S *JOURNEY TO ARMENIA*

I have made use of two separate texts. Next Editions, of London, has issued a beautifully produced edition of Clarence Brown's translation (copyright 1980) of *Journey to Armenia*—I take my citations from that. The other available version, translated by Jane Gary Harris and Constance Link, can be found in the Ardis volume: *Mandelstam: The Complete Critical Prose and Letters*. This book includes the "Addenda" material that Mandelstam did not use in the final version.

I stress repeatedly that *Journey to Armenia* cannot be paraphrased; indeed, it seems calculated to rebuff all reductive or analytic strategies. This is, finally, a part of its great charm. However, it puts the essayist/commentator in a tough spot. I urge my reader to read the *Journey* first.

Journey was, incidentally, the last of Mandelstam's works to be published in his lifetime. It appeared in 1933 in the Leningrad journal *Zvezda* (The Star)—the publisher subsequently lost his job.—SB.

"I had only one book with me, Goethe's *Italienische Reise* in an expensive leather binding, as worn from use as a Baedeker."
—From the "Addenda" to *Journey to Armenia*

In the Spring of 1930, Osip and Nadezhda Mandelstam set off for an eight-month trip to Armenia. So might run the deceptive syntax of the "shilling life." But as any reader of Nadezhda Mandelstam's *Hope Against Hope* or *Hope Abandoned* knows, there was no such propositional simplicity in their lives—ever. They did go to Armenia, yes. But it was a going attended by tremendous symbolic and circumstantial complexity. In retrospect, the journey would, like Goethe's abrupt flight from Weimar to Italy, stand for a great deal more than a set of remembered particulars. Armenia, with its sun and its ancient simplicity, was a gift bestowed upon one whose life was being clipped "like a coin." Before it could be viewed in retrospect, however, it had to hover before him as a prospect, a dream to hold against the anxious pressures of the present.

For the five-year period between 1925 and 1930, Mandelstam, without question one of the most gifted lyric poets of our—or any—age, wrote no poetry. As these were the ripest years of the poet's maturity—he was in his mid-30's—this barrenness could only have had the most devastating inward effects. Of course, there is always a danger in trying to account for creativity, or its absence. But we have some warrant for considering the political and cultural situation of the day and Mandelstam's relation to it. Nadezhda Mandelstam reports, of the period in question, that her husband was trying, against his own instincts, to align himself with the attitudes and purposes of the emerging Soviet State. He believed, she writes, that his "oath to the fourth estate obliged him to come to accept the . . . regime." Whatever his outward demeanor at the time, it's not unlikely that the barometric pressure in his soul was dropping steadily.

In 1929, the storm broke. A journalist named David Zaslavsky accused Mandelstam publicly of having plagiarized a translation of *Til Eulenspeigel.* Mandelstam had, of course, done nothing of the kind. But the fury with which he was attacked, and the promptness with which official favor was withdrawn, showed him how things really stood; and, given the distribution of lines of force, how they were likely to continue to stand.

Mandelstam knew that his public career was scuttled. Privately, however, he appears to have experienced a tremendous liberation. Freed from a despised obeisance, sure now that his writing was for the drawer and not for the censor's eye, he felt a resurgence of creative energies. In December of 1929, he wrote his *Fourth Prose,* a declaration of independence—and a pledge of self-allegiance—which still reads as if it had been seared into the page with an acetylene torch:

> It was all as terrifying as a child's nightmare. *Nel mezzo del'cammin di nostra vita*—midway along life's path—I was stopped in the dense Soviet forest by bandits who called themselves my judges. . . . It was the first and only time in my life that Literature had need of me, and it crushed, pawed, and squeezed me, and it was all as terrifying as a child's nightmare.

In the decade remaining to him, Mandelstam would write not only the *Journey to Armenia* and the *Conversation About Dante*—the most remarkable work of poetic interpretation ever written—but also some of his finest lyrics.

The Armenian journey began just a few months after the discharge of *Fourth Prose.* Arrangements and permissions came through the office of Nikolai Bukharin, Mandelstam's sole remaining ally in power (Bukharin would be executed a few years later in one of Stalin's purges). If Mandelstam had any specific premonition of his fate, he did not confide it to the page. The *Journey to Armenia*, composed a year after his return, is almost pure celebration. The land, the people, his own rekindled senses—everything is heralded with energy and enthusiasm. Only in the very last passage does he remind us of the pitched battle between the poet's vision and will of the tyrant; only there does he reveal what he knows—that a happiness so pure will never come his way again.

*

If *Fourth Prose* represented Mandelstam's liberation, his acceptance of his poet's destiny, then *Journey to Armenia* is perhaps the first great bursting of the vocal pod. It is, like some of Mandelstam's other ventures into prose, utterly singular. Though we get all kinds of vivid glimpses—sensory and anecdotal —of Armenia, we could not really call the work a travelogue. It is as much about Impressionist painting, naturalism, chess and music as it is about places, customs or people. In its midst we find oddly-proportioned vignettes about the poet's Moscow neighbors. What's more, while some parts seem to be addressed to the general reader, other parts retain the intimate address of a personal letter; in fact, Mandelstam wrote sections of it for Boris Kuzin, a biologist he befriended in the course of his visit.

Journey to Armenia cannot be summarized or circumscribed in any fashion. The closest resemblance is to a writer's workbook. Reading through it for the first time, we suspect that the poet has culled through his insights and observations and has put them together pell-mell; that he is hoping to hold his reader through force of style alone. With a lesser writer we would absorb what pleasures the prose could offer and continue on our way.

But this is Mandelstam, who just a year later in his *Conversation About Dante* would write: ". . . where there is amenability to paraphrase, there the sheets have never been rumpled, there poetry . . . has never spent the night," and who would demonstrate in that work an unrivalled understanding of poetic structure.

Anyone who thinks I'm exaggerating should hasten to read this *Conversation*—it makes scholars, prosodists and literary critics look like lumbering primates. Anticipating wave-particle theory, Mandelstam grasped that the *Divine Comedy* was *simultaneously* a crystalloid construction of astonishing complexity and a sublimely energized system of flowing sound-waves. On one page he can liken the whole to a "thirteen-thousand-faceted form" created by bees with a stereometric instinct, on another explore its "genuine kinetic ballet." Should we imagine, then, that Mandelstam was capable of tossing off a loosely-stitched quilt of notebook entries? More likely, we should give the *Journey* a second look.

If we read the work as we would a poem, attentively, not once or twice, but many times, and if we allow its casual-seeming elements to exert their magnetic waves, we begin to discern a most striking non-linear cohesiveness. Indeed, not only is the *Journey* not arbitrary in its construction, but it proposes an entirely new kind of prose—a poetic prose which is not merely the result of a poet applying himself to a new *metier*; but a prose which utilizes on a very refined level many of the associative dynamics of poetry.

*

Even the first-time reader of *Journey to Armenia* will be struck by Mandelstam's great interest in Impressionist painting. We are only a few pages into the work before he introduces an enthralled—and seemingly irrelevant—passage on Signac (later there will be several pages devoted to his reactions to an Impressionist exhibition). The whole section is, in fact, a flashback; Mandelstam is still in Moscow, anticipating his trip, when he finds a book which contains Signac's theory of optical blending. Mandelstam's was something more than a momentary enthusiasm. He writes: "I felt a shiver of novelty; it was as if someone had called me by name. . . . In all my long life I have seen no more than a silkworm."

There is no trace of silkworm blindness in the *Journey*. On the contrary, it is as if Mandelstam is seeing, *really seeing*, for the first time in his life. His own elastic simile, which introduces the later encounter with the Impressionist masters, conveys this excitement: "I stretched my vision like a kid glove, stretched it onto a shoe-tree, onto the blue neighborhood of the sea. . . ." The prose is studded throughout with the most exuberant sightings: ". . . the light-blue policemanly phizzes of giant trout . . ."; poppies "bright to the point of surgical pain . . ."; "a lacquer painting the colour of blood coagulated with gold . . ."; "a swampy parade ground the colour of billiard cloth . . ."; tea-roses "like little scoops of yellow ice-cream. . . ."

But there is something more involved here than just a celebration of the visual sense. Mandelstam did not insert the Signac passage casually. Rather, I believe that he discovered in Signac's book the clues, or justifications, for a new compositional method for prose, and that the disruptive placement of the anecdote is meant to alert the reader.

"The author," writes Mandelstam, "explained the 'law of optical blending,' glorified the method of working with little dabs of the brush, and impressed upon one the importance of using only the pure colours of the spectrum." What the Impressionist attempts with color in three dimensions, Mandelstam will essay with units of prose—in four. The former destroys the tyranny of the subject in order to reveal the process of visual perception; Mandelstam explodes the linear and subject-centered progress of narrative so that he can expose the phenomenology of memory. His kind of impressionism has nothing of the slackness of arrangement that characterizes the efforts of second-rate talents. It is not a means of avoiding the structural imperative; rather, it implements a far more demanding—and poetic—organizational mode.

The key phrase in the above quotation is: "the importance of using only the pure colours of the spectrum." As the writer cannot refer to an objectified spectrum, as his working materials are nowhere near as distinct as colors, the only criterion for "purity" is subjective. For Mandelstam, the pure was that which his poetic sensibility had naturally seized upon and preserved. However unprepossessing its outer contours—and many of Mandelstam's observations and anecdotes are strangely oblique—the event or observation had to have survived in memory with its aura intact. He was forcing himself to keep faith with the actual grain of his experience; heightening or artificial foregrounding were forbidden.

If we think of the *Journey* as a work of impressionism, then we have to think of each passage, each quotation, as a pure color, as a patiently-distilled dab applied to the narrative plane. And just as one does not *see* an impressionist canvas except by stepping backward in space, so one cannot gauge the effect of the *Journey* without allowing for an equivalent removal in time. Only as we recede from the actual reading can we see the work for what it is: a portrait, not of a place, but of an experience. Its larger life only begins in our after-image, as it did for Mandelstam in memory.

In the Addenda material that was ultimately deleted from *Journey*, Mandelstam set down a particularly revealing observation about prose composition:

> Reality has the character of a continuum.
> Prose which corresponds to reality, no matter how expressly and minutely, no matter how efficiently and faithfully, is always a broken series.
> Only that prose is truly beautiful which is incorporated into the continuum as an entire system, although there is no power or method to prove it.

No finite prose, then, can match reality, just as no bounded canvas can faithfully represent a countryside. The creator (writer/painter) must not only select from among his perceptions, but he must arrange them so that they form a self-contained system. For the Impressionist painter, that system will be structured to the proportions and perspectives of the natural world. But for Mandelstam there is no discernible paradigm. His "system" need only correspond to the structure of the lived experience—rather, to the structure of the memory. Even though it is subjectively determined, however, it is not arbitrary. The distribution of elements—"although there is no power or method to prove it"—obeys the same psychic necessity that poetry does. And here we may add that poetic composition was, for Mandelstam, more a process of listening and discovering than of invention. "The poem," he wrote, "is alive through an inner image . . . which anticipates the written poem."

For all of this, we would nevertheless be wrong in trying to call *Journey* a poem in any sense. Though we find compression, metaphor, and a progress through association, the central propulsion does not come from the word-unit. This, for Mandelstam, was the one essential attribute of poetry: its process was philological. Whatever power was released by a line came from collisions of strata in the individual words; semantic coherence was a secondary by-product. Prose, however, was forced by its discursive nature to build itself up from semantic clusters—phrases and sentences. It is, therefore, axiomatic that prose will be more diffuse. Its echoes and cross-stitchings can only approximate those found in a poem. Still, working within these natural limits, Mandelstam created something not altogether unlike a poem.

*

In *Journey to Armenia*, Mandelstam has given poetic/symphonic development to a specific array of elements. By this I mean something more than just an implementation of patterned recurrence. For Mandelstam was interested, above all, in transformation. His dynamic is Ovidian. The "pure colours" that he has gathered from his experience move in a force-field animated by the currents of his obsession. He does not thereby distort his remembered account; if anything, he penetrates right to the springs of personal memory. In its overt particularity, *Journey* denies the very possibility of objective reportage.

At the beginning of his Dante essay, Mandelstam hails his subject as the "strategist of transmutation and hybridization," and as "the master of the instruments of poetry . . . not a manufacturer of tropes." And on the very next page, he describes poetic discourse as "a carpet fabric containing a plethora of textile warps differing from one another only in the process of coloration, only in the partitura of the perpetually changing commands of the instrumental signalling system." What Mandelstam has supplied, perhaps unwittingly, is a most astute characterization of his own prose in the *Journey to Armenia*. It is, assuredly, a most intricately woven carpet, abounding in pattern and detail, and free of the autocracy of a governing figure.

The carpet analogy is quite useful, a means of access to a work almost entirely closed to analysis. With it we can make sense of the bewildering assortment of unconnected sections that comprise the opening pages. For if we keep in mind that any woven fabric, however complex, can be traced back at its borders to isolated threads—its constituent elements—then these disparate notations turn out to have a purpose. They present, often very subtly, the materials that will eventually undergo "transmutation and hybridization"; they are, to take an analogy now from 12-tone music, the tones in the tone-row. Not until Mandelstam has laid out his separate notes is he free to begin working them together. But where music instigates its transmutations through the perpetual shifting of harmonic tension, Mandelstam's prose enacts its changing commands through the use of metaphor.

Metaphor was, for Mandelstam, less a device than an imperative; it was the mainspring, not the accompaniment, of his thought. This may derive from a clearly discernible polarization of sensibility. We find (and the following discussion will bear this out) competing drives—toward the structural and static, and toward the morphological and dynamic. We get simultaneously an absorption in the fixities of natural form *and* a fascination with the process of evolutionary change; archaeology and the live anarchy of the present; living speech and philology. In addition, we find recurrent reference to music and chess, both of which represent structure and change in their most intimate dialectical incarnation. As we shall see, Mandelstam's metaphoric transformations are the result of an incessant maneuvering between the poles of his own nature.

*

Mandelstam begins *Journey to Armenia* by locating himself, without any preliminary explanation, on the island of Sevan (Lake Sevan is Armenia's largest lake), where he "spent a month enjoying the lake water standing at a height of four thousand feet above sea level. . . ." We expect, perhaps, a leisurely description in the best 19th-century manner. But we get nothing of the kind. Instead, the very next paragraph gives us a startling image of trout feeding at sunset, causing the water to roil up "as though a huge pinch of soda had been flung into it." And the following paragraphs rapidly catalogue wind conditions, the ubiquity of mischievous children, tall "juicy" grasses ("one felt like coiffing them with an iron comb"), and—everywhere—the "fiery red slabs of nameless graves."

We have scarcely begun to take in these descriptive cues when Mandelstam shunts us off onto another track. Quite abruptly, he begins an account of an expedition he took to a recently uncovered burial site. He introduces a certain Professor Khachaturian, "whose face was stretched over with eagle skin beneath which all the muscles and ligaments stood out, numbered and with their Latin names." But of the visit itself we learn little, except that Mandelstam carried away in his handkerchief "the porous calcified crust of someone's cranium."

The sections follow in quick succession. More uncentered anecdotes, more single-stroke characterizations. On another of his day-trips, Mandelstam notices the completed frame of a barge and remarks upon its "fresh musical proportions." On yet another occasion, a visit to the Institute of Eastern Peoples, he reports, without much explanation:

Owing to my incorrect subjective orientation, I have fallen into the habit of regarding every Armenian as a philologist. Which is, however, partly right. These are people who jangle the keys of language even when they are not using them to unlock any treasures.

And a few paragraphs later, we find him staring at the enormous head of one Comrade Ovanesian, musing all the while about the Armenian etymology of the word "head."

It is then, in the section entitled ZAMOSKVORECHIE, that Mandelstam retails his discovery, while still in Moscow, of Signac's book on Impressionism. Next, continuing the Moscow interlude, he devotes short passages to the toppling of an ancient linden tree, to his friend B.S.K. (Boris Kuzin), to a confused going-away celebration where the conversation is compared to "the knight's move, always swerving to one side. . . ." Narrative considerations, we now realize, will be irrelevant to the *Journey*. What possible link could there be between the remembered farewell and this subsequent insert:

> When I was a child a stupid sort of touchiness, a false pride, kept me from ever going out to look for berries or stooping down over mushrooms. Gothic pinecones and hypocritical acorns in their monastic caps pleased me more than mushrooms. I would stroke the pinecones. They would bristle. . . . In their shelled tenderness, in their geometrical gaping I sensed the rudiments of architecture, the demon of which has accompanied me throughout my life.

However brilliant the prose—and already we have seen innumerable flashings from Mandelstam's quartz-light—we cannot quite shake the impression that these are inspired jottings. They simply do not add up to a narrative or a portrait, whatever their local merits. But now, one fourth of the way into the text, something begins to happen. Mandelstam, it seems, has finished arranging his threads; he is ready to begin working them together.

"Only last year on the island of Sevan in Armenia, as I was strolling in the waist-high grass, I was captivated by the pagan burning of the poppies." The perplexing Moscow interlude is done with, and we are returned to our point of origin. The grass is again mentioned. And the poppies, as Mandelstam goes on to describe their astonishing color, recall for us the "pure colours" of Signac. Then, in the very next sentence, Mandelstam describes the flowers as "gawking butterflies" that grow on "disgusting hairy stalks." From now on, virtually every phrase will plait together with something else. The butterfly, for example, returns a few pages later. Observing a particular specimen, Mandelstam notes that its thorax "is strong, shaped like a little boat." We recall the skeletal barge with its "fresh musical proportions," not to mention a half-dozen other boats that have been mentioned in the narrative. As for the poppy's "hairy stalk," it reverberates perfectly with his later characterization of the Abkhazian language—with its "gutteral compound sounds . . . one might say it was torn out of a larnyx overgrown with hair." Mandelstam's repertory of sensory and imagistic crossings is inexhaustible. I have space to sample only a few.

"I gratefully recall one of my Erevan conversations . . ." writes Mandelstam. "The talk turned around the 'theory of the embryonic field,' proposed by Professor Gurvich." Then:

> The embryonic leaf of the nasturtium has the form of a halberd or of an elongated, bifoliate purse that begins to resemble a little tongue. It also looks like a flint arrowhead from the Paleolithic. But the tension in the field of force that rages around the leaf first transforms it into a five-segmented figure. The lines of the cave arrowhead get stretched into the shape of an arc.

Further along in the same passage, he asks: "What Bach, what Mozart does variations on the theme of the nasturtium leaf?"

The associative tensions move in every direction. A few pages earlier, for example, Mandelstam remarked of a fellow visitor: "The little children would show him their slender little tongues, sticking them out for an instant like slices of bear meat." We cannot read his description of the nasturtium leaf without a quiver of recollection. So, too, the flint arrowheads from the Paleolithic call up the visit to the burial site and the "crust" of cranium that Mandelstam wrapped in his handkerchief. The arrow itself materializes a few sentences down the page: "A plant in the world is an event, a happening, an arrow, and not a boring, bearded development." (It was for this innocuous-looking line, rumor goes, that the publisher of *Journey* lost his post; the offending words were "boring, bearded development," taken by authorities as a swipe as Karl Marx.)

The "force field" is taken up and re-shaped in the very next section, where Mandelstam digresses on a chess game that he observed:

> But these little Persian horses made of ivory are immersed in a solution of power. The same thing happens to them as happens to the nasturtium of E.S. Smirnov, the Moscow biologist, and the embryonic field of Professor Gurvich.

Two subsequent observations then tighten the warp. "When the rays of a combination focus upon the chess figures," he writes, "they grow like mushrooms in Indian summer." This, of course, recalls the earlier passage where Mandelstam remarked on his reluctance to pick up mushrooms. It also exemplifies the poet's penchant for images that not only convert immobile artifacts into organic entities, but which impose dynamic potential upon the stationary. Fascinated as Mandelstam is by inorganic structure, he nearly always finds a way to blow a living breath upon them. Even the pinecones, architectural paradigms, were given a "shelled tenderness."

Still on the subject of chess, Mandelstam asserts boldly: "The (chess) problem is not solved on paper, and not in the camera obscura of causality, but in a live Impressionist milieu in Edouard Manet's and Claude Monet's temple of air, light and glory." This peculiar statement directly anticipates his visit to the Impressionist exhibition, where, among other things, he will call Cezanne the "best acorn in the forests of France," and say of Matisse—in a beautiful phrase reminding us of his opening image of feeding trout—"The red paint of his canvas fizzes like soda." Again, the delight is in the unexpected synaesthesia, in the conferring of motion and tactile sensation upon an objectively stable color. In essence, it is the Impressionist credo: Paint not the thing, but the effect it produces.

As for "What Bach, what Mozart . . .", the musical motif comes to infiltrate nearly every section in the work. On the naturalist Pallas: "Whoever does not love Haydn, Glick, and Mozart will never understand a word of Pallas." On Lamarck: "He hears the pauses and syncopes of the evolutionary line." And: ". . . I love it when Lamarck deigns to be angry and smashes to smithereens all that Swiss pedagogical boredom. Into the concept of 'nature' bursts the Marseillaise!" Still later, in the brashest of synthetic metaphors, he will describe the environs of Erevan thus: "Then suddenly a violin, sectioned into gardens and houses, divided up according to the system of the whatnot—with spreaders, interceptors, dowels and bridges." Even Tzara would have been tickled!

One could go on and on. The associative patterning is as subtle as that in the finest of Oriental carpets, yet it possesses the transformational fluidity that Mandelstam celebrated in Dante. We have to wonder whether the poet had it in mind to render

Armenia in terms of a figured tapestry, or whether that impression is just a fortuitous by-product of his aesthetic. As I have said, I don't believe that Mandelstam set out to compose a portrait; he was just as much interested in getting into words the subjective sense of self-rejuvenation. The place and the event were most happily interfused.

*

Journey to Armenia begins with a laying out of fabric threads. It ends with a most affecting parable. On the last two pages—breaking with the prose pattern he has initiated—Mandelstam tells, in numbered sentences, the legend of Arshak and Shapukh. If we read past the accretions of legend, Arshak is clearly Mandelstam, Shapukh is Stalin, and Darmastat is, very possibly, Bukharin. I excerpt:

1. The body of Arshak is unwashed and his beard has run wild.
4. His tongue is mangy from jailer's food but there was a time when it pressed grapes against the roof of his mouth and was as agile as the tip of a flutist's tongue.
8. He (Shapukh) commands my hair and my fingernails. He grows me my beard and swallows me my spit so accustomed has he grown to the thought that I am here in the fortress of Aniush.
13. A certain Darmastat, the kindest and best educated of the eunichs, was in the center of Shapukh's army, encouraged the commander of the cavalry, wormed his way into his master's favor, snatched him, like a chessman, out of danger, and all the while remained in full view.
16. When the time came for his reward Darmastat inserted into the Assyrian's keen ears a request that tickled like a feather:
17. Give me a pass to the fortress of Aniush. I want Arshak to spend one additional day full of hearing, taste, and smell, as it was before, when he amused

himself with hunting and saw to the planting of trees.

No problems with interpretation here, especially from our vantage in time. How closely that last section recalls Hölderlin's petition *To the Fates*: "Grant me just one summer, you mighty ones,/And one autumn to ripen my song,/So that my heart, sated with sweet playing,/May die more willingly." Mandelstam still had eight years to live, but he did not have to be a prophet to know that he would be harried to the limit of his endurance—and over it—by Shapukh. His well-known lyric, written just one month after his return from Armenia, marks the end of the idyll and the beginning of the odyssey:

LENINGRAD

I returned to my city, familiar as tears,
As veins, as mumps from childhood years.

You've returned here, so swallow as quick as you can
The cod-liver oil of Leningrad's riverside lamps.

Recognize when you can December's brief day:
Egg yolk folded into its ominous tar.

Petersburg, I don't yet want to die:
You have the numbers of my telephones.

Petersburg, I have addresses still
Where I can raise the voices of the dead.

I live on the backstairs and the doorbell buzz
Strikes me in the temple and tears at my flesh.

And all night long I await those dear guests of yours,
Rattling, like manacles, the chains on the doors.

Translated by Bernard Meares

SVEN BIRKERTS

SNAPSHOTS FROM AIRPORTS

1 *A Little Girl*

I don't remember what she really looked like. Soft hair, a short dress (for the heat poured from all sides over the landscape and the people), playful eyes, freckled chirping—all of this will be to the point. For the girl was lively. For the girl was like any girl. All will be to the point. At the airport in Orlando or Los Angeles, I don't remember.

song for a girl: little flirt go on
                    wrap around your waist
                    summers springs and falls
                    and mornings of goodbys

For the girl was seeing her father off. For the girl was proud. She danced around him, embraced him—she wanted everyone to see her tall handsome father in uniform. Circling she wished to wrap around her waist the whole world.

song for a soldier: o soldier march away
                      spreading for the worms
                      your greatcoat and your bones
                      in the morning mist

2 *A Boy*

He had a few minutes left before the flight. The boy held a girl by the hand and she kept on talking to him, smiling. The boy was sorry to part with her. She was not beautiful, she only smiled pleasantly. But the boy was sorry to part with her. Maybe he liked her naked body, making love to her. Maybe they never made love. Maybe he loved her smile, loved her. I don't know. It was too hard for me to cross those few steps into their souls.

song for lovers: when your youth
                   comes down like dew
                   make love before
                   life swallows you

3 *A woman*

Those few minutes before the flight dragged on. The wife was seeing her husband off. Husband and wife, wife and husband—they stood in silence. For all words had been said and answered. All words had been used and misused. When the minutes came to the end, they plastered light kisses on each other's lips and separated. The kiss was unpleasant to both of them.

song for married couples: no need to be bored
                                     time goes by too fast
                                     go and wash your words
                                     go and rinse your hearts

4 *An Old Man*

Time rushed and the old man rushed, but couldn't keep up. He held onto a shaky arm of his old woman, but couldn't keep up. Those few minutes before the flight passed quickly. Though there was no need to hold hands, no need to kiss, the old man couldn't keep up.

song for the old: though wrinkles crawl and flow
                                     down your trembling hands
                                     hold on like once upon
                                     or—for—ever—end

LETTERS

New York, Sept. 11

We are strangers, because nobody defiled you with a name. We met on the night's black waters, you came over the soft path of a dream. Waters trembled and receded like a tide. And I don't know you, because nobody defiled you with a name, woman. You are pure. For a name is a stain, blurred with many meanings. I'm glad I do not know you.

Hartford, Jan. 1

The hours elbow me, but I don't want to go. It's frightening. The hours push and shove me out the old year, but I refuse to go, hold on to my memories and think of you. It's frightening to step into the unknown. Remembrance is closer to us than life, which stands like a strange person on the road. I'm scared by the unknown. The Creator did not give Us a shred of His heart.

Washington, March 11

The season reminds me of you: green buds rise through the black shirt and disturb me with the smells of spring. Vegetation swells with sap, yearns to grow—for just one spring, one summer! Oh, what a narrow time! But my spring is only a memory. My spring is you. Maybe it is better that you remain a memory, because we don't know how to forgive, as a woman's beauty wears down with age.

Sarasota, Aug. 1

Heat. Excess of sun wrongs and scorches. Biting fruits, we infect our mouths with a taste of death; smells of late love. I never bit your mouth. The songs of your hips are also unknown to me. After having drunk a loved woman, do we really lose our deepest feelings for her? I don't know, I never wronged your lips, we never knew the smell of late love.

New York, Sept. 11

I was looking for you on the streets of New York. But in vain, in vain. The streets choked with faces, swelled with weariness, boredom, stale loves. Time smeared the faces with sweat and wrinkles, drove them closer to the end of the last street. You were not there. Time cannot mark a dream by age. You will never change. You will be young.

BOHDAN BOYCHUK
Translated
by Mark Rudman
in collaboration
with the author

WHERE WE ARE; OR GETTING THERE
IS ONLY HALF THE FUN

Travel comes to an end. We get to there
wherever it claims to be, or home again,
and it's over. That's all of that. Travel assumes
that place is different from place, though everyone knows
(even the traveller knows) the assumption is made
mostly to make the trip, to offer excuse
for it, for what we want: the travel, the steps
from here to there, the demands, their peremptoriness,
preemption. Dear God! That something engage us, that we
be busy at something, wars or careers, enroute!
Going somewhere. Moving again so as not
to have time for here, not to be stuck with it.
With here. Look at it! At here. Let's go!

POLAR PROJECTION

The *National Geographic Magazine* sends me a projection
of North Polar regions.

Mercator would stretch it but, always thinking of other
things, Mercator misses.

I am astonished how vast it is; how it has places in it,
lots of them.

They say the people are perishing because of us. Well,
it is probably true.

They are no more important than we are. We kill each
other; it doesn't matter.

Oh, it matters at first to a few: sad. Afterwards, it
is all forgotten.

The vastnesses! We are all so little.

WILLIAM BRONK

from THE SPIRIT OF MEDITERRANEAN PLACES

ISTANBUL

I woke up in the train, which was still moving. I lifted the curtain and looked out. I had never in my life seen such desolation. Rain was falling on the Thracian plain where not a single tree grew, only small thorny bushes and asphodels among its pebbles. Here and there, inside barbed wire enclosures near their sheet metal camps, Turkish soldiers watched the railway cars go by, coming from the West. We were already several hours late. I closed the curtain and went back to sleep.

The next thing I saw was the long stretch of suburbs on the banks of the Marmara, the airfield and the beaches, then the great golden gate with its two cracked towers of white marble, the maritime ramparts through which we slowly snaked our way, the tall houses of gray wood, the irregular squares, which were not level but littered with rubble, the rising streets, the swarming crowds, the minarets like great pencils.

It was hard getting out of the station. The platform was being repaired, and I had to make my way among piles of stones. The weather had cleared a little.

As soon as I emerged onto the square, I was caught up and deafened by the stridency of the city, by the noise of its taxis and red, yellow or green tramways with their grinding switches, and the large billboards proclaiming the merits of different banks wherever you looked on the black facades of this Oriental Liverpool.

It was lucky for me there was rain and fog the first time I crossed the floating Galata Bridge, which breathes gently under your feet every time a tugboat goes by. This bridge is in fact both a bridge and a railway station with two levels, with many iron stairways, bordered by loading quays with landing steps, for the Bosporus, the Prince Islands or Eyup; with ticket windows, waiting rooms, shops and cafes, congested with a crowd of fishermen dropping their nylon lines, leaning on the railings or crouching on the edges, and with travellers carrying their baskets, or people walking by, dressed in European style, except for their fur caps, but mostly with profoundly foreign faces, with olive skin, wide cheekbones, a slow and uncertain gait.

The coast of Asia was barely visible. Soaked to the skin, worn out because I had been walking for so long, I sat down to drink a glass of tea at a little square green-painted table. In the room, which was decorated only by advertisements in Turkish, other customers were also drinking in silence. Like me, they watched the people walk by, serious in their dark and dull suits, passing between us and the overloaded river busses coming alongside, the small boats in which men were frying freshly-caught fish over a cooker and then stuffing half of each fish into a round bread, other small boats painted and even sometimes sculpted and hung round with old pieces of tire to cushion the bumps, large caïques with sails, long strings of black barges, to the left the big ships that ran to Smyrna and Alexandria, to the right the cranes, the smoke from the trains, the trees of Gulhane Park, and, above the roofs of the seraglio with its odd bell tower like a French church, the cupola of Saint Irene, then the Sophia looking as though it were floating, as though it were being borne away in a very slow, imperturbable flight by its four enormous buttresses.

It may be that I never again felt so profoundly the effect of this immense and solemn spectacle, this animated maritime crossroads, this unfolding ceremony, as I did during that disagreeable and Nordic arrival which so amply emphasized the sad and gentle savagery of those ancient nomads who had forgotten their horses amid the wails and whistles of the steamers, the dull tumult of the cars, the knocking of boathooks and oars, the splashing, the cries of the gulls above all this; and yet as I watched it I was delighted by the pearl and amber light that was so wonderfully diffused, reflected, set in motion by the shimmer of the omnipresent water, I was delighted by all the minarets on the hills like the tent poles of some sumptuous camp, or like reeds in an angel's pool, then, in the evening, everything becoming transfigured in the contagion of the sky's dripping gold, flashing back from that immense luminous horn that plunges into the interior of Europe, dyeing the domes and the depots, dyeing the eyes of men, entering their blood, entering my blood, entering my hands which I no longer recognized as they squeezed the railing which had not only turned to bronze but become the trembling limb of a sleeping wild animal.

Three cities are superimposed on one another, and as one wanders one unravels them, three cities of profoundly different structure, three cities born of three invasions. Let us continue to dwell on the last one, the industrial one, the banking one, the black one, its tramways, its signs, its "tunnel," the underground train that lifts you from Karakoy to Pera, and the Istiklal Caddesi, a long winding thoroughfare, too narrow, overcrowded, with its shops and its bars, that follows the ridge of the hill as far as the immense Taksim square, let us dwell on its traffic lights, its aviation agencies, its bookstores, its restaurants and garages, its effort to make itself secure, to deliver itself from the past, to transform itself and to grow healthier, but let us also dwell on its gummy mud, in which one sinks up to one's ankles on rainy days, its disorder, its gangsters, on the deep feelings of insecurity that it exudes, on its doors barricaded very early in the evening, on the unpleasant loneliness of its streets at night, on the sort of terror that lurks around its gardens and casinos.

This Oriental Liverpool, which grew up so vigorously on the left bank of the Golden Horn, has insinuated itself into old Istanbul on the other side of the river, into the great Ottoman city which has been rotting away for centuries, and it has in some sense put down roots there, suckers in the interstices of its worn and loose fabric, draining its strength. Little by little, concrete buildings, incomparably more solid, are replacing the large houses made of slate-gray wood with their balconies, their innumerable windows set obliquely in relation to the pebbly and gullied street, their little twisted columns, their exterior stairways, their corbels pierced with trefoils, their inscriptions in arabic characters above the entrance, those old houses that are burning, cracking, eaten by worms, that stand in the midst of kitchen gardens, cemeteries, and wastelands where children run back and forth, pulling on endlessly long strings to raise their kites higher and higher, up into the region of air where another kind of kite, the bird of prey, turns and turns, until suddenly it swoops down on some scrap of refuse.

An encampment that has settled, but without solidifying completely; huts and shanties that have been enlarged and improved, that have been made comfortable, but without ever losing their ephemeral feeling. Turkish Istanbul is a superb

101

abortion, it is truly the expression of an empire that collapsed on itself as soon as it stopped growing. In the great bazaars the canvas had become the roof, and especially on the tops of all the hills, raising them even higher, crowning them, finishing them, had been built those great crystallizations, the imperial mosques, and in the lower part of town, their delicate sisters with their facing of faience and their great gray facades. What a city was built during those epoques of grandeur and audacity in the wake of victory, the victory of Mohammed the Conqueror, the victory of Suleiman the Magnificent and his architect Sinan, at the end of the 15th and during the 16th centuries, out of a desire to equal the city in whose ruins it sat! It was more advanced than anything being done in Europe at the time, as we can see from the two splendid groups of buildings named for those two sultans, that of the conqueror having been reconstructed during the 17th century, but more or less on the old plan.

Then, suddenly, the wind went out of the sails. The tradition certainly extended into the beginning of the 17th century with the blue mosque of Ahmet, an attempt was certainly made to revive it in the 18th century with the mosque of Nuruosmanye, and the Tulip Mosque, but these were only isolated efforts, increasingly rare, less and less confident, and the two great islands of order never came together. While the ruins of Constantinople continued to crumble, to subside, earthquakes were already damaging the new buildings.

Let us come now, therefore, to this ghost city, this city whose rubble we stumble over at every step—with its brick sub-structures, its ramparts, the large rectangular holes which were once open cisterns, and lastly the churches, which have become sorts of caverns; this city whose very prestige was the cause of its loss—a prestige that remained intact despite its ruin, its dimi-nution; a city which, even while remaining so unknown, since this immense excavation site is still almost entirely unexplored, soon effaces, in the mind of the visitor, almost everything that followed it.

This city was at the origin of everything, it has left its mark on everything. The city itself, we might say, chose this extraordi-nary site, because it did not come into being as a development of Byzantium, but through the deliberate transferral, to this spot, of the capital of the Roman Empire as it extended into the East. Its large church, the Hagia Sophia, which is hardly at all denatured by the four minarets that only accentuate its structure, and which reigns incomparable, immediately recognizable, haunted Ottoman architects. After having for a certain length of time prudently avoided imitating an edifice so very expressive of the civilization which they wanted to replace, they found themselves obliged by this irrecusable presence to adapt its structure to their taste, to take it as the basis of their researches, attempting, henceforth, all possible variations in order to tear themselves free of its influence. What are these delicious pools of calm, the mosques of Rustem Pasha or Sokullu Mehmet Pasha, in all their refinement, in all their perfection, compared to the silence that descends on you as soon as you pass under the mosaic of the Virgin between Justinian and Constantine, a humming, gilded silence which has swallowed up in itself the rumbling of thunder, the rustling of leaves in forests, the breaking of waves on shores. The distinction of those slightly broken arcs, all that precise, rational, refreshing elegance, all that good breeding—how much is it worth compared to this magical depth encircling you on all sides and yet fleeing from you? And against this background of splendor, at Fethye Djami or Kharie Djami, we are further humiliated, we are more completely bewitched, by the addition of these figures of grace mysteriously receding in their narrow cupolas.

Little by little the dream assumes a form, when one gathers together all these fragments, when one measures these distances; and above these wastelands, through all these minarets, rises the mirage of Constantinople—the Church of Saint George of Mangana is reconstructed, and once again its gold, as though leaping up from a central spring, flows over its entire surface, as in the description left us by Psellus; once again, it is surrounded by arcades, horses, fields, canals, basins, groves and pools; Salomon's throne sits once again in the palace of the Magnaure; the Chalce is covered once again with its bronze tiles, the cisterns fill with water, the hills recover their terraces and their steps—the mirage of this city which from its very beginning was threatened by everything that came from the plateaux, from the interior of the continents, this city which had already been living such a very long time in its own ruins when the breach was made in its walls, this city which safeguarded with such great difficulty a few caverns of the old amber in the midst of the deserted quarters, in the midst of the immense, abandoned, crumbling palaces, this city, more and more solitary, which has itself become the Empire.

Galata Bridge breathes under my feet; I haven't left it. Night is falling. I watch the cranes and the railway cars, I watch the fog coming from Asia, I watch the lights floating on the strait, where the *Argo* still sails, this teeming strait so full of splendor, joy, and apprehension.

MALLIA

I was in Crete, and the day was December 31. I had taken the bus early in the morning in Herakleion to come to this village, a village all of white cubes which lay on the north coast between a mountain covered half way up its slope with olive trees, and orchards that went down to the sea.

I had spent a long time photographing the ruins of an ancient Minoan palace, the circular bases of columns surrounding the courtyard, the several steps, the ball of stone in the middle, all of which was scattered with small white and violet flowers. I had had lunch in a cafe on the side of the road, and I had returned to the bus stop to wait for the bus, well before the hour when it was supposed to come by.

All of a sudden I saw it throbbing towards me through the dust without slowing down, its roof heavily loaded with bags and baskets. Using the few words of modern Greek that I knew and that I've since forgotten, and throwing in various scraps of other languages that the people I was talking to might have heard, I asked what was happening, if there would be another bus later in the afternoon to take me back to the island's capital. I was told that since this bus was no doubt already completely full, it couldn't take on any new passengers, and that no doubt a second bus would be following along after it. I sat down again. An hour went by.

Then someone explained to me there was no more hope of a bus that day, it was New Year's Eve, and the bus service would be disorganized until the next day.

I couldn't possibly walk back to the city—it was thirty-five kilometers away. The light was going from the sky. The white houses were turning blue.

Some young men went off to one of the largest houses in the village to look for its owner, a rather plump man, by now rather old, who had been to Europe, as they say in Greece, and who apparently spoke English. We had a great deal of trouble understanding each other: what I wanted to find out was where I was going to sleep. It was at this point that everything began to be quite wonderful.

The man in whose cafe I had eaten my bread, mutton and olives that day at about one o'clock had an enterprising son who was dividing the second floor of his house into rooms to be rented during the coming spring and summer; the first room was clean and ready.

I went off down a path with him, and he did the honors of his orchard for me, having me taste all the different kinds of oranges he raised, while the wheel of the windmill above our heads hummed softly, pumping up clear water.

At nightfall, we went down into his basement diningroom, where he had me eat dinner with him and his wife and his two daughters, who were about six and seven years old (I was facing the entrance, I saw the steps covered with moonlight, and I have a confused memory of a large pitcher or a face in the stones—I can't remember any more—watching me like some huge, unmoving owl). Then, since it was New Year's Eve, the last night of the year, we played a game with a small six-sided top, betting dried beans, and hardly speaking, naturally, except to pronounce the few simple words, quickly learned, that were needed for the game. We played for several hours, and it was only when the children began to have trouble keeping their eyes open, in spite of their excitement at the presence of a stranger, at the unusual events of the evening, that he took an oil lamp and led me up a creaking outside stairway to the new and very cold room whose windows I could not close.

At dawn I opened the shutters. Below me the leaves of the orange trees trembled in the breeze; the grey sea soughed in the distance.

In the church there was a beautiful iconostasis of gilded wood; I had no film left for photographing the village; at the end of the morning the bus for Herakleion arrived, at the appointed hour, and I got on, keeping safe in my memory, like a talisman, Mallia's hospitality.

MANTUA

For months I had said to myself: this summer I will go to Rome for my vacation, to check certain details there, to steep myself in it more, I can't go anywhere else for my vacation; but all summer I worked on *La Modification* without leaving Paris, and when it was finished, when the proofs were corrected, and because I was tired after this long effort and needed a change of scene, needed to soak up some sun, I actually did take a vacation, and I actually did go to Italy, but not to Rome, because this trip could not have changed anything, and because for the past year and a half, one part of me at least had been in the train the whole time, going in that direction, travelling toward that destination; and so I took the train to Milan, where it rained so hard all day that after visiting the new museum in Sforze Castle with the amazing room which was painted with a canopy of interwoven trees under Leonardo's direction, and without even having been able to get into the Sant'Eustorgo Chapel decorated by Foppa which one of my friends has talked to me about so often and for which he feels such undoubtedly justified tenderness, and which I miss every time I go through, I left that very evening for Florence, where for three days I didn't really do anything but sleep, going out only to eat and to shut myself up in a movie theater in the late afternoon, thus seeing, in succession, *I sogni nel cassetone*, the detestable remake of the already detestable *Elle et lui*, and *Les Nuits de Cabiria*.

On the fourth day, I felt rested and it was wonderful October weather, the sun's golden, horizontal rays picking out the hills which I was contemplating from the fortress of the belvedere above the Pitti Palace, this fortress having been restored, cleaned up, completely renovated for an exciting exhibition of detached frescoes; but the very next day I had to go back up north, because I was absolutely determined to see Mantua, stopping off in

106

Modena, a town whose ancient heart spreads out in little winding streets bordered by arcades around one of the most singular and wonderful of all the Roman monuments,

in Mantua not only because of the *camera degli sposi*, but also in order to try to penetrate the secret of the name, which I had encountered so often in books or conversations, and which was marked by an obscure magic that I wanted to understand.

There you are—I would have liked to talk to you about Mantua, about the splendor and desolation of this city a little off from the main roads, without modern buildings or stores, but I don't have either the time or the tranquillity necessary, this evening, to be able to produce anything but the most rudimentary indications, in other words, that it is one of the places, outside of Rome, where the preoccupation with Rome is most obvious, the sort of despair that seized Europe when it began to feel, because of the taking of Constantinople and the discovery of America, that the image of the empire as unifying the world began to shatter finally, desperately trying to disguise this absence by a prodigious imitation of "Antiquity," no longer as the foundation of Christianity, the preparation for it, but for the first time as a completely other world from which one was horribly separated and which had to be reconquered (in this respect Mantegna played an exemplary role, as we know).

How violently one is struck when one emerges for the first time, after the long preparation of the narrowing Corso, into that dark red group of connecting squares, punctuated by high towers, one of the most remarkably varied of the internal organizations of urban spaces left us by the Middle Ages, through the triumphal arch to the right, of dazzling white marble, which Alberti provided as a porch to his basilica; almost more significant and even more impressive is the other one, sinister, unfinished, of powdery brick, on the square that so correctly bears his name. But only within this labyrinth, at once gloomy and magnificent, so sumptuous, so dilapidated, only when we come to the festive and absurd, disorderly pile of rooms, courts, and gardens which is the Gonzagas' palace at the tip of the city, among the swamps, with its complement on the other side, the Te Palace, does the preoccupation turn into madness and obsession, all the architecture becoming stage sets, with false marbles, false stones, trompe l'oeil,

never enough, never satisfying, the superabundance only accent-
uating the deception, stage sets in which the life of an entire
family, of an entire court, is gradually transformed into theater,
"scenes after the manner of the ancients."

And I would have liked to show how the peculiar weight of
the Roman theme on Mantua at the time of the Renaissance can
be connected to the "spirit of the place" that, for this city, has
consistently remained Virgil, represented by a very moving
medieval statue in the center:

> *e li parenti miei furon Lombardi,*
> *Mantovani per patria ambedui.*

> *Nacqui sub Julio, ancor che fosse tardi,*
> *e vissi a Roma sotto il buon Augusto,*
> *al tempo degli Dei falsi e bugiardi.*
> *Poeta fui, e cantai di quel giusto*
> *figliuol d'Anchise che venne da Troia*
> *poi che il superbo Ilion fu combusto.*
> (*Inferno*, I.)

primary poet of Latinity, not only because throughout the
Middle Ages he was considered to be the "pagan prophet," the
figure representing par excellence what, in imperial Rome, permitted Christian Rome to exist, but also because his principal
work concerned the very origin of Rome, was an attempt, at a
time when the latter was realizing that it had become the center
of the world, in the place of so many other older cities, to give a
mythological justification to this amazing privilege.

At last, leaving Mantua, I rejoined the Orient Express at
Verona, another city with beautiful connecting squares.

FERRARA

*Here is a text which pretends to be no more than a description of the text
that might have been, but is nonetheless a text. And perhaps deliberately,
perhaps not, the text as rough sketch, as written with a vision of something
greater and future, mirrors exactly the city itself as the text gives it to
us.*—LD.

Forgoing, for the moment, for today, writing this text on Ferrara as I would have liked to write it, because in order to be specific and illustrate what I want to say I would have to consult documents which are not immediately available to me, for example Roberto Longhi's book *Officina Ferrarese*, which would have provided me with valuable information about the whole group of painters who fascinate me, would have provided photographs, at least, of some of their pictures, which are so rare and so dispersed, of a quality often higher than that of the details of the marvellous *Room of the Months* at the Schifanoia palace, allowing us, therefore, to reconstruct much more correctly and more convincingly— taking as a point of departure the architecture as a whole that it suggests to us—this ancient mental world which is so close to us, so rich for us, so precious in its urgent enigma,

documents on the Este family, the nucleus of this whole movement, the nucleus of what can well be called the civilization of Ferrara, documents on all these figures, so singular, and their relations with the masters of the other Italian cities,

on the extinction of this family, on the passing of this city into the hands of the papacy, which signified its final death as place of originality and culture, but which was also no more than the retribution for a long agony that began early in the 16th century, the contamination by the power of Rome, by Rome's seductive artifices, of that spirit which was so profoundly free, so distant from all counterreformation,

I am resolved to give you only the broad outline of an invitation to discover this place, only my way of using Ferrara, to present you only with fragments of a future text which, if it ever exists, will be somewhat different, as you well know, from what this sketch promises.

We ought to start with the reverberation of the name Ferrara, with the resonance it has had for several centuries in the minds of men who are generally so obscure to us despite their celebrity in schools, who are intelligible only with such difficulty (and this by our own fault, because we knowingly neglect a whole part of their environment), men to whom we apply the quite deceptive name of "classical"; we ought to take Goethe's Torquato Tasso as our starting point and go on to show the prominent role played by two great writers of Ferrara—Tasso, and before him Ariosto—in the literary equilibrium of Europe, which is to say, in the mental structure of all cultivated Europeans, and, in Italy, of the people too, from the 16th century up to the 19th century, and show that the revolt of someone like Boileau against them in France was an incomparably more serious business than a simple question of taste:

> *The terrible mysteries of the faith of Christians*
> *Are not susceptible to gay ornaments.*

There is, in fact, in their poetic practice, a suspension of belief in Christian dogma, which is treated as mythology. In Ariosto, the awareness of this suspension leads to an astonishing irreverence, in the midst of the magical world he describes to us, something that obviously would need to be shown with citations.

This amazing country that one finds in *Orlando Furioso* is the very same one displayed on the walls of Schifanoia, so much more present. We should, therefore, now turn towards its great quattrocento masters: Tura, Cossa, and Roberti. Clearly, a long commentary on the *Room of the Months* and its philosophical paganism ought to be inserted here.

There is someting in the civilization and spirit of Ferrara that was not followed, a direction that took a sharp turn, stopped abruptly, and found itself in wonderful harmony with certain of our needs, as though all we had to do was to take up this light, which was so bright and which over several centuries gradually darkened, before becoming manifest to us again—as though all we had to do was to take up this light again in order to go forward.

And I will end with what is perhaps most moving about this city, something that will only be discovered by an attentive and patient reading of it: the fact that the group of ancient monuments that draw us to it, for the most part unfinished, and almost all signed by Biagio Rosetti, are really the ruins of a city, but the ruins of a future city which never took place, Ferrara's prosperity abandoning it under pressure from the other states, its boldness becoming blunted, then, as the spirit of all Europe took a different turn, in a direction different from its own, all those neighborhoods planned at the time of its expansion remaining empty, those palaces, designed to form the corners of lively squares, remaining isolated in the middle of wastelands, incomplete stage sets for absent pageants.

Here, then, are real pieces of a dreamed-of city, and among these admirable indications, the traveller's mind may wander as freely and fruitfully as it may wander before the surprising perspectives of the so completely deteriorated paintings of the Schifanoia palace.

MICHEL BUTOR
Translated
by Lydia Davis

THE RAINS OF NEW YORK

New York rain is a rain of exile. Abundant, viscous and dense, it pours down tirelessly between the high cubes of cement into avenues plunged suddenly into the darkness of a well: seeking shelter in a cab that stops at a red light and starts again on a green, you suddenly feel caught in a trap, behind monotonous, fast-moving windshield wipers sweeping aside water that is constantly renewed. You are convinced you could drive like this for hours without escaping these square prisons or the cisterns through which you wade with no hope of a hill or a real tree. The whitened skyscrapers loom in the gray mist like gigantic tombstones for a city of the dead, and seem to sway slightly on their foundations. At this hour they are deserted. Eight million men, the smell of steel and cement, the madness of builders, and yet the very height of solitude. "Even if I were to clasp all the people in the world against me, it would protect me from nothing."

The reason perhaps is that New York is nothing without its sky. Naked and immense, stretched to the four corners of the horizon, it gives the city its glorious mornings and the grandeur of its evenings, when a flaming sunset sweeps down Eighth Avenue over the immense crowds driving past the shop windows, whose lights are turned on well before nightfall. There are also certain twilights along Riverside Drive, when you watch the parkway that leads uptown, with the Hudson below, its waters reddened by the setting sun; off and on, from the uninterrupted flow of gently, smoothly running cars, from time to time there suddenly rises a song that recalls the sound of breaking waves. Finally I think of other evenings, so gentle and so swift they break your heart, that cast a purple glow over the vast lawns of Central Park, seen from Harlem. Clouds of Negro children are striking balls with wooden bats, shouting with joy; while elderly Americans, in checked shirts, sprawl on park benches, sucking molded ice creams on a stick with what energy remains to them; while squirrels burrow into the earth at their feet in search of unknown tidbits. In the park's trees, a jazz band of birds heralds the appearance of the first star above the Empire State Building, while long-legged creatures stride along the paths against a backdrop of tall buildings, offering to the temporarily gentle sky their splendid looks and their loveless glance. But when this sky grows dull, or the daylight fades, then once again New York becomes the big city, prison by day and funeral pyre by night. A prodigious funeral pyre at midnight, as its millions of lighted windows amid immense stretches of blackened walls carry these swarming lights halfway up the sky, as if every evening a gigantic fire were burning over Manhattan, the island with three rivers, raising immense, smoldering carcasses still pierced with dots of flame.

I have my ideas about other cities—but about New York only these powerful and fleeting emotions, a nostalgia that grows impatient, and moments of anguish. After so many months I still know nothing about New York, whether one moves about among madmen here or among the most reasonable people in the world; whether life is as easy as all America says, or whether it is as empty here as it sometimes seems; whether it is natural for ten people to be employed where one would be enough and where you are served no faster; whether New Yorkers are liberals or conformists, modest souls or dead ones; whether it is admirable or unimportant that the garbage men wear well-fitting gloves to do their work; whether it serves any purpose that the circus in Madison Square Garden puts on ten simultaneous performances in four different rings, so that you are interested in all of them and can watch none of them; whether it is significant that the thousands of young people in the skating rink where I spent one evening, a kind of *vélodrome d'hiver* bathed in reddish and dusty lights, as they turned endlessly on their roller skates in an infernal din of metal wheels and loud organ music, should look as serious and absorbed as if they were solving simultaneous equations; whether, finally, we should believe those who say that it is eccentric to want to be alone, or naïvely those who are surprised that no one ever asks for your identity card.

In short, I am out of my depth when I think of New York. I wrestle with the morning fruit juices, the national Scotch and soda and its relationship to romance, the girls in taxis and their secret, fleeting acts of love, the excessive luxury and bad taste reflected even in the stupefying neckties, the anti-Semitism and the love of animals—this last extending from the gorillas in the

113

Bronx Zoo to the protozoa of the Musuem of Natural History—
the funeral parlors where death and the dead are made up at top
speed ("Die, and leave the rest to us"), the barber shops where
you can get a shave at three in the morning, the temperature that
swings from hot to cold in two hours, the subway that reminds
you of Sing Sing prison, ads filled with clouds of smiles proclaiming from every wall that life is not tragic, cemeteries in flower
beneath the gasworks, the beauty of the girls and the ugliness of
the old men; the tens of thousands of musical-comedy generals
and admirals stationed at the apartment entrances, some to
whistle for green, red, and yellow taxis that look like beetles,
others to open the door for you, and finally the ones who go up
and down all over town like multicolored Cartesian divers in
elevators fifty stories high.

Yes, I am out of my depth. I am learning that there are cities,
like certain women, who annoy you, overwhelm you, and lay
bare your soul, and whose scorching contact, scandalous and
delightful at the same time, clings to every pore of your body.
This is how, for days on end, I walked around New York, my
eyes filled with tears simply because the city air is filled with
cinders, and half one's time outdoors is spent rubbing the eyes or
removing the minute speck of metal that the thousand New
Jersey factories send into them as a joyful greeting gift, from
across the Hudson. In the end, this is how New York affects me,
like a foreign body in the eye, delicious and unbearable, evoking
tears of emotion and all-consuming fury.

Perhaps this is what people call passion. All I can say is that
I know what contrasting images mine feeds on. In the middle of
the night sometimes, above the skyscrapers, across hundreds of
high walls, the cry of a tugboat would meet my insomnia, reminding me that this desert of iron and cement was also an island. I
would think of the sea then, and imagine myself on the shore of
my own land. On other evenings, riding in the front of the Third
Avenue El, as it greedily swallows the little red and blue lights it
tears past at third story level, from time to time allowing itself
to be slowly absorbed by half-dark stations, I watched the skyscrapers turning in our path. Leaving the abstract avenues of the
center of town I would let myself ride on toward the gradually
poorer neighborhoods, where there were fewer and fewer cars.

114

I knew what awaited me, those nights on the Bowery. A few paces from the half-mile-long stretch of splendid bridal shops (where not one of the waxen mannequins was smiling) the forgotten men live, those who have let themselves drift into poverty in this city of bankers. It is the gloomiest part of town, where you never see a woman, where one man in every three is drunk, and where in a strange bar, apparently straight out of a Western, fat old actresses sing about ruined lives and a mother's love, stamping their feet to the rhythm and spasmodically shaking, to the bellowing from the bar, the parcels of shapeless flesh that age has covered them with. The drummer is an old woman too, and looks like a screech owl, and some evenings you feel you'd like to know her life—at one of those rare moments when geography disappears and loneliness becomes a slightly confused truth.

At other times . . . but yes, of course, I loved the mornings and the evenings of New York. I loved New York, with that powerful love that sometimes leaves you full of uncertainties and hatred: sometimes one needs exile. And then the very smell of New York rain tracks you down in the heart of the most harmonious and familiar towns, to remind you there is at least one place of deliverance in the world, where you, together with a whole people and for as long as you want, can finally lose yourself forever.

ALBERT CAMUS
Translated
by Ellen Conroy Kennedy

Milan, June 6

(Brera Gallery)

But the most astonishing of the paintings is the Piero *Madonna dell'Ovo*, newly restored. Surrealism is an old story in European art. Consider that egg suspended from the scallop-shell ceiling over the Mother's head. Or the four epicene angels standing beside her, each different, different, all gazing at us with unearthly eyes, blank features, a complex jewel fastened to the ringleted hair above their foreheads. The Infant sprawling to one side on her lap, a coral Sacred Heart dangling with its arteries from his neck. The downcast gaze of Mary, contemplating the burden of Mystery. The motionless pose of the attendant saints, with their decipherable attributes, including St. Peter of Verona, with his bleeding skull, split by a machete. The marble stillness of all present makes for much of the strangeness. But also the color and tonality. Did Piero mix a little gray tempera with all his colors? Everything seems muted, dimmed, as with a faint layer of chalk dust; and somehow the general *grisaille* comes to be ontologically fused with the fraught immobility that has marble-ized these heavy, round-limbed statues—which, however, are done, as the Parthenon frieze once was, in polychrome.

(Castello Sforzesco Museum)

Then, the "Rondanini" Pietà of Michelangelo. His last work, and unfinished. But I think its "unfinish" was integrated into the meaning. Least detailed is the figure of Mary; she stands, very much in the ascendant, supporting—or is she engulfing—the dead Christ. One reads her, finally, as Mother Nature, Matter, she who gave her son his fleshly, mortal frame—which is now being reclaimed, dissolving into the looming mass of her amorphous volume. The figure of Jesus is almost done, with a convincing limpness to legs and arms. But then, oddest detail, standing out from him, attached by a mere stem of stone, is an extra arm, complete, ideally rendered, and polished. An accident, a pentimento? Maybe, but I read it as: the pietà allegorizes Michelangelo's waning powers and approaching death. He no longer has the strength to realize his conceptions, which, from his youth among the Florentine Neoplatonists and up through his sonneteering maturity, always retained a marked bent toward idealization. This "idea" of an arm hovers like a dream near the actual, failing body, cruelly out of reach. . . .

Sabbioneta, Lombardy, June 12

On a bench in the public garden opposite the Galleria degli Antichi. The bus back to Mantua won't leave for nearly an hour. If I do this now, I can nap at the hotel.

When the Ufficio di Turismo opened at three, we were assigned a pretty guide, who took us to the Palazzo Ducale on the square at the town center. Cool inside, unrestored, and empty of furniture. You have to rubberneck to see what there is to see—the soffits, made of cedar of Lebanon, carved and painted. Also, four equestrian statues of the Gonzaga, Ludovico to Vespasiano, the same who first left Mantua to come to this village and transform it into a "Piccola Atene." Better to be first in a tiny Iberian village than second in Rome, or second to your older brother ruling in Mantua. Vespasiano's arms bear the device *Libertas*.

Our next stop is the Teatro Olimpico, done by Scamozzi after he finished the Palladian one in Vicenza. This one's smaller and hasn't a trompe l'oeil stage. It does have a pantheon of statuary above the Duke's gallery. And frescoes, some imitated, we're told, from those of Veronese at Villa Maser. Also, views of Rome; and busts of emperors. Vespasiano clearly wanted to emphasize his Roman aspect; his name is a daunting one to have to live up to.

The Palazzo Giardino was a short hike away, across the very park where I'm now sitting. Vespasiano's refuge from the great house, it is built in comfortable dimensions, with frescoes, *stucchi*, soffits, and ornaments in *stilo grottesco*, copied from Pompeii. Frescoes by Campi depict scenes from the *Aeneid*, including a handsome Trojan horse with hoof gracefully lifted; and Aeneas ushering Dido into the cave, his sword drawn and flashing. Laocoön. Aeneas bearing Anchises on his shoulders. *E così via.*

The Sala degli Specchi differs from others so designated in that the featured mirrors are set in the soffit, not on the walls. Dancers (this was the ballroom) could gaze upward and catch a glimpse of themselves, upside down, executing the measure. It must have been startling—and wouldn't you fall out of step?

We finished up with two churches. Actually, the first, the "Incoronata," was the private, octagonal chapel of the Gonzaga. Vespasian's tomb stands to the right of the altar, himself dressed in dark bronze, the robes of a Caesar. Clearly an imitation of the Medici tombs, but with a smaller sarcophagus and colored marble insets. Noticing a similarity between the galleries of the theater and the chapel (where, high up, Vespasiano heard his masses), I wondered whether divine service was simply one more spectacle for Vespasiano. How did he get to the altar to receive the sacrament? Was it brought to him? Did he not bother? Quite possibly his was no more than a humanist's religion, classical in flavor, stoic, marco-aurelian. The liturgy would be then a dutiful performance, with what condescension viewed, who can say?

The thing to see in the Assunta church is Bibbiena's side chapel (not sure if this is the same Bibbiena who did stage design. But it must be, considering the effects here.) The roof is domed, painted sky blue and seen through an ornamental lower dome of latticework. Windows not visible from below throw light on the blue ceiling; it looks like a twilit sky. On either side of the chapel and glass coffins with—not the bodies of martyrs but *effigies* of them. What's more, up in the dome, just below the latticework were what looked like marble sarcophagi—but only trompe-l'oeil. On closer looking, you see that they are stage flats: death and the memorials of it shammed, a bit of stagecraft. Italy, O most theatrical, O most operatic of nations! I remember talking to Mario C. about his translation of "Promised Land Valley." What was the Italian for "imagine," in the full, Romantic sense? "Fingere," he said, which also means "feign" or "disguise as" (think of the *Finto matrimonio*). So if in Italy you must feign in order to live life at full strength, perhaps dying requires some of the same stage magic in order to take place, in order not to be left listlessly half alive.

And if an Italian asked me what our counterpart in America to the program of "fingere," what would I say? I suppose, that our great thing is telling the awful truth, stripping away illusion, finding out what we *really feel.* . . . And when we can't manage that, feigning to, most likely.

Venice, 17 June

It must be near 6 o'clock, but with the solstice less than a week away, still bright. I may not be able to get a nap. CLANK-CLANK go the bells of the Gesuati. Opposite the bed is an armoire with doors painted (inexpertly) in tan, green, and brown—a path among birch trees (descended from Corot's grayer ones). Next to that, a big white sink whose faucet gives an occasional phlegmatic drip. The taps gleam dull silver and ponder their reflections in the facing mirror, where they also see a glass holding upright two toothbrushes, one red, one white, and a shaving cream aerosol. Light at the window is filtered through muslin. Also, the contrapuntal argument of dozens of birds, a layer of filigree over the human—Italian human—vocalizing on the street below. Tree branches are muslin-pale green through the curtains.

Venice puts anyone into an impressionistic mood. Several times daily I climb the Accademia Bridge to see what the light is doing now to the Canal, the palazzi, and La Salute. It seems a full occupation to stand and stare, registering the dust-brown of the buildings, the verdigris of the water, the ash-white of the Gothic arches, the vaporetti as they skid into their turns, the bright stripes of the mooring spiles sprung up before the old addresses—Vendramìn, Contarini, Grimani—against whose algae-carpeted steps a floating grapefruit rind knows no better than to wash up and be rebuffed. The weather is fine, bright, yet still cool.

Yesterday we were to see the Carpaccios at San Giorgi degli Schiavoni. The last painting of the series includes an inscription, "Victorius Carpathius fingebat." You would expect "pinxit" instead—"painted," in the perfect tense. *Fingere* again. But what is the "fiction"? One half of it is easy enough: St. George's vanquishing of the scaly beast. And the series links that fabulous act with the conversion of the pagans. Next, the Agony in the Garden, "Not my will, but Thine be done." Then to St. Matthew's renunciation of his life as a Jewish publican. Now for the more difficult part. The story takes up with St. Jerome, beginning with his returning to the monastery with a pet lion. The monks flee in faithless terror, and Carpaccio wants us to laugh at their fears. The "beast" in us must be conquered but not eradicated. This message would have been appreciated by the little Dalmatian colony who commissioned the work. Living in Venice as they did, still they wouldn't want to become indistinguishable from the super-civilized Venetians. The next painting in the series, St. Jerome's death, shows his lion in the background, couchant, and gazing up into the clouds whither the soul of the saint has departed. Then, the final painting, the one identifying the painter, brings in St. Augustine, who is meant to, among other things, stand in for Carpaccio. The saint is writing a letter to his colleague Jerome; when suddenly he becomes aware that the addressee has died. At the same moment, he is given the solution to a theological problem that had been troubling him. St. Jerome has become fused with the light pouring through the window that Augustine faces, and with an invisible light streaming into the soul as well. Not far behind, the saint's little white terrier sits on the floor looking at him, trying to understand what his master is feeling. Undragon-like, unlionlike as he is, still an *animal* is present here, a companion to theological events, which, I suppose, must always take place within an incarnational context. In the lower right corner of the painting, so far in the foreground as to seem flush with the surface plane, is a sheet of music (a figure here for the art of painting), where we read the signature inscription: "V.C. fingebat."

ALFRED CORN

TO REITERATE

Michel Butor says that to travel is to write, because to travel is to read. This can be developed further: To write is to travel, to write is to read, to read is to write, and to read is to travel. But George Steiner says that to translate is also to read, and to translate is to write, as to write is to translate and to read is to translate. So that we may say: To translate is to travel and to travel is to translate. To translate a travel writing, for example, is to read a travel writing, to write a travel writing, to read a writing, to write a writing, and to travel. But if because you are translating you read, and because writing translate, because travelling write, because travelling read, and because translating travel, that is, if to read is to translate, and to translate is to write, to write to travel, to read to travel, to write to read, to read to write, and to travel to translate, then to write is also to write, and to read is to read and even more, because when you are reading you read, but when reading also travel and because travelling read, therefore read and read, and when reading also write, therefore read, and reading also translate, therefore read, therefore read, read, read, and read, and the same argument may be made for translating, travelling and writing.

LYDIA DAVIS

CAPTAIN COOK

So often had he sailed the world in dream
That even the first voyage was more like homage
To the gods of repetition than like discovery.

The day the landbirds perched in the spars
After months of empty seas could have been many days.
Again through mist the steep headland
Or the same flat beach at dawn when the sky cleared
Or darkened. Always the excited crowds on shore,
The flotilla of canoes, the eager swimmers,
Young men and girls laughing among the ropes.

Today he may call their home New Zealand,
Tomorrow the Society Islands or Friendly Islands.
And this is Mercury Bay, Hawke Bay, or Bream Bay.
Time again for patching the wound in the main keel,
For refilling the water casks and exchanging cloth and nails
For pigs and fruit, rock oysters and yams.

Always the same trouble with island thieves,
The spyglass missing again, the quadrant, the anchor buoys,
More shovels, pulleys, bolts, and screws,
Till the worst offenders are driven off with small shot
Or flogged, and the sailors are flogged again
For not watching their muskets carefully.

Today as before the Captain rows after two deserters
And climbs the hill again to their leafy hideaway
And drags them from the arms of the weeping island girls
Back to the ship, and again the sailors wail
Like Odysseus's sailors dragged back from the Lotos fields.

This captain is no Odysseus, no raider of cities.
He takes no booty as he claims an island
For the King, trying simply to fill
The white spots of his map with dots and lines,
Unseduced by a hunger for experience,
By the gospel of growing whole,
Patient like a man who's been everywhere
When the chief rows out to deliver his long
Incomprehensible speech of welcome,
Willing to hear him to the end and make in return
His own incomprehensible speech
And then rub noses, as is the custom there.

Not a part of all he meets, though no one is readier
To taste the boiled South-Sea dog and the worm stew,
No one more impressed by the night-long paddle dance.
It doesn't matter to him how much or little his heart
Is written on by adventure as he writes in his log
His reckoning of the latitude, practicing the same skill
He practiced before in the same Pacific
Under the numbered phases of the moon
And the wheel of stars.

LETCHWORTH STATE PARK

Because she pauses awhile
In the middle of the shaky footbridge
To look down at the spume,
Not listening as you mention the refreshment stand
And the options for the evening movie,
You needn't assume she's sorry she's come with you
And would rather be pausing elsewhere
With someone else.

Maybe it doesn't even mean
She thinks of you as a stranger
Though it shouldn't surprise you if she does.
Dig down past your opinions;
Empty your mind for a minute of thought;
And what's left? Only a hollow place,
A gorge whose slopes and bottom are not visible
As they are here, no spruce, no river.

Put yourself in her place.
Think how thousands could have given the speech
You gave on the drive down
About Honduras and El Salvador,
How we keep backing the rich few
Against the poor many, staining the flag.
Thousands, and how can she be sure
Your words betoken a love of justice,
Hours of lost sleep,
Not spoken merely to fill the ride up?
And how can you be sure?

It can't be reason you want from her,
A bridge more rickety than the bridge she's standing on,
Swaying over a deeper gorge.
It can't be meager honesty.
Something without questions must help unstintedly
If she's to cross over and greet you
As friends greet friends on the dock
After a long voyage.
"Let me look at you," they say.
"You look good. You look wonderful."

CARL DENNIS

We stand still. "And Kafka?" I say.

"Kafka is not buried here."

"No? Because I thought— What I mean is the lady at my hotel's tourist information desk—the Intercontinental over there—and the one who sold me the ticket now, both told me—"

He's shaking his head, looks at me straight-faced. It's up to you, his look says, if you're going to give me anything for this tour. I won't ask. I won't embarrass you if you don't even give me a crown. But I'm not going to stand here all day waiting for it.

"Here, I want to give you something for all this." I look in my wallet. Smallest is a twenty note. Even if I got three-to-one on the black market, it's still too much. I feel the change in my pocket. Only small coins. He's done this routine with plenty of people, that's for sure, and I'd really like to not give him anything. "Come, come," he said.

"You understand? For Kafka's grave?" I said. "Just as I told the lady at the ticket window, I'm sure the other parts of this ticket for the Old Synagogue and the Jewish Museum are all very interesting—maybe I'll take advantage of it some other time—but what I realy came to see—"

"Yes, come, come. I work here too. I will show you."

I followed him up a stone path past hundreds of gravestones on both sides, sometimes four or five or I don't know how many of them pressed up or leaning against one another. He stopped, I did and looked around for Kafka's grave, though I knew one of these couldn't be it. "You see," he said, "the governor at the time—it was the fourteenth century and by now there were twelve thousand peopld buried here. He said 'no' when the Jewish elders of Prague asked to expand the cemetery. So what did the Jews do? They built down and up, not outwards, not away. They kept inside the original lines of the cemetery permitted them. Twelve times they built down and up till they had twelve of what do you call them in English, plateaus? Places?" and he moved his hand up in levels.

"Levels?"

"Yes, that would be right. Twelve of them and then the ground stopped and they also couldn't go any higher up without being the city's highest cemetery hill, so they couldn't make any levels anymore."

"So that accounts for these gravestones being, well, the way they are. Belowground there's actually twelve coffins or their equivalents, one of top of—"

"Yes, yes, that's so." He walked on about fifty feet, stopped. "Another governor wouldn't let the Jews in this country take the names of son-of anymore. Son of Icaac, Son of Abraham. They had to take, perhaps out of punishment, but history is not clear on this, the names of animals or things from the earth and so on." He pointed to the stone relief of a lion at the top of one gravestone. "Lion, you see." To a bunch of grapes on another stone. "Wine, this one. And others, if we took the time to look, all around, but of that historical era."

"So that's why the name Kafka is that of a bird, if I'm not mistaken. Jackdaw, I understand it means in Czech. The Kafka family, years back, must have taken it or were given it, right? Which?"

"Yes, Kafka. Kafka." I didn't think by his expression he understood me. "Come, please." We moved on another hundred feet or so, stopped. "See these two hands on the monument? That is the stone of one who could give blessings—a Cohen. No animal there, but his sign. Next to it," pointing to another gravestone, "is a jaw."

"A jaw?" The stone relief on this one was of a pitcher. "Jar, do you mean?"

"Yes. Jaw, jaw. That is a Levi, one who brings the holy water to wash the hands of a Cohen. That they are side by side is only a coincidence. On the next monument you see more berries but of a different kind than wine. Fertility."

"Does that mean a woman's buried here? Or maybe a farmer?"

"Yes. Come, come." We went past many stones and sarcophagi. All of them seemed to be hundreds of years old and were crumbling in places. Most of the names and dates on them couldn't be read. The newer section of the cemetery, where Kafka has to be buried, must be in an area one can't see from here. I remembered the photograph of the gravestone of Kafka and his parents. Kafka's name on top—he was the first to go—his father's and mother's below his. It was in a recent biography of him I'd read, or at least read the last half of, not really being interested in the genealogical and formative parts of an artist's life, before I left for Europe. The stone was upright, though the photo could have been taken many years ago, and close to several other upright stones but not touching them. The names and dates on it, and also the lines in Hebrew under Kafka's name, could be read clearly. It looked no different than the gravestone in an ordinary relatively old crowded Jewish cemetery. The one a couple of miles past the Queens side of the 59th Street Bridge where some of my own family are buried.

He walked, I followed him. "Here is the monument of Mordecai Maisel. It is much larger than the others because he was a very rich important man. More money than even the king, he had. The king would borrow from him when he needed it for public matters. Later, after he paid it back, he would say to him 'Mordecai, what can I give you in return for this great favor?' Mordecai would always say 'Give not to me but to my people,' and that did help to make life better in Prague for the Jews of that time. He was a good, wealthy man, Mordecai Maisel. Come, come."

We stopped at another sarcophagus. Hundreds of little stones had been placed on the ledges and little folded-up pieces of paper pushed into the crevices of it. "Here is Rabbi Löw. As you see, people still put notes inside his monument asking for special favors from him."

"Why, he was a mystic?"

"You don't know of the famous Rabbi Löw?"

"No. I mean, his name does sound familiar, but I'm afraid my interest is mostly literature. Kafka. I've seen several of his residences in this neighborhood. Where he worked for so many years near the railroad station, and also that very little house on Golden Lane, I think it's translated as, across the river near the castle. A couple of places where Rilke lived too."

"So, literature, what else am I talking of here? *The Golem.* A world-famous play. Well? Rabbi Löw. Of the sixteenth century. He started it. He's known all over."

"I've certainly heard of the play. It was performed in New York City—in a theater in Central Park—last summer. I didn't know it was Rabbi Löw who started the legend."

"Yes, *he, he*. The originator. Others may say other rabbis might have, but it was only Rabbi Löw, nobody else. Then he knocked the Golem to pieces when it went crazy on him. Come, come."

We went on. He showed me the grave of the only Jewish woman in medieval Prague who was permitted to marry nobility. "Her husband buried here too?" I said. "No, of course not. It was out-of-religion. The permission she got to marry was from our elders. He's somewhere else." The stone of one of the mayors of the Jewish ghetto in seventeenth century Prague. The stone of a well-known iron craftsman whose name he had to repeat to me several times before I gave up trying to make it out but nodded I had finally understood him. Then we came to the entrance again. After he told me Kafka wasn't buried here and I give him the twenty note for the tour and he pockets it, I ask if he might know where Kafka's buried.

"Oh, in Strašnice cemetery. The Jewish part of it, nothing separate anymore. It isn't far from here. You take a tube. Fifteen minutes and you are there," and one of his hands moves off the other like a train going straight out to it. "It's in walking distance from the station. On a nice day unlike today, the walk is a simple and pleasant one. And once you have reached it you ask at the gate to see Kafka's grave and someone there will show you around."

STEPHEN DIXON

HARSH THUNDER

Over drumlins thunder lasts, rolls through time: black sky a thick skin shaken. The highway is numbered but the number doesn't matter. Only the storm he walks into, and the moments before the storm when air starts to crack and hum.

What was is behind him: years that never happened. He dreamed the bright skin of women, legs and thighs like lightning, muscled as fast cars, and found children, and a job that went from nine to five, and dusty weekends, and nights asleep in his clothes on furnishings that owned him.

So this highway that leads to other highways that cross the country claims him, and he leaves tracking New York mud through Pennsylvania, West Virginia, Kentucky, heads south and west for warmer weather, dreams again of where the road will take him, of bodies that open for him, of meals served in a home that mounts a hillside, cars, planes. As does: The Mexican walking toward him two thousand miles distant. The Vietnamese colonel who boards a foreign plane. A black kid, waits under the Atlantic City boardwalk. A white man, turns away from a Georgia farm.

Evening approaches and they all grow hungry.

The sky flies out over all of them, and holds them together in its relentless weather.

EDWARD FALCO

A PARIS SUITE

1

Sometimes the clouds run off and the stone lights up
cascades of contrast on the old facades
you think will last forever it's so deep
and old: old European light
someone called mother-of-pearl.
You cannot cross the rich grass of the past
you have to come from behind
on your narrow path, in your heavy coat
while your heavy breath tries to rise.
So leave it for the primrose and impatiens.
If summer comes
the all-pervasive issue of the moment
—clouds or sky, water or clear air—
dissolves in the general windlessness
and the bricks of the Place lie flat in the sun
and the old question re-occurs
(it does even tonight beneath the snow
that lasts just as long as it takes to cross it):
something about yourself and the powerful
lord on his high unimpeachable horse.

2

From the top of the mountain today you can suddenly see
the towers surrounding the city.
The walls don't exist any more
but we could be medieval citizens
in our winter cloaks and boots
the kind of scribe
who sits at home and copies in weak light
or wanders on the cobblestone and straw.

The day wastes itself.
Only your red umbrella
enlivens the aquamarine bedspread
till the Alsaciennes next door start laughing
and the courtyard lights are lit:
it's Parisian night.
Then you come in and we go out
to watch the French stars dodging the rooftops.

3

The strongbow you draw back when you enter the garden
is aimed at the heart of the palace guarded by soldiers
who are younger and stronger than you.
The vista almost stretches out of sight
but you walk it, you bring it to its end
halfway between the rows of upraised fists
and the male and female gods
symmetrically disposed at the points of the compass.

Man is everywhere in his divine
aspect: his cold white flesh
is stark against the winter green
as you scatter the lovingly raked sand in the twelve directions,
proud to be something disordered and out of place,
foreign, like the tree that leafs out of season
the one fountain that someone is playing.

4

The sad gaiety of the hand organ
if you hear it
changes the afternoon
into something with a depth
a wound you can get into if you want to
or a screen with a life behind it
like the smoky blue of the sky that reminds you of elsewhere
where you felt less circumspect, or less divided.
Paris is another word for home
but not in your language.
for you it is the sample in solution

the skin dyed radioactive.
You hold it up against those semi-abstract
pictures the sky keeps painting
kaleidoscopic forms that imitate
the drifting crowds around
the post-electric building.
And the rain falls in your oysters, thins your wine
so you walk the locked-up streets, not really cold
till something develops, you go inside
and one of you is finally big enough
to cancel the other.

                            5
Then finally the gentle moment comes
or seems to come.
The air is the same temperature you are
or seems to be,
a little wind just barely stirs the leaves
that have appeared.
At night you walk along a wall
and sense a garden on the other side.

It will be cold again, the sun will be
impossible
(even today he seems to threaten to)
and the rain will return with its storms
to shatter the roofs long after you're gone.
But something in the moment promises
a kind of truce
a way of life that isn't always
terror and compromise.
Like everything it always breaks its promise
and comes back to remake it not even abashed
not even with its tail between its legs.
Yet tonight the royal alleys blaze around us
under a half-open sky. The constellations blink
in the light fields over the clouds—
a sign, a dare,
a rearrangement in the air.

Another piece of the world
that says it fits and does because it says so
offers its exaltation here and now.
We're brave for once tonight,
stare back and take it in,
watching the glare of winter disappear.

JONATHAN GALASSI

EVENING IN BANGKOK

The perimeters of light behind Wat Pho,
the long-boats working upriver,
and flowergirls, not twelve years old,
emerge in the traffic with fragrant strands,
bell-like and pungent as gardenias,
in hands more delicate and eyes
black as prayer.
Garlands sewn by their keepers
to embrace a wrist
or dangle from a rearview mirror,
adorn the Buddha on the dash.

The light changes.
You buy her flowers.
You're moving now.
You want to give her something more,
perhaps to say forgive me.

DAN GERBER

WAITING IN THE AIRPORT

On the same journey each of them
Is going somewhere else. A goose-necked
Woman in a flowered dress
Stares gravely at two businessmen.
They turn away but carry on
Their argument on real estate.

Lost in a mist of aftershave,
A salesman in a brown toupee
Is scribbling on his *Racing Form*
While a fat man stares down at his hands
As if there should be something there.

The soldiers stand in line for sex—
With wives or girlfriends, whoever
They hope is waiting for them at
The other end. The wrapped perfume,
The bright, stuffed animals they clutch
Tremble under so much heat.

Lives have been pulled cross continent.
So much will soon be going on
But somewhere else—divorces, birthdays,
Deaths and million dollar deals.

But nothing ever happens here,
This terminal that narrows to
A single unattended gate,
One entrance to so many worlds.

INSTRUCTIONS FOR THE AFTERNOON

Leave the museums, the comfortable rooms,
the safe distractions of the masterpiece.
The broken goddesses have lost their voice,
the martyr's folded hands no longer bless.
Footsteps echo through the palaces
where no one lives. Consider what you've come for.

Leave the museums. Find the dark churches
in back towns that history has forgotten,
the unimportant places the powerful ignore
where commerce knows no profit will be made.
Sad hamlets at the end of silted waterways,
dry mountain villages where time
is the thin shadow of an ancient tower
that moves across the sundazed pavement of the square
and disappears each evening without trace.

Make the slow climb up the winding alleys.
Walk between houses shuttered close for midday
and overhear the sound of other lives,
the conversations in the language you
will never learn. Make the long ascent,
up to the grey, stone chapel on the hillside
when summer is a furnace open to the world,
and pause there breathless in the blinding sun
only one moment, then enter.

                    For this
is how it must be seen to understand:
by walking from the sunlight into darkness,
by groping down the aisle
as your wet skin cools, as your eyes adjust,
by finding what you've come for thoughtlessly
shoved off into a corner, almost lost
among the spectacle of gold and purple.

Here in the half light, covered by the years
it will exist. And wait,
Wait like the stone face of a statue waits
frozen in the moment before action.
Or like a mirror in an empty room
whose resolutions are invisible
to anyone but you.

                    And so
standing there face to face, without a guide
in a place you have never been before,
you will discover how you have returned.

THE WORN STEPS

But if the vision fails, and the damp air
stinks of summer must and disrepair,
if the worn steps rising to the altar
lead nowhere but to stone, this, too, could be
the revelation—but of a destiny
fixed as the graceless frescoes on the wall—
the grim and superannuated gods
who rule this shadow-land of marble tombs
bathed in its green sub-oceanic light.
Not a vision to pursue, and yet
these insufficiencies make up the world.
Strange how all journeys come to this: the sun
bright on the unfamiliar hills, new vistas
dazzling the eye, the stubborn heart unchanged.

                              DANA GIOIA

138

ONLY METAL: CROSSING THE DESERT

Before setting out again upon this journey, once a very private experience, now about to be swapped, like a story, with readers whose parallel or diverging paths I can only imagine, a few prefatory comments will be helpful. To begin with the inevitable irony of time's passage. Subjectively, I both am and am not the woman who kept the journal which, as natural verbal counterpart of this sort of experience, seems its inevitable presentational format. Indeed, without the journal, there could be no conceivable replay of the journey itself. Yet nine years have intervened, during the course of which our complementary inner desert in arid patch after patch has been unerring disclosing itself, so that the consciousness of the narrator seems rather thinner in texture than her dutiful editor (me) might wish. Meanwhile, the outer desert crossed has tragically encroached upon those lands, watered by the River Niger, which were her/my destination. The ragged figures begging at the passes of the Adrar des Iforhas were victims of the drought of 1973, now seen as harbinger of so much worse to come a decade later. Which processes, keeping pace, exemplify that mysterious relation all travellers feel between lay of the land and disposition of thoughts and feelings.

Originally, my dictionary tells me, "travel" and "travail" were synonymous—hard work. For women, the lexicographer adds, "travil" is a being-in-labor. Which is certainly true in this instance. As I kept best track I could of that desert crossing, something new was being born in me—a new accountability for experience. Though I had been places before, how I arrived, the route taken, was always expediential. The desert crossing was different. To be sure, I was going to Africa, for the second time and for a protracted stay; but this time the route to be taken had its own integrity, to be experienced as such. Which is to say that the process of "crossing the desert," all absorbing, imposed itself as task. Even now I cannot entirely account for its meaning; but certainly, never before or since, have I been so aware of "travelling" as in the course of those fifteen days in the early fall of 1976 which led me from Rome to Gao.

Part of the hard work of that passage, its subtext, had to do with accomplishing a major transition in my life. Since I didn't dwell in the journal upon the painful context of my leaving, nor upon those left behind, for this I mistakenly thought, would have been to abrogate responsibility to the immediacy of the undertaking, I allude to this situation here to account for a certain tension, extraneous to the going-concerns, making itself felt between the lines.

Further *lavore stanca* is implicit in automobile travel, not my usual way of getting anywhere. But having a car in Africa that year-to-come seemed of the utmost importance at the time. Upon reflection it seems almost comically obvious. Not only did the little landrover of which I became immediately so fond symbolize the stirrings, after much black inertia, of a hopeful motility, it also promised to be a transitional mobile home of my own to replace the broken-up familial. But the trouble with a car, apart from any potential mechanical problems, is that you're stuck in it. Though a car protects, ensuring a certain comfort together with the efficient gaining of one's destination, it also insulates its occupants, isolates them. Which, under certain circumstances can be a good thing, under others, not. A car has doors, perhaps even a tail gate, but no exit.

And with the work of the car into the story comes the young man I have called Stephen. As soon as the research grant enabling the trip came through, my aunt sent me a marvelous new-age book called *Everything I Know About Cars* by Stephanie Judy. I was tempted to take time out to read that book thoroughly, then to study the landrover manual I eventually ordered for Stephen. Moreover, I was tempted to study mechanics on location with one of those blue jump-suited artesans who people Italian garages. It wasn't simply lack of free time and mental space; in my heart of hearts I chickened out. Being born too soon, and perhaps also of too compliant a disposition for true liberation, all but the simplest gadgets continue to mystify me. The list of automobile parts eventually put into the landrover even now fills me with amused wonder as I come across it pasted onto the back cover of the sturdy *Registro* in which I kept log, diary, and eventually field-notes.

Stephen, then twenty-four, was the eldest son of old friends in the States. Ever since boyhood, Stephen had been a natural mechanic, which disposition was leading him into a career of

140

metal sculpture making. At the time, though, he was free to travel, indeed delighted to be asked to cross the desert with me. We had always enjoyed what we both took to be a mutual understanding—that of honorary aunt to nephew. But alas, as it turned out, our temperaments did not mesh well under stress. That he was by then less mature than I had assumed he would be is true; but by the same token I proved incapable of negotiating the relationship. As I read back over the journal, I am apalled by my deep unwillingness fruitfully to empathize with Stephen on the personal, as opposed to the archetypal level. Imprisoned not so much in a car as in an interlocking of complexes (containing the seeds of both our subsequent liberations), somewhere along the road I actually gave up hope of explicit communication between us. It is in this regard that the "me-now" most radically parts company with that "she" who crossed the desert, ailingly, by his side.

Finally, as is true of all journeys worth the taking, there is the questing, or mythological aspect. And here we venture on rather unknown territory. It was Odysseus who travelled. Penelope stayed at home. So very little has been written on this adventuring aspect of feminine consciousness. Mary Kingsley was an astonishingly intrepid and observant African traveller, but it's hard to know how she more deeply felt about what she was up to. The women of the Annapurna expedition were aware of much more than a Victorian traveller could be, even if she were not only intrepid but a mystic, like Alexandra David-Neal.

I'm not all that intrepid, and if mystical, it's in a different way than that of the truly remarkable French Tibetanist. The resolve to cross the desert, separate from that desire for a car, which could quite logically have been purchased in Bamako, Niamey or Lagos, numinously uncovered itself in a poem inspired by the following lines from Sophocles (Fitzgerald translation).

Then, suddenly,
A storm of dust roared up from the earth, and the sky
Went out, the plain vanished with all its trees
In the stinging dark. We closed our eyes and endured it.
The whirlwind lasted a long time, but it passed;
And then we looked, and there was Antigone.

The resolve, therefore, had to do with death, burial, defiance of "Creon," and. . .

During the end of that long waiting period, with its ritualized visits to the post office, among the guests who showed up in the Trastevere apartment on a friend-of-a-friend basis was a youthful Jungian analyst, who made his entrance into the conversation with a theory about Pavese. "My" Pavese. Apparently he had failed to establish contact with the *anima* (his female principle) except in his poetry where, taking the face of Death, She eventually led the poet to suicide. Hmmmm. I remember saying rather testily, "You, all you people are so preoccupied with the Great Mother in all her guises. Tell me, Concetto (for that was actually his name, "Concept,") how does the *animus* manifest itself to a woman in nature?" "As desert," he replied quickly, without thinking, "or, more particularly, as a dry wind from the desert. A woman never goes alone into the desert," he added, as if reading my mind, "It is the man who goes alone into the desert and receives his vision there." The conversation drifted into another direction. But as he was leaving, this Concetto looked me in the eye and remarked, in an undertone, "It would be a tragedy, Signora, to go into the desert with your son."

Thus, in an eerie way, were foreshadowed certain mythological components with which the author of this travelogue must struggle in partnership with the sly voice of the *I Ching*, which consistantly reminds of the obligation to maintain moral balance. I did not consult the Chinese oracle that evening, when the frightening lineaments of the mask my *animus* might be wearing adumbrated themselves in the course of Concetto's conversation. For the resolve had already been made. However, when the go-ahead arrived from America on the Ides of March, I did throw the coins. The result was hexagram #15, "Modesty," with moving lines in first and second places. It furthered, the sages said, "to cross the great water," but one must proceed carefully, with disciplined sincerity of purpose.

It was at this juncture that I sought help, or perhaps more truthfully found myself in the office of Dora Bernhard, who was surely the only person in Rome who could have helped me realize the crossing, however it would present itself. From that room, perched high on the Trinità del Monte, I looked out upon the earthly city with a new mode of detachment. Then I looked at her, this very old little woman, whose husband had originally brought Jungian concepts across the Alps to Rome, and knew, for the first time, mutely, what true courage could be. As viaticum came the following dream: "There were twin red and white anchors—lively things, rather like Senufo ancestral spirit-masks with small hinged legs which, as I watched, unfolded and dug themselves firmly into the desert sand." Only now, with the help of an Ephemeris, have I begun to probe the meaning of that dream, but then the visceral message was all I needed: Since we're here, digging in and steadying, you can let go, truly give yourself to the journey.

Tuesday, August 31, eve of departure. André Szabo, that Israeli from FAO, called to say "I like you." Thanks André, I'll admit I need that sort of thing amidst this total collapse of all the old structures. Even my desk has been moved out of the studio. There remains the bouganvillea outside on the *terrazza*. This I shall remember always. You say you like me, André, because you know Mali and wish you could be going back, and because we share a certain mad-cap energy, which I've battened down with a thousand and one tangible precautions, including your own last-minute advice about the springs.

We went back to Suriano's garage. He was magnanimous. If we don't use the spare front spring, it can be returned to him eventually without charge. A loaned spring! Pleased to see how Stephen had painted "Suriano, Landrover Services, Roma," on the cab, the maestro took pictures of the rig, which he has good reason to be proud of.

Three generations of Surianos, aided by blue jump-suited apprentices, had been working for over a week on the second hand, 1968, 88" wheel-base, hard-top diesel landrover I named MAMY WATEH. During this time, under Suriano *filho*'s inspired supervision, out of thin iron strips they had constructed a fanciful superstructure called the *porta-bagagli* and four heavy sand ladders. These accoutrements were painted cream-white to match

143

the solid metal flaps of the pick-up. MAMY's stalwart body was a lovely color—greyish green, with lots of white and a tinge of blue in it.

The early pages of the journal are filled with columns of addition, tiresome evidence of how dogged I was from the very beginning by financial concerns—one-third of the modest grant already gone by the time I left the shop—centered in the car, whose maintenance, once the Surianos provided their best, had been entrusted to the young man, Stephen, as though to a recalcitrant, however creative, part of my own unconscious. The camping equipment and tools of documentation (film, tapes, etc.) were my conscious responsibility, gladly taken on.

In the beginning, then, there were lists, which gradually materialized into things, each in its place, ready to engage in dialogue with terrain, event, and personality. In the beginning there were also cosmic signs. The MAMY WATEH's top panels were emblazoned with cheerful esoterica, including the sequence of geometrical patterns with which upper Niger canoe paddles are inscribed, hexagram #15 in its block of mostly short lines, a spiral turbulence like those depicted on weather maps to symbolize the African goddesses Nyalè and Oyá, and the words "Niger-river" run together like that in black lettering.

Out of the shop, the miraculous vehicle was parked in Signor Pellegrini's lot, behind a big wooden door on the Vicolo del Piede, just a few steps from the Trastevere apartment through which I moved now like a ghost of the already-departed. For the past couple of days Stephen, two Roman kids and I had been painting and loading the MAMY WATEH in the sole company of stray cats, sunlight and festive banners of laundry suspended from trolley lines originating in the kitchen windows of environing tenements. Now, as we brought her back with two spare springs from her final visit to Suriano's garage, another car was parked there—a stubby sister Toyota belonging to a Dottóre who, Signor Pellegrini informed us, had only last May returned from his own Sahara crossing. "Why this is astonishing! Where does he live?" "Wait a little minute, Signora, and Il Dottóre will arrive to pick up his car."

Not only had he crossed the Sahara in that spiffy little Toyota, but he had taken the so-called *Bidon Cinque* route,

144

which I had chosen as being, though not picturesque, the most direct. Yes, one can see the *bidons* (oil cans) at intervals, and so avoid getting lost, the Dottóre confirmed. But there are few other travellers. Instead, an immense solitude. *Confronto da se,* he specified, with metaphysical relish. He had driven for nine days without speaking to anyone (except himself, I suppose, reflexively). Why had he gone—this vital, robust little man with grey hair and tanned skin? Solely for the sake of the *confronto?* This is precisely the question not to be asked of strangers who wear their privacy like a cloak—of the type worn by messengers from the gods in old time travelogues and odysseys.

Tuesday, September 2. Nine am, waiting in line for the Tunis ferry. Our take off yesterday was so natural, I can't believe it to be the result of so many months of anxious planning and preparation. A few shouts, wavings of hands as we roared out of Pelligrini's parking lot, taking a hard left where the street's foot arches, and that was that. A few more manoeuvres through narrow cobblestone streets and already we were on the Lungo Tevere. We might have been going on a simple jaunt to the beach for the day. No tumultuous feelings. These are buried too far beneath my own crank shaft. Instead, in a holiday mood we cruised slowly down to Naples on 28 litres of *naptha.* Stopped off for a swim in Gaeta with Carlo Cassola, looking like Neptune, his grizzled chest barreled from much swimming. Around the promontory often, he says, always alone, a four hour stint— weather permitting. Out on the billows he led us, so buoyantly, across great swells and treacherous currents he knows so well that it's impossible in such company to fear them. Mutter, aged 87, was there watching—a wisp on the shore. "I don't mean to live past 90,"she said in Italian. "I've lived long enough, don't you think?" Never long enough for me, Mutter; surely you are the most beautiful person on earth. Katinka was friendly. For the first time I was conscious of her vulnerability, of her dependence on Mario. "Why is it," Stephen observed when we were out on the highway again, "that for all his love of the ocean, the water line in his paintings is like a barrier? And the water itself static as a mirror?"

We charged the rover up and around the hills of this energetic city (touristic tour for Stephen) before settling for the night on the docks in the shadow of a closed customs office. Stephen on the roof (bumpy, he said); me in the cab (procrustian). Drunken American sailors straggled by during the night in twosomes and threesomes. Now they are leading immense semi-trucks with names like KYLMAKULIETUS or RASIMELLI & COLETTI. Soon MAMY WATEH will be wedged into the hold like a porpoise among elephants.

Saturday, September 4, early morning. Leaving M'Daourouch (not on the map), having filled our water cans at a spring.

Thursday we spent on the ferry—a terrible place, bureaucratically run. Forbidden to walk around, to eat except at specified moments, etc. I escaped for a round of barre exercises on the top deck in a stiff breeze. Anyhow, we survived that day and the next were in Africa! But aha, then ensued hours of bumbling through Tunisian officialdom. Had to get car insurance, even though we weren't going to be in that country for more than a few hours. Drank coffee and ate bread standing up in the rain at the open-air counter of the Bar du Port, before rattling off over mountainous roads for the Algerian border, which we crossed at Ghardinaou.

Though the Tunisian countryside is prosperous, the people glimpsed along the road beautifully dressed in bright dyed wools and heavy woven cottons, the Tunisian customs house is a nondescript cement-block structure; whereas the Algerian frontier station, entered through a lush garden and loggia set with blue and white tiles, announced paradise to come. . . ? We were asked to take an official passenger on down to Souk Ahras, where we treated ourselves to a delicious dinner at the hotel restaurant before setting off in a downpour. Who knows where we were headed? Anywhere. . . . The mountain roads became increasingly treacherous and the squall turned into a violent thunder storm. Flashes of lightning indicated a low cement block house with a tin roof. We stopped, ran inside to look around, and quick as thought the owner, with a plastic tarp over his head, appeared. He gave us permission to spend the night on his unfinished aggregate floor (very uncomfortable, but dry). As soon as it was light we drove on down the M'Darouch road to a stand of pines, where we stopped to get breakfast and discovered a fresh mountain spring. My little kerosene stove is entirely inadequate. I'll have to buy a good one in Biskra. Top priority. Also eight big plastic water jars for the crossing. Would that they all could be filled with pine spring water!

Sunday, September 5, on the way down from Biskra to Ourgala, an ancient caravan city, situated (according to the map) in a trough between two giant ergs. Sunset: exactly 5:55 pm. We have stopped for supper at a little restaurant in Tougou, where the count-down is now taking place. It is Tabaski, the Moslem equivalent of Lent. No food may touch tasting lips until the precise moment of the sun's passing below the horizon. In the center of the room there's a table of men, spoons humped over the edges of their soup bowls, waiting for the announcement to arrive via short wave radio. At another small table like ours an elegant young man sits alone reading a photo-romance. Stephen's reading the landrover manual.

In Biskra we met Hadid Abdemalike, twenty-four years old, who took us to a coffee house with a friend of his who, having gone to Koranic school, speaks no French. Hadid spent two years at the *lycée* in Algiers before being summoned home to support a family of ten brothers and sisters. His father is over seventy. When Hadid has time, he likes to participate in Party affairs— demonstrations and the like. Afterwards, he helped me buy a huge camping-gas stone, sky blue, for 139 dinars (about $35). "Why don't you fast, anyhow, even if you aren't a Moslem?" suggested the guy in dark glasses from whom I bought the stove. "It is good, Madame, the discipline." Ah, perhaps; however. . . . I couldn't explain to him the stringency I'm in the midst of, constantly. It's a curious inner thing, reflected back at me from mileage meter and gas gauge, from the cramped muscles in my legs. So eating well becomes of great importance. In the Biskra market there was delicious bread for sale, and tomatoes, and those sticky honey-dipped fried pastries first encountered in Souk Aras. The fields outside town are being cultivated by tractors.

Monday, September 6, almost evening, entering the oasis of Ghardaia, 50 kilometers ahead. Today we spent the morning hanging out in Ourgala. It is a white walled city with a vast empty space in the center.

The light is dazzling. Without dark glasses the light would be impossible for blue eyes to bear. An army band is rehearsing behind a high fence. Behind a low latticed concrete wall Koranic school is in session. Supervised by an older boy, an obstreperous group of kids recite pell-mell off their wooden slates. Restlessly I pace the perimeter of this absurd parade ground, with its pompous reviewing stand, empty of everything but glare. Pacing along the edge, grateful for whatever scrap of shade, I become more reconciled to, even in a pitiful way defiant of whatever it is that stalks, with the hot breath of lions, beyond the unseen outer wall—on the other side of Koranic school and army barracks. Yes, it's there all right, carniverously keeping exact pace with me. "It is good to fast, Madame; the discipline—you need it out here."

Early this morning we were given a gift of dates by an old man the fenced edge of whose orchard we awoke to find ourselves camped against. The little basket was covered with bamboo leaves. "Otherwise the flies will follow you everywhere," the old man said.

So we spent the morning hanging out in Ourgala. It was odd. As if under separate spells, Stephen his taciturn gloom, me my restless bout with Allah's prowler, or whatever it was out there, we went our ways. Who knows where Stephen gravitated? Out of my sight, for sure; I got out of his.

Then, wouldn't you know, leaving, finally, at high noon, we got ourselves stuck in the sand. Unhooked, for the first time, Suriano's ladders.

It's strenuous work. As ladder-bearer you have to run behind the car, haul one up into place, then two, while the driver lumbers, heavy-tired in low-low gear, across the bridge made by the initial pair. As soon as you've got them placed, you run back for the pair the car has just rolled over, pushing those ladders down, almost burying them in the sand. So you have to take each one up with a quick prying motion. And they're worth their weight in iron, all right, Suriano!

We weren't the only ones to have gotten stuck there outside Ourgala. Sunken bodies of army cars, like surfaced porpoises, gleam here and there as brown as the day, decades ago, they were first impatiently abandoned. Still amazingly intact. Nothing rusts in the desert. Somewhere, lightly covered by a dune, one might come upon a Roman chariot. For time also stays stuck in an incorruptable present tense, so thick it would take a blow torch to dissipate a single moment.

Tuesday, September 7, leaving campsite south of Ghardaia, a magical city which appeared all blue as we drove down into its hollow last evening at dusk. Actually, Ghardaia is a conglomeration of several fortified towns, each walled to its own hill; but all the buildings are painted light blue, and the whole glows from a distance with electrification. When was that installed? Could oil lamps once have produced the same enchantment?

We wandered around from 6 to 8, because in Ghardaia every enterprise shuts down just before sunset during Tabaski so the inhabitants can eat at home. Down in the wholesale produce market we were given our second gift from the desert by an old man in a white turban, guardian of the goods, who sat on a sack of melons making that sweet mint-flavored tea, called Touareg tea in Mali which all men and boys whatever their origin brew and drink. We sat there on melon sacks beside him as he brewed the traditional three pots from the same leaves. Three shot glasses ceremoniously filled with that frothy amber nectar, as we sat, smoked, and philosophized the way travellers before small camel dung fires used to socialize in the open-air caravansarai which Ghardaia once was. Knives sheathed beneath their robes, backs to the chill desert winds, the original tea drinkers of Ghardaia would have sat on through the night; but we said good-bye to the old produce-watchman who, in exchange for a package of Marlboros, insisted on giving me five succulent tomatoes.

An hour or so later we stood in a crowded bar and drank two miniature Turkish coffees, one right after the other. Beside us a man in a red and white wool ski cap conversed in authoritative-sounding Arabic to his European-looking son while a beautiful black man, over six feet tall, his friendly face swathed in a deep indigo turban, looked on.

Camped outside of town later on Stephen announced that he would like to study Arabic. He was born in Egypt; and the sounds of the Muezzin must have coiled themselves about his inner ear at such an early age as to make English talk, his father's constant discourse on topic after topic, seem unaccountably harsh, incomprehensible, eventually, I suspect, inaudible. Yes, I encouraged him; it would be wonderful to learn Arabic.

There was a moon, which came up well past midnight to illuminate the barren knoll upon which the tent was so fragilely pitched, as upon a withered sea whose droplets, one by one over the centuries, had been surreptitiously replaced by specks of gravel.

Wednesday, September 8, leaving campsite between El Golea and Adrar. I had wanted to take a little excursion to In Salah, where, according to Viviana Paques, a possession cult still flourishes among descendents of a black enclave once enticed (or driven) there to perform agricultural labor, which desert tribes both disdain and are no good at. But Omar Abdellah, night watchman at the Hotel El Bustan in El Golea, told us the track between In Salah and Reggane is very bad, downright dangerous at the moment. A T.V. cameraman died there last week. Apparently he got lost following French army car tracks, fossilized in reconnaissance more than thirty years past. His companion survived, though, Omar Abdellah added, as sweetener to this depressing intelligence.

No way, said Stephen's up-hunch of the shoulders. And I concurred, on ethical grounds. His life is his to risk, not mine. Still, it's difficult to evaluate this information. Omar Abdellah is such a gloomy fellow to begin with: a man from the south blaming the northerners, who run the government, for exploiting the people. Whereas, had we been talking to Hadad Abdemalike of Biskra, we might have been given a different version of the incident. Maybe the T.V. cameraman was drunk. What was he up to, anyhow, in In Salah?

Anyhow, as if to compensate for the abandoned excursion to In Salah, Omar Abdellah offered to guide us on a pleasure jaunt to an artesian water spout forty kilometers away. Mute diffidence this time on Stephen's part. Come on, you'll see, it'll be fun. So what if it's slightly off the track. We've got a guide, and a conservative one at that.

Well, it was a joy to put on a bathing suit and kneel beneath the gush from a pipe propped on a tripod five feet above a shallow pool, really no more than a wide puddle so fast does the water sink into the sand. Behind the pipe gush, on slightly lower ground, was a green swamp in which two donkeys grazed, fetlock-deep. The two men stood by at a discreet distance, arms folded, in identical attitudes of amused tolerance as I bathed.

Word got out around the El Golea market that the European woman wanted to buy eggs; and within five minutes a small boy was by my side handing me a stiff little opaque plastic bag filled half-way with reddish sand. Nestled carefully were five pullet eggs. What an ingenious container! I have it not up front with me in the open glove compartment, where it rides steady as a bean bag.

18, Ku, with a moving line in second place, says the *I Ching*, cast early this morning. When "gentle indifference" of the wind meets "rigid inertia" of the mountain, this is what one gets: "Decay," repairs needed. A three day cautionary period is called for, following which, "assertive action" is suggested. That should take us right up to the "starting point" at Reggane. Uncanny. But which is which? Or are both somehow in me? Were this an African oracle, a sacrifice would be prescribed to facilitate the reparation process. When we stop, I'm going to crack all five precious eggs into the pan and dedicate an omelet.

Trab is the Arabic word for sand. *Fasa* the green, green leafy branches sold in the market as provender for donkeys. *Zlabia* the name for fried sweets.

Friday, September 10, camped on the soft sand, sparsely palmed, just outside the village of Mansouria, Wilaya d'Adrar. Arrived here late Wednesday. Thursday spent a frustrating day vainly trying to cash a travellers check. But the night was magical—for a while.

Stretching out on a blanket in the warm, gentle darkness, suddenly: the unmistakable sound of a drum. And as if in answer to a thought, Mahoméd. A young boy, intelligent almond-shaped eyes set in a thin face, framed by a gleaming new turban, emerged from the shadows into the light of the lantern set on the tail gate. He would take us there, half a kilometer across dim sand, through a clay arch into the heart of his village: secrecy spilled into a labyrinth of quiet clay walls. A diffused glow from a late rising moon sufficed, until a lamp indicated the narrow passage to an inner courtyard, upon whose sand two huge red and green wool rugs had been spread.

The space was alive with tittering young girls. A thin, dark, elder sister of about seventeen was playing a washtub drum, up-to-date version of the ancient palmwood and goatskin *tobal* Viviana Paques describes. Earth-sound of the *tobal* fecundates the listening womb, she says. As the drummer rotated palms and fingers upon galvanized metal, deeply resonating to the touch, resounding against the high, thick walls, the little girls clapped sharply x-x-x-xx; x-x-x-xx: the ubiquitous clave pattern. Then the drummer began to sing, the clappers to respond in chorus, and here we were: an oasis of black music in the midst of Islamic austerities. Two older girls emerged from the group and asked the stranger to join them. Hip-rolls, shoulder shimmies, feet shuffling flat upon the firm rugs with their vibrant African colors. Mohaměd had led Stephen to join the small audience of boys sitting against the innermost wall. A single older man wandered in; a few others looked down from the top of the opposite wall. Otherwise the place was entirely given over to the young girls and their music. I sat down amongst the clappers, whose pattern became more intricate as the drummer picked up her pace, threw herself into furious virtuosity which belied her shy, slender appearance. . . . Suddenly we were raided by the police. All dissolved in confusion. Mohamed adroitly fled over the wall. Green-uniformed men tramped on the carpets, sought us out, examined our passports, talked among themselves while our hearts sank, then mercifully decided we weren't worth arresting. Somehow we managed to get out of the courtyard, back through the laybrinth and into the open. "Why did that happen, Mohaměd?" "Some time ago," he replied, "a Moroccan had been hiding in the village. The police found him out. Now they have it in for us. And they are always suspicious of strangers."

During the night three grim beggars showed up at the campsite wanting diesel fuel. It was difficult to get them to go away. Much later, about two o'clock, Mohaměd returned with a note, painstakingly composed upon squared school notebook paper, reminding us of his name and address, of his desire for a postcard, eventually, from Italy, together with a well-illustrated geography book.

Nine months later I sent him these things, together with a photograph taken the following morning of Bakhadda, Mohamĕd, Ben Abdellah, holding the horns of his little pet goat. He is the unusual one, who looks beyond the walls of his own world. There was no response, but I didn't really expect it. By now he must be twenty-one. In the army himself, perhaps, or if fortunate, bent over his books at the lycée in Algiers.

The moon never did rise over the wall fully to illuminate the hidden courtyard, so the laughing, clapping girls remain shadowy figures in white dresses and scarves tied at the nape of the neck: gypsy moths of a September night caught by chance in one of those mysterious *culs de sac* that lie along the twists and turns of memory.

Saturday, September 11, on the outskirts of Reganne. I am sitting under a small thorn tree with delicate, feather-fern leaves, greyish green. I am sitting under this small rain of shade provided by what I take to be an African Acacia. A few dark brown pods pause gently on the sand beneath the tree. Though my butt and feet dig in, for this moment sharing their space, I do not disturb them. Several meters away stand thick, reddish walls enclosing the last Palmyrie before the desert, like an angry grey sea, triumphs over all containment.

The walls are made of little slabs of baked mud set in a herringbone pattern: an intricate texture of stresses and counter stresses with which to resist weight of sand, sting of wind. So far we have been merely toying with the desert. Now begins the real thing: "starting point," according to *I Ching. Michelin* No. 153 shows 1,600 desolate kilometers to Gao. Stephen is afraid; and since I am unwilling to countenance that fear of his, not one word beyond the reach of common courtesy can pass between us. He is greasing the rover in the open air garage across from the frontier station while we await permission to leave, which will not be given until a convoy collects at the gate; and this could take hours.

It is beautiful in this maze of palm gardens wrested from oblivion. The town outside, if town one can call it, is a graveyard of rubber sandal soles and crumpled tin cans. The local water, running along in a clay trench, tastes like milk of magnesia. I hear a cock crow. Would there be an egg or two to place in my sandbag container?

I was hoping last night as we drove along the washboard road from Adrar, sandladders, only two now, terrible in their clanking against the metal flanks of the MAMY WATEH, that today we would be in that state of "Keeping Still" towards which the moving second line of "Decay" was suggestively nudging us. Well, this page is still, but the pen moves and the wind is unceasing. Here, at the very edge, a mind slowed down to almost-still takes inventory.

One bleached bone in the sand before me, a piece of green glass fallen from somebody's shades, a few reddish sticks, some pieces of clay blown loose from the wall, and, even less substantial than these, a shifting pattern of miniscule twigs and leaves. Is there some mantic art by which to read them? Ah, as if following this tentative thought, something additional now shyly discloses itself: a bit of palm frond stripped and tied by string in three places. Minimal human endeavor. To protect? Against *that*?

Clattering along last night, I was thinking of writing a comic piece entitled "Getting out of Adrar," which sure isn't easy if your wants don't jibe with their scheme of things. While Stephen was flushing out the radiator, again I went to work trying to cash that travellers check. Last chance to buy fuel, which is not available down here in Reggane, everybody said. But the fuel-seller simply would not cash the check, and the bank, in principle open on Thursdays, and on Friday mornings as well, remained unaccountably closed. Maybe the bank president, someone suggested. I located his house and found him in his pajamas not at all disposed to make whatever effort required to open that bank. Maybe the customs officer, somebody else suggested. Maybe, yes. He was personally willing, went so far as to open the door and enter it; but the functionary who had taken the offical stamp and rubber ink pad home on Wednesday evening could not be found, so there could be no authorized exchange. With apologies then and a shrug of the shoulders, the customs officer returned home.

We drove to the airport to have lunch away from stifling futility, only to discover that everything was shut down, bolted.

154

The only shade to be found was in a construction hollow, flies buzzing around. The great stove from Biskra refused to boil water for tea. What's going on? Napping there, or any place, was impossible. In this heat, there's got to be shade, and—for me at least—privacy. So we returned to Agoudjil's prosperous fuel station where, in the public shade of a cement-block wall, we spent a leisurely afternoon arranging our gear and awaiting fate. Maybe Agoudjil would eventually relent, defy procedure, risk an unauthorized exchange. Or who knows what. My will gave up, exhausted; and I began to enjoy life.

Near the fuel tanks was a strenuous water tap to which I repaired often to dunk my head beneath as though it were a waterfall, or artesian spout. Of course no one else was doing this, but it felt marvelous. Then, from my vantage point against the wall, there was the delight of long, mental pan shots taken of grey trucks roaring into the station, amid bravado whirls of dust, dissipating to reveal their *chiech*-wrapped drivers (tattered turbans of black or grey) leaning out of their high cabs as once their ancestors must have bent down from lead camels.

Finally, at dusk, along came the prosperous merchant from Gao, his low-cut yellow burnous unveiling the beginning swell of a mature stomach. Smooth of skin, of manner, was he, with a slightly boisterous chiefly style, externalized by a troop of rather down-at-the-heel retainers. He had heard we wanted to sell a tire. Did we? (Whose inspired idea was this? Agoudjil's? Stephen's?) Of course! I offered it to him for more than I had paid in Rome. He cut off most of my profit. We conclused the deal for 250 dinars, which would fill three jerry cans with diesel. (These, with the three full cans we already had would probably suffice; but two more would be preferable.) Then the well-fleshed merchant of Gao suggested that a couple of sand-ladders might be a good load off the already heavily weighted little car. I hesitated, knowing how helpful four had been in the drifts outside Ourgala, hesitated also for sentimental reasons, thinking of Suriano's devoted craftsmanship. "Come on, now they are only pieces of metal," said the philosophic merchant from Gao. And I laughed. Even Stephen laughed. We all had a laugh. How could anyone resist?

A blissful feeling of lightness came over me from relief at being able to sell something, after all the haggling purchases made, after all the penciled hassles with myself over expenses. Here was clear gain. Of course, "only metal."

Spreading things out against Agoudjil's wall like a gypsy, I prepared a sumptuous meal while Stephen finished with the jerry cans. The stove now worked to boil water for spagettini, then to fry onions, garlic, and the last remaining tomatoes in thick green olive oil carried in its wicker-covered sea-glass jug. Cooking dinner as Mario swam in the swells off Gaeta—buoyantly.

Sunday, September 12, 6:30 am. Difficult to say where we are. Just saw a sign: Bordj 500 km. That's the Algerian border: Bordj Moktar. Had one strayed off this permissive route too far twenty years ago, one might well have come to grief in the midst of atomic explosions being set off by the French. Burning bush, pillar of cloud. So this is how the entire earth might look a hundred years from now? So much for *animus*. We're at sea on ochre sands grooved chaotically with parallel, often intersecting tracks—as though this were all one vast technological memory of our human presence on this planet, a presence beginning with footprints. No sign of them, of us. Absurd race course. Average speed 28 mph. Where are the other contestants?

After waiting all day. . . Stephen decided in the iterim that we really ought to change the rear spring, for help with which task we paid the local mechanic a pair of light blue corduroy pants. We're getting the hang. . . Finally, at dusk, they sent us off into the unknown with a little ceremony. "*Roulez!*" exclaimed the sleezy un-uniformed frontier guard in his bright yellow T shirt. Yes, that's exactly what he said, "*Roulez!*" with accompanying down-stroke of right arm, minus the flag. But the blue-gowned vizier of the ancient Berliot truck, which was to be the substantial member of our convoy, didn't move an eyelash. There he sat in state on a blanket, his wrist watch neatly laid out before him, while his turbaned and tattered retainers lolled about in the now unnecessary shade of the chassis. Above them, bloated querbas (goat-stomach water-bags), spring shaped, hung suspended.

"*Le problème,*" confirmed the guard in an undertone, "*c'est plutôt morale que mechanique.*" Indolent mutiny. Did the guard

156

think such summons to a race would move that seemingly implaccable merchant to offer more money to his men?

"*Roulez!*" he said for the third time. The French dashed off, dune buggy in the lead, followed twenty seconds later (as though programmed by stop watch) by the twin Peugot 404s, both of which, white painted, clownishly came to grief in loose drifts. So the dune buggy had to circle back. Ah, the stupid, but from a distance, rather endearing French, off to sell their second-hand 404s in Niamey.

On the spot I determined to have as little contact with them as possible en route. Not so Stephen, who, watching them founder, completely lost his nerve. Too shy to have bantered with them at the gate, he had been counting on them, it now turned out, really counting on them for support.

Still within sight of the few lights beginning to flicker back at Reganne, Stephen double-clutched into first gear, found a stiff patch of sand beneath the treads, and stopped altogether. Furious, though I can't say I was unprepared. The lines of perspective have to meet somewhere, and this was it. It was stupid of officialdom to send us off at nightfall, but we had been sent. *The Red Badge of Courage, Lord Jim* sped to mind. At such moments one has to summon what sustenence of culture one can. But I did not quote chapter and verse to him. Taking a deep breath, I simply tried to reason him into the inevitable position he already in fact was in. And I could only hope then, as I hope now, that when it seemed obvious he had no choice but to go ahead, the decision finally came not by implant but truly from within.

Monday, September 13, 9:30 am, leaving Borj Moktar. Arrived 3:30 am, having crossed the worst of the desert during the night. Stephen drove steadily, with but one brief intermission, from 4:50 pm on. The crossing became his, beginning with the newly rigged head lights, set so that we could see almost a kilometer broadside in each direction. Keeping my feet up on the dashboard, all I did was look out on the left for those *bidons* so erratically spaced, buoy-like in the midst of that track-rippled sea. When we stopped to refuel, he went up on the roof and handed down the heavy can; I took the empty up and secured it with a bike strap while he checked the tires. That was the rhythm of it, performed for the most part in complete silence, but not a sullen silence now, something more like superstitious silence, as if, holding our breath, we were fleeing tiptoe across a sleeping monster so as not to awaken it.

Since Adrar we have used up five 20 litre containers of *ghazwal* (gas-oil, "diesel" in Arabic); but we have only about 100 miles more to the Malien customs station at Tessalit, where they say fuel's available. Since we're getting 18 miles to a gallon, this means another can and a quarter. If nothing exceptional happens, we can probably make it to Gao with what's on the roof, thanks to the happy, yellow-gowned merchant.

We hadn't originally planned to drive all night. But having the side lights work so well as searchers was thrilling. Around ten o'clock "the car really started to perform," (as Stephen put it this morning). After midnight we passed the dune buggy and the twin Peugots parked by a *bidon*, all drivers cocooned in their sleeping bags. "Shit!" Stephen exclaimed, as we roared past; but by then he wouldn't seriously have considered stopping for anyone.

"The car really started to perform." And so did he. The cool night and the blood flowing out of me was energizing him. *Manhood*—there's that book by Leiris. It's as though the bull in me had finally allowed itself to be slaughtered in the ring. No other way to disequilibriate the situation and allow him to take hold. And the odd thing is: unconsciously I knew it, which is why, though hemorrhaging badly at some points during the day. I wasn't afraid. I treated myself with salt tablets, bouillon by the cupful boiled when we stopped for lunch, bouillon in a canteen. Trouble was, that magnesium water picked up at Reggane would make an iron clad stomach sick. And they say that in the desert you're supposed to drink a gallon *per diem*. So how, with your period gone berserk, to avoid dehydration when you can't really stomach the water? During the worst bouts of bleeding I retreated into the pickup, head down, knees up, feet pressed against the tail gate. Trouble is, there's so much stuff back there. I drove a little, on and off during the day, to spell Stephen. And at night, feet propped on the dashboard, I acted as pilot on the left side, appropriately enough. So with Stephen at the wheel we made it.

158

Here gently begins the valley of the *oued* Tilemsi, former source of the River Niger. This source dried out, geological ages ago; but miraculously the great river itself survived, through "capture" by another stream, originating in the rain-blessed mountains to the south, seeking an outlet for its swollen waters. . .

Several months after the "crossing," a Canadian pilot, flying out of Gao for a Japanese prospecting company, took me up in a two-seater. While the fancy equipment in the rear of the little plane automatically decided whether or not there was uranium down there, I scanned the sweep of the valley with delighted eyes. From such perspective one could see the ancient watercourses marked in meticulous detail by their own hydraulic history. Like winter trees against grey sky, their minutest ramifications formed a delicate, fossilized tracery upon flat yellowish-brown sand, apparently undisturbed for centuries.

. . . And so life begins anew on the Tanzerouft. First the mirages. These misty, pale blue mirrorings of the sky appear to be water, but aren't, as everyone knows from childhood tales about stragglers in the desert, who, overwhelmed with thirst, suicidally exert themselves to arrive at such illusions. However, having seen mirages now at first hand, I am thrilled to report an unsuspected truth about them which would have astonished neither Keats nor Coleridge. That mirror doesn't mock the thirsty viewer with nothingness, but with nostalgia.

Where a mirage occurs, there *was* water, and could be again. Taking rise in depressions mirages form in concave recollections of abandonment. Here in the Tassili N'Ajar the matrix of the mirage is a scaley mud flat. We saw a stunted acacia growing in the midst of one of these imaginary lakes. Nearing, as the water vanished, the tree remained to validate the site.

Further on towards Tessalit the mirages give way to pale strivings of recognizable plant life. In the cracks tiny succulents are growing. There are three types of these blessed plants. The first, low to the ground and shaped rather like drab turnip greens, is bitter to the taste. Thus reality's condiment, after a long diet of illusion. The second is wispy—a premature grass. The third, grey by grey-green on the compass of colors, is a miniature thorn bush with four spines at every stem juncture and only two leaves. Future shade tree—well defended!

159

Tuesday, September 14. Spent last night in Tassalit. The mountains of what they call the Adrar des Iforhas are black as the gowns of the Touareg clan for whom they are named. Along the road, early this morning, we saw lavender flowers growing in clumps. Convolvulous of some sort—nomadic morning glories.

After the "formalities" had been taken care of, we spent a couple of hours relaxing here and there about the customs compound, which consists of several rooms along parallel verandas—one looking out on the auto park, the other facing an adobe village. Leaning on the sill of the former, I watched the goings on atop a *gros camion*, piled high with bags of dates serving as pillows and mattresses for an itinerant population gowned variously in blue-black indigo cloth or brilliant patterned cottons from convivial markets down south. As I watched, enjoying the collaborative comfort, all at once the people began to crawl under a concurring tarpaulin, pulled across the top of the truck until that was all there was to be seen. Without my realizing it, the late afternoon light had been thus pulled behind a dark and rather ominous cloud cover. Sure enough, a few drops pocked the dust, and soon there was a curtain of rain between truck and watcher.

Last night we ate with "the French," who bumptuously showed up as Mahomet, the customs station cook, was preparing to serve the rice and green sauce he had been patiently cooking over charcoal most of the afternoon. (All those amazing, bright fresh vegetables simmered into a sludge! I wanted to eat handsful, raw, or barely steamed, as in a wok, but didn't dare intrude upon his careful process.) The leader of the French group, the one who drives the dune buggy, owns a discotheque in Zinder.

Newsflash: Stephen has stopped the car and gotten out to take his photograph of the trip. Subject: a metal bridge, Eiffel-tower vintage, spanning the *oued*.

He was moody and difficult last evening: something, but only superficially, to do with the French. My animation? No, again, it's not that simple. After supper I had a great time washing everything—dust-laden clothes, caked and grimey plates—in unlimited water. Scrubed the tail gate, then by lantern light thereupon consulted the *I Ching*. #48, "The Well." The Well contains the common source of human life. Again, as in "Decay," there is danger in not penetrating to the source of the malaise.

To leave one's deepest needs, including those of one's associates, unfathomed, makes a mockery of all surface attempts to set things to rights. Yet such sounding of the depths is not without its own perils. The rope might break, or the earthenware bucket.

Intermittently during the breezy night up there in my crows's nest among jerry cans, trunk and tire, I could hear voices of the customs station community, all male, intent upon their poker game, intermingled with silly songs like "Fly, Robin, Fly" coming in over the wireless, a texture further complicated by distant sounds of an African guitar from the village. Up by cock crow at five am. Imagine, cock crow! I had almost forgotten such domestic sounds existed. Yet it's been only three days since Reggane. Is that possible? We are going to Gao by way of Bourem because the shorter, easterly route is flooded.

Wednesday, September 15, driving south-southwest from Arafis, outside of which, on a pebbly hill, we camped last night. On the way to Bourem, and by nightfall to Gao. I felt yesterday morning how easily this trip could lose itself in the going. The ride through the high grassy plains of the Adrar des Iforhas was beautiful. White grasses. Then, a tree green as Caribbean grape with plump kidney-shaped fruits about six inches long. When popped, the insides are like milkweed. Then there was the exciting task of driving through sheets of blue water. Luckily, I was at the wheel. A road of shallow blue water over gravel. But there have been sinister touches. Along the most desolate stretches of the Adrar one begins to see blue-black hooded figures standing like spectres along distant sheer walls of sandstone through which, with little lee way, one has to pass. At the approach, small boys standing beside these desperate beggars merge with the ochre dust. All traditional pride starved out of them, Touareg victims of the drought. Frightening as a scene painted by Goya.

In the afternoon we allowed ourselves to be led through a by-pass of certain rumored dunes by the Goddard-like French. I really can't say it was entirely Stephen's fault, for I could have exerted by veto of leadership, but didn't. We came to a flooded pond. It took nerve to gun the motor and race on through, even with a diesel set-up. I waded out first, to test the depth—hip-level. Ragged figures lined the road—like those at the pass, but with turbaned men among them. Same story: the dune buggy made it, but not the 404s. Thus, with much theatrical joining of tow rope to chassis frame under water, we began the process of getting them out. It took hours. Night came on. A sticky-sweet marsh smell invaded the place. Frogs were jumping all over the road. Insects dove around the headlights. The French used us and every relevant piece of equipment we had—Stephen's wrenches, my flashlight, not to speak of the rope, not to speak of the sturdy, road-worthy MAMY WATEH herself. By the time we finally got out of that swamp at 10 pm, my patience was frayed to the breaking point, as the *I Ching* might be said to have predicted.

Why did that happen? Now in retrospect I realize that what you can't face within, is inevitably encountered without. Somewhere, along unexplored reaches of my own Sahara, those irresponsible, ill-equipped, parasitic Frenchmen-of-fortune continue to careen in their Peugot 404s, guided by an athletic, bearded trickster whose dune buggy will never get stuck, come sand dunes or high water. Nor are they the only Saharan shadows lurking in my unsatisfied nether regions. That night, camped high and dry on soft gravel outside Arafis, I had a violent dream. One of those black, tattered figures, waiting to waylay us in the pass or along the road leading to the ford, stepped out of the darkness to pee right into the corner of our tent. How's that for insolence of the unacknowledged?

Thursday, September 16, Gao, writing at the bar in blacked-out hotel. Arrived yesterday, decided to crash here for a couple of days *de luxe*. After a long drive over white salt flats, animated by occasional cows—cows!—there at last was the river. Today, markets. And people, shaded by ample trees, seated people enjoying life. Had a long talk today with André's friend Hamid, who is *Chef des Eaux et Forêts*—that marvelous title. He advised me to take the Hambouri route down to Mppti, leave the car there for a while and go up to Lake Debo by steamer. He says from now on, whenever we visit Gao, we can camp in the *Eaux et Forêts* compound. So the desert crossing is over. Tomorrow we catch the early morning ferry across the river and start off on the Hombouri route, reportedly rough but beautiful. Sent a telegram to Rome: ARRIVED SAFELY. "Gratefully," would be closer to the mark. This beer is so cold and good. Well, that's that; here's mud in your eye, MAMY WATEH!

JUDITH GLEASON

JOURNEY'S START

From La Via Evangelica to La Medicatura to the Pension Sucre.

It becomes an obsession in this heat to travel South. It is not the pull of the Equator nor the names of the towns as they vanish. It is the movement away from time and the suction it creates. It is loss that both attracts and exhilarates. And the night sky about to crack. Close to the first full moon of Spring and the sky should be clear and blue. It should be a tourist's sky by day, filled with just enough clouds to frame it. It should be brilliant and hard; elusive and infinite. Mediterranean and sexy. But this sky is white like steel, and like the earth, now brittle and cracking, now heaving and gasping for just a drop of water. The driest time and flames are eating it everywhere.

And so all the way South earth burned and fed sky with smoke.

From the mission to the hospital to the Hotel Sucre.

THE TRAVEL DANCE

The Ye'cuana is a small, Carib-speaking hunting and gathering tribe living in the headwaters of the Orinoco River in Venezuela.—DG.

Travel literature, especially that of the "true explorer," inevitably exploits danger at every bend in the river. The "first white man ever" is a real-life, self-proclaimed matinee idol, whose serialized adventures often bear as little resemblance to the truth as those of his cousin up on the screen. Yet the "dangers" these heroes face are always real in one sense: they are physical, peopled by flesh and blood savages wielding deadly weapons in inaccessible and remote landscapes beyond the reach of a Greyhound bus. The fear of the unknown which keeps readers flipping pages is not meant to be inhabited by spirits. If it is a psychic journey through a new barrier of consciousness, then it is probably not a work of travel but of psychology. For the Ye'cuana Indians of the Upper Orinoco, the terror inspired by travel is just the reverse: journeys into an unknown universe beyond the "peopled" one mean contact with the invisible. It is a move toward chaos and vulnerability. The dangers conjured up by "travel talk" skirt the physical world and dwell in the one behind it.

A traveller goes out expecting trouble, and goes prepared. He paints himself with pigments known to keep bad spirits away. He carries herbs that can be used to frighten snakes. Herbs that can be thrown into waterfalls to calm the *mawadi* that live there, upsetting canoes and sucking their passengers down to be used as slaves forever. He brings presents for the owners of animals or plants he might kill or use. He sings and plays the flute, putting their minds at ease. He carries small gourds called *tiritojo*: women's magic filled with centuries of wisdom grown in their gardens. Only they know how to handle these: *woi*, the avenger herb, *awana*, to ward off snakes, *dihusi*, for rain and thunder, and *tiritojo* itself, sliced up nice and thin. All these are stored in the gourds which a traveller carries, shaking them as needed against clouds or rapids, against the howl of a spirit as night begins to fall. The gourd itself hung at the end of a hammock, its small mouth plugged with a resin said to keep jaguars away. A resin which the twin heroes once heated up and poured down the first jaguar's throat to kill him. That's why jaguars won't come near.

But the biggest danger is not to hunters seduced by animals or to women carried off by water spirits. It is to children with no residue of power to defend them in this new terrain. Parents know this and take precautions. They wash their children with *yawoodi* to make sure Wiyu, the giant anaconda and water mother, won't come near. They cover the tops of their heads and the soles of their feet with *wawanaka*, preventing cuts or any other injuries from occurring. The pigments they paint them with are mixed with special herbs to make them sleep and to stop their crying. And then, just as they cross the mouth of a new river, they take *wenaña* and squeeze it in their eyes. For the traveller is also threatened by what he sees, and new sights may bring fevers.

Villages along the Upper Orinoco are spaced far apart, making journeys long. A three month trip is short, while that of a year quite common. Such was the case in the 18th and 19th centuries, when Ye'cuana traders regularly crossed into northern Brazil and from there into Guyana to trade with the Dutch and English at Georgetown. Other trips may not be for trade or visit, but to set up camps deep in the forest where canoes are made and animals hunted.

All travel, though, exposes one to the wilderness and possible contamination. In the world beyond village and "man" (i.e., Ye'cuana) things adhere. A traveller might be possessed by a bad spirit without even knowing it. Kanaima, it's said, empties the body like a sack and climbs in. The traveller's return is as delicate as his trip out. He is "wild" with the landscape he has passed through. Returning means making one safe again. One is cleansed just as poison is pressed from the yuca root before being eaten. To do so, the village calls a dance and starts to sing.

The travellers send a runner ahead to warn of their approach. They never surprise the village. They give them time to make new drums and liquor. As they wait in the forest, the travellers catch game and fish, and weave them into bundles with loops to drop around their wrists. When they do return, it is with loud conch blasts and shrill whoops. Those who have remained in the village go down to greet them singing, the men beating drums and the women carrying gourds full of fermented yuca called *iarake*. The first to touch shore are the young men. They walk slowly toward those who have come to meet them. And then suddenly, men their bundles up easily while others fight on for twenty minutes attack them. They pair off trying to throw one another to the ground. The port is suddenly filled with dust and mud as arms and legs are flying everywhere. Twenty men are engaged in *watahanya*, the "fast way" of fighting. Later on will come another.

As the fighting ends, those returning are left to empty their canoes and the others to return to the village. They climb back up to the round-house singing and drinking, laughing about the matches that have just occurred. Not long after, a file of the newcomers approaches. They are the same young men who have just wrestled at the port. Around their wrists fresh packets of game dangle like purses. They circle the house. Once, then again. And as they come to the beaten plaza in front of the house a second time, the young women of those who have not travelled suddenly attack, grabbing at the game. The men have the loops twisted tightly around their wrists. Three women struggle after one packet, yanking and pulling with all their might. Some men give their bundles up easily while others fight or for twenty minures or more. But in the end, all game changes hands, from men to women and traveller to resident.

Now a new round of fighting begins: *fowade*, "the slow kind." As the men and women form two separate galleries at the edge of the plaza, an elder calls out the name of one who has remained in the village and one who has just returned. They walk to the center of the plaza where first one and then the other picks up his opponent and, from a stationary position, tries to flip him over his shoulder and onto the ground. To the great amusement of all, these matches continue until all the young men have fought several times. Some of the pairings are quite humorous: a thin little man trying to overturn an enormous fat one. Other match-ups provide better odds. But all of them share one thing: they pit a man who has not left the village against one who has.

The men now go off to bathe and search for the costumes that give the travel dance its name. They go into the surrounding forest to cut leaves from the enormous *wasai* palm. From each long shoot of this cokerite palm, a full-length skirt and headdress

167

is fashioned. The skirt, which rattles like an instrument with each step its wearer takes, is called *ani*. This is the same name as the masters of the *Wasai*, the Aniana. These "Skirt People" are forest spirits, dangerous and malignant. When the dancers dress up they become just like them, "outsiders," "wildmen." It is said that if a child so much as touches one of these skirts, it will die. When the men dance into the village several hours later, it is as travellers from a far-off place. The jungle is still on them, wild and contaminated, foreign and dangerous. The dance and the song that goes with it will purify them. But it will take time; the *Wasai Yadi Ademi Hidi*, "The Palm Leaf Song," takes three full days and nights to perform.

The dancers approach at dusk, weaving their way up from the river, each man with his right hand on the left shoulder of the one in front of him. The lead dancer holds a tall baton which is topped with pods and hoof caps that rattle as he beats the rhythm. In his other hand he carries a four-foot-long bamboo flute, the mate of the one held by the man behind him. The fresh cut palm skirts glimmer in the last rays of the sun, forming an enormous screen that waves with each step. A separate band walks along at their side. These are the drummers, a skirtless, chaotic escort that beats and trills as it leads the dancers into the village. For three days and nights these drummers will stand apart, goading the dancers on with their wild shrieks and ecstatic rhythms. The line of dancers circles the round-house and enters the plaza. Now the women break into their ranks and begin to dance as well.

As darkness falls the dancers move inside, continuing their steps around the center-post. Women circulate inside the circle, thrusting gourdfuls of *iarake* into the dancers' hands. In no time, the floor is wet and slippery with the excess of alcohol and vomit. The drummers move ahead of the dancers, wild and coquettish, first forward and then backward. They are like lures pulling the dancers along, teasing and coaxing, encouraging and taunting. They pull the dancers out of themselves. They howl and roll as their flamboyant and sexy movements set the tone.

It is late by the time the singer steps forward and the instruments are set down. The dancing continues but at a less frenzied pace. The first chant lasts two hours, telling the story of the palm dance and how it came to be. Each verse the singer chants is picked up by the dancers and repeated; not as a single chorus but in rounds, a type of syncopated responsive. This first chant is an introduction. When it ends, the drums and flutes resume.

In no time at all, the dance is back to its same feverish pitch. It continues like this through the entire night, casting a spell on everyone there. The incredible resonance of the instruments, the huge quantities of alcohol, the lack of sleep, the incessant circling, the strange shadows thrown up on the wall, the secret language of the chants—all of these transport the dancer to a different state. They turn him upside down and the world with him. Reality changes places. Profane becomes sacred, outer becomes inner, the contaminated wanderer becomes the safe villager. Later, the process is intensified as men dress up as women and join the dance with the tools of women's work hanging down their backs.

In the morning, two drummers and two flute players go to rouse all those who have drifted off to sleep. They play a serenade by each household's door, waiting till a woman emerges to smear *parakare*—the fermented yuca mass before it is strained— onto their lips. Howling with laughter, they march off to the next door and repeat the scene.

When the dancers reassemble, the men have huge bundles of roasted fish dangling from their arms. They dance like this for some time. And then suddenly the women attack them, taking away their prizes. Soon these are returned on enormous woven trays. And now the village feasts.

For the next day and a half the dancing continues without a break. It is only in the afternoon of the second that the singer returns and the drums and flutes are set down once again. The dancing does not stop, but the only accompaniment now is the beat of the leader's baton and the verses of the chant as they are passed back and forth. The Song of the Cokerite Palm is now sung in earnest: the story of how it came to be and how all things foreign were decontaminated. The dancers move as though in a trance as the singing goes on throughout the night and into the third day. The composition of the dancers may change now but the dance itself does not. A family slips off to get something to eat. A young man exhausted collapses in his hammock and falls asleep. Women disappear to make fresh *iarake*. The lead dancer

169

decides to rest and hands the baton to the man behind him. Even the singer, at an appropriate break, may be replaced by another with sufficient knowledge. At three in the morning there may be three or four dancers. It doesn't matter. Fresh ones are sure to arrive. They go on circling the center-post with their slow steps, repeating the singer's verses and emptying the gourds handed them by the women.

As the sun rises, the line of dancers swells. By noon, the entire village is there once again. At four, when the dance is nearly seventy-two hours old, the column weaves its way toward the door and moves outside. Back in the plaza where the dance began, the pace revives. Perhaps it's the sun or the knowledge of its finish. The steps become sure and quick, crouching down and moving backward. Those not dancing shout encouragement and howl. It's as if they'd just begun. And all the time the singer chants and the dancers answer.

Now the women drop out, leaving the men to dance alone, just as they had when they'd entered from the river. They start to close their ranks and form a circle. Their steps change. They go on moving toward the right, but hopping forward and back. Now one kneels in the center and takes off his skirt. No longer moist and fresh, he lifts it to a torch. As it catches fire, he adds his headdress and takes the skirt of another dancer. Soon all the dancers are removing their palm skirts and headdresses and throwing them on the pyre. As the flames give way to coals and ashes, small children of eight and nine reach in and pull them out. Still hot, they stuff them in their mouths and swallow. Mothers come with paddles to scoop them out and feed them to their infants. What was poison just three days ago is now a charm. The *wasai* has been sung over and has the power of the song. Instead of killing children, it now protects them. The dancers too are safe. As the last palms are burnt, the circle nears the fire's edge. Their feet start to touch it as they lunge forward and then retreat. But the dancers are invulnerable. The circle shrinks with the fire now beneath them. But they don't feel the fire. They raise their arms and stamp it out. Children reach in to grab what's left. The dancers howl. The circle closes. The travellers have returned.

DAVID GUSS

THE BORGO PINTI SONNETS

1. Primavera

O my harbinger of the equinox,
your season drenches me in Florentine
rain. The Arno and the streets are green.
Iva helped Liana fix a box
from the greengrocer's for the pregnant cat
who's due to drop a litter any minute.
They put wood shavings and torn papers in it
and hid it in a corner of the flat
(two stories, quattrocento) where she might
hunt it out and claim it for her own.
Perched on an antique escritoire, the phone
doesn't stop ringing: friends of friends who bring
seasons of messages. Yours was the spring.
Lie down with me before midsummer night.

2. Il Cibreo

White tablecloths in front, for fêting raises
or anniversaries. Go in the back
door, though (marked Vini e Olli, round the block
in one of those unmapped alleys like mazes)
and there's a room behind the kitchen: wooden
tables, straw placemats, anemones in jugs.
Students in dufflecoats eat there, with hugs
and backchat. The young waiter plunked a good and
toothy unlabeled red down for a start.
Iva, who opts for life in lieu of art,
and looked on Petrarch (frescoed, twice life-size
in the Uffizi) plain, looked in my eyes
with round-cheeked candor, and said what she thinks
we *do*, offhand. No wonder Mommy drinks.

3. After the Telegram

My eyelids fly open like windowshades
minutes before the birds, before the bells.
My hand is on my own right breast, which swells
to the touch, to the month. (Getting laid's
not on my mind, but is it under my skin!)
My gut's reminding me about my last
dinner, when—yes, it did happen, that fast:
the note taped to our door, your voice on the phone,
me rolling with my wine on the parquet,
Julie, still rumpled off the train from Rome,
sure she'd walked into an eighteenth-century
madhouse. From behind the sliding door,
Liana's voice drew Iva's, reassur-
ing her she'd still find her own home, at home.

4. Instamatic

Julie and I are sitting on the grass
in the sun, in front of a cathedral
closed for lunch. Beneath a tetrahedral
obelisk, young Europeans pass
post-prandial booze, barefoot, *bandes dessinées*
in hand. *She* has my poems in hand, and yours.
As the basilica opens its doors
the kids pack up their wine and file away.
"You guys are crazy, but it's great," she said.
(We've put up with each other through a lot
of moods, mileage and meals; we've swapped and read
first drafts where no one for kilometers
read English—so I am itching to know what
hot crit's cooked now behind that frown of hers.)

5. March Wind

I almost came in my new herringbones
in the Via degli Alfani, just
imagining your *socks* off. Wind, you must
blow me back to my own one, though the stones
of Florence glisten in late March sunshine.
If I were here a month, and home tomorrow,
with you tonight, but with a week to borrow
between shops' reopening and bedtime,
(if you, O if you, if you O were here)
I wouldn't abridge this season by an hour.
I taste the morning light with such desire
as I will (say I will) take from the flower
of you, touch as I will learn your entire
country these tender hills seen from some tower.

MARILYN HACKER

BETWEEN WORLDS

1

Where were the evenings and the afternoons?
The years in Greece, in retrospect one long
bright morning, bright illusion:
world without death!

No, just that I was young.
Death lived there too. Nickólas
lay propped one April in a narrow coffin
showered with clods and roses

and women sat and keened and rolled out wax
candles, long and flabby,
yellow between their palms: a grief
molded to form and gesture

utterly alien to the fearful loss
I seemed to have retreated to what seemed
the world's end to recover from. An edge.
A sheerest skirt of continent. Not deep.

And every morning was a lip of light
full to the brim; and every day was morning.
An old man sat on his iron-railed veranda
waiting to die. I walked by fast

between the balconied facade and sea.

2

Bonfire on the beach
smell of woodsmoke
ten years later:
signallings through fire.
I reach to grasp
sky from the edge of sleep,
pull down a bird:
struggling, it flies to vapor.

Daily notations, dutifully promised
records of hope, change, fear
unuttered in the slow dyslexic zone
between the worlds.

3

Moon just past full. The house
brims with various breaths.
Freedom so far: the phases of the moon;
to sleep or snuff the raspberry dark
stain of its red-pale light on greyish grass;

the limited freedom of a house of cards
turned helix, then turned stone,
halfway unwound, still falling.
Do not allow it all
to fall, instructs the genius in the blood.

Turn over, sigh, and wait,
shoehorned into a bed, a room, a house,
dovetailed into the middle of a life. . .
Middle? The blood pods ripen,
prepare to fall like fruit.

4

Going for milk one rainy autumn morning
I glide to sudden sunlight; skip; stumble
over a pile of skulls in the walled
garden behind the cathedral;
then leap the long way home
over more bones—all polished, neatly piled
and gleaming (khaki teeth
grin at the glare of daylight).

And where in the world to find milk for the baby?
I am myself the source; must feed out hope
like lifeline, improvise a changing self
over the swollen breasts, the belly hard with bone.

5

It wasn't death. It wasn't even love.
But unexpected tears,
but hasty exposition,
spates of confused narration.
Impatient puppies sniff ahead, loop back,
inquisitive but all at a remove.
There was no neutral ground where we could meet.
The rutted path of language was the toll
and tool; the shard; the medium; the cost
of finding *there* now *here*, now face to face.
And yet it felt like shyness, boredom, loss.
Waiting to part, our talking marched in place
over a tamped-down soil,
an earth worn thin with use and again use.

6

Exactly what was all the sobbing for?

Travail of ages shaken in a centrifuge,
the burden of belatedness—no.
Most of it, although not all, was spoken.
We let it all hang out,
knotted and netted into great morose
hempen festoons that somehow covered your
central bruise of loss.
Filmy curtains billow
outward from blackened windows.
Mist is rising. Veils
flutter in a wind
whining over impossibilities
there's somehow never time enough to mourn.

RACHEL HADAS

HISTORICAL ROMANCE

I. *Alis Ubbo*

Hard rain pummels the Avenida da Liberdade.
The Rio Tejo is swollen
dark with silt and new hillside soil.
This same rain fell on the Phoenicians
who called this
Delightful Little Port
so many hundreds of years ago.

Even the beggars in the Praca do Rossio
have clothed their twisted limbs
and gone wherever beggars go.

We walk beside the Fountain of Maximilian,
rounding the square,
three of us arm in arm,
unaware that by morning
the Algarve would be closed,
the Costa Verde
a veritable island,
all the bridges north and south
swept away downstream or out into the Atlantic.

Perched on its topmost hill
and growing darker by the hour,
the old gray stone Alfama,
eight stony centuries of blood
blackening its towers. We climb
the high walls and walk
its perimeter together,
pausing to search the city
from dank parapets at its corners.

Nothing but poor, black-shawled women
hanging out their laundry in the alleyways
of tenements,
nothing but a few old men with canes
and memories of war,
nothing but a few dirty children
throwing stones at alleycats or running through the rain.
Nothing changed in eight hundred years
but the bare bulb glow of shabby rooms
one afternoon in autumn.

II. *Capela dos Ossos, Evora*

"*Laborare est orare.*"
Saint Francis, forgive them.
How can they know what they do?
Pillars of skulls, walls of human bones,
and in your name, they pray.

And when I asked the old priest I'd spoken with on the street
how the chapel came to be built,
he pretended he didn't speak English;
and when my daughter asked in pure clear Portugese,
he said he didn't know.

We stood inside a whole afternoon
in a silence heavy as a syrup, the bones of the fearful
or of the unafraid
five hundred years in their plaster, five hundred years,
and the terror they promise is eternal.

Outside the rain continued to fall.
Someone came in, knelt before the little altar,
and lit a single candle.
Being pantheist and pagan,
we knew it was time to go.

All night, hammer-blows of rain
rang on the cobblestones.
Cold in the Spanish dark,
I screamed myself awake,
dreams of fire and bones and blood

shattering my sleep.
To the south and the west there are seas,
calm beaches with gentle
evening breezes in the olive groves,
a history of so long ago it seems

almost like mercy, a pain so remote
we think we can embrace it,
naming it History, or Helenism, or Love.
I cannot sleep.
"Labor IS Prayer,"

Tree repeats, and says a chapel built of bones
is a natural thing,
"the temple," she says,
"is neither in the bones nor of them;
they are the instrument through which it sings."

The same bread soup bubbles on a stove.
The same streets reek of fish and urine.
The same gray light stains everything
it touches, rich and poor alike.

A few swallows sail in the rain
over black slate roofs
as they did over Moors and Romans.
Barges and boats float slowly
down the huge brown river, round the bend,
and vanish.

We who have traveled across centuries
from a world we think is new
think this poverty is nostalgia,

that we don't belong to it.
My daughter speaks to them by name
and tells them about Brazil.
Because it is far away,
they think it must be better.

And we go back through evening light
and heavy rain,
back to our hotel to drink alone in the bar.
My daughter takes my face in her hands
and holds it like a mother.
And says,
Don't worry,
tomorrow we'll take the train
to Evora, it's the only line that's left.

And my partner says,
And if that's not enough,
we can ride the bus all day
in hard-backed seats
to take in a juerga in Seville,
we can visit the Moorish gardens in the Alcazar,
and search the bookstalls Saturday
for Spanish editions
of Lorca and Alberti.

And if it's literary history you crave,
we'll take a single yellow rose
to throw into the river
for all the Spanish poets
who haven't any graves.

III. *Plaza de Espana, Sevilla*

Riding all day on a cold bus through broken fields
and hills of wild flowers,
past the relics of failed rancheros,
there were birds we couldn't name
slumping down gray skies

180

above huge, black Andalusian bulls
standing aloof and dark,
watching nothing, like sullen, indifferent gods
about to embrace their wounds.

And then, evening coming on and the first glimmer
of sunlight in a week,
rolling down from easy hills, the city lights
soft in the east like sunrise,
the city before us like a postcard from the true country
of a dream: huge cathedral black against the sky,
its belltower lit from below
like a masked face on Halloween
with a candle beneath the chin
to frighten all the children.

We eat gazpacho and chorizo and wander the city streets
like any good turista. The Torre del Oro
rises dark and shining
from the banks of the Guadalquivir,
and everywhere, we think,
we hear music. And I want,
suddenly,
to learn the names of all the flowers in Spanish,
I want to visit
my ancestor's grave in Venice,
to bring him a defeated rose from Spain.

Turning back
down narrow corridors leading toward our room,
our feet, unaccustomed to cobblestone,
ache and ache. And something else,
inside,
cold and hard
like a stone inside the heart. But just before
I fall asleep, I think: Sevilla, Sevilla,
and call it softly, feeling with my mouth—
"*Sevilla, . . . Sevilla, . . .*"
thinking it harsh and beautiful, beautiful and harsh
like love.

Dawn arrives with its wagonload of gold—
a clatter in the street below,
and yellow sun so bright
even fine gauze curtains
can't protect my eyes.

The night's waves washed over me
and carried me out again to dream:
a memory of music in the hills,
distant music and bawling sheep,
an old man with stubble on his chin
remembering the guns,
the black boots
of the Generalisimo
on the plaza, forty-five years ago.

Walking in the warm December sun
between two lovely women, why do I remember
only dreams of martyrs,
our unaccountable failures,
our national greed?
The great cathedral built on the wreckage of a mosque
tolls the morning hour:
nine o'clock.

By ten, we're in the plaza:
the river, still and blue,
curls slowly under bridges
along the colonnade.

We walk along
looking at the coats-of-arms,
remembering what we can
of the failed revolution
till we come
to the Capitania General—
two military guards with burp-guns

stand outside the hall.
The first steps forward
and waves us on our way.
His eyes are dead.

Beyond the river, in the Parque
de Maria Luisa,
there are jasmine and rose-trees,
narrow lanes among the fountains,
and a monument to the poet, Gustavo Adolfo Becquer, con
with Cupid and swooning girls—
the dream of a past before the past we see.

Soon, we will fly all night
in a drone above the Atlantic.
We will bring back everything
we were given.
Who has heard the sound of bootheels echo
on the flesh-colored tile of the plaza
will remember. And remember roses
in December
purchased from a pushcart in the plaza,

and the myrtle labyrinth
and infinite corridors
of the Alcazar.

It is autumn in a city we have dreamed.

The maple leaves are turning red, the nights
grow long and cold.

We will fly west until we vanish in the sun.

It is beautiful and sad
the way we, dying,
make monuments of the dead.

SAM HAMILL

SIDE ROADS:
JOURNEY TO THE EXTERIOR OF THE SYMBOL

Semite: to find a way for myself
George Oppen

Is what I am setting down here concerned with travel, with going on a trip, a voyage, *voyeur* to see? To be a tourist. Well that, we know, may involve the banal vicariousness of the subject rather than his or her object. What is more unspeakable than to feed at the trough of another culture, to acquire photographs, beads, charms, geegaws, to hoard sights and smells, to expand on the confirmatory slide show of one's memory bank? Will it do, at death's door (which I often imagine to be the boarding gate in the corner of an airport passenger lounge), to shuffle photographs, go over one's atlas with a magic marker, ticking off in dayglo red, France, Burma, the Galapagos? Before redemption, Walter Benjamin tells us, every day must pass muster as judgment day, including the final one. Will mine be spent undergoing the transit of recollection?

This I know: certain images, correlatives or correspondences, somehow, after the fact, speak to me. I will let the cofferdam of memory open, the torrent flow by; the heteroglossia of potential remembrances will cling to the mind, in effect, mark their own passage, these hard turds of experience which it is almost a sadness to evacuate. Give me back the memory. For my travels, if nothing else, will give me eyelets and hooks, reference points of there and there and there. The tour is in a sense a chronicle against non-existence, a scroll of sometime being, the filled-out bank check against my own dying.

Possibly the literary model can be useful. We, who go on the tour, have not yet reached a state of Literature, by which I mean that we are not yet as characters in a novel whose lives and actions demonstrate significance at all points forward and backward through the spans of a book. In the best fictions, a character's 'reality' is co-terminous with his or her 'symbolism'. At best, we travellers have reached the life of the Prologue or Exordium, in that there is both the need for and the possibility of meaning, and that the tour is chosen so that we may complete

184

ourselves, eradicate our lacks in Time if not in Being. We will compel our *as-if* histories toward fullness; our durations on the tour then are meant to be philosophically satisfying, to be no less sufficient than necessary. Emerson referred to this as "the superstition of Travelling" (at the same time as he was reminding Americans that "the soul was no traveller").

Memory. I even store an image of sucking at my mother's breast. Let me make this clear: I don't see *me* doing this, but see her, the long slope of her shoulder, the curves, the aureole, the black hair flowing like a torrent down her shoulder.

Hence I am easily capable of sinking a paltry twenty years back into the memory hole. I still taste by mere induction the dust of the powdery rocks of Spain that lay beside the roadway, and feel the bright sun as I came into the hilltop town of Frigiliana, walked to the cafe for a *vino de terrano*. I am now going to sit in the cool darkness, listening to the click of the dominoes. The man next to me accidentally drops a coin onto the sawdust-covered floor. I watch him take another coin off the bar and holding it between finger and thumb, grovel in the sawdust for the coin he has lost. The one in his hand will 'attract', will guide him to the other, he tells me.

Like that coin, I will travel. I will be pulled out of my self-made pocket. I will voyage not for the 'new' but for myself, for the self I do not (nor perhaps want to) know.

If so much happens on my travels: separations, break-ups with old friends, the weird self-involving metaphysics of identity, does the coin of personality by the act of transfer become something else? In the Orient, where all spiritual transformation is a path, a journey, still one returns to the self-same self. So travel, the tour, is also the recombinant acquisition of one's lost or emptied heritage, is a reminder that the vessel is incomplete or inferior, indeed, that its very inferiority is based on its having missed something.

At the very beginning, wasn't there also a key? The freighter which left from New York had been at sea for eight days, a loose, various, unplanned time for the passengers, people wandering in and out of one's cabin, parties and song through the nights. And then one morning, with the coast of North Africa a smudge on the horizon, to be called into the dining room by the ship's purser who returns our passports and hands each of us our cabin room keys and says, "Here, you'll need these now that you will be back among your own kind."

Characters in a novel? They are stamped with such immensities of assurance, such consistency, that even their innocence or lack of foreknowledge is simply another of their traits. And I must admit that we see, in our travels, those 'hip' tourists of the world whose coolness would seem to express a certain self-confidence of Being, the sort of confidence which a living of life-as-literature might embody. One does not deny that particular book, but finds it trivial, for close inspection shows this confidence in the service of presuppositions, of bestowing a kind of honor on indifference among those who carry their cultures forever with them, who, if we look closely are indistinguishable as they sit at their cafes or on their beaches in no matter what country of the world.

The truth of the matter is that few serious tours are taken with confidence (and by this I mean that the absence of confidence concerns one's self, not what is to be seen). My subject is this very lack. To be a tourist, to venture forth, yet to be aware of emptiness and anxiety as the root of the search itself. To be, as Baudelaire put it, "one whose desires are shaped like clouds," whose characteristic way of being in the world is not in the sense of attainment but in the paradoxical continuities of the search.

Now the contemporary tourist is certainly not on the way to Canterbury or Mecca. His pilgrimage is without an identifiable locus, without an imagined state of grace. Rather he or she is in the grip of an almost biological panic which is curiously eased by travel. We hear travel's relief almost as a sigh. Isn't this what we hear in Rilke's first sentence of the *Malte Laurids Brigge* as the poet-narrator first arrives in Paris: "So, then people do come here in order to live." He espies the Hotel de Dieu, whose inhabitants go to meet their Maker, the ultimate trip. As long as you are dying, you are living; as long as you are dying, you are still on a journey.

Concomitant with Rilke, however, came Freud's accomplishment: the inward world falls victim to science. If Rilke could imagine an ultimate parity between what lives and what feels and thinks, in Freud, we find displacement—the hand of God toward which the dying moved was just another opiate of travel. The journey must be borne with the knowledge of rationalizations. So one senses, no matter where, that one does not belong. Freud transforms the wanderer into the stranger, the one who is 'alienated'. The contemporary tourist then is suddenly some admixture of Sisyphus and Tantalus (whom we remember were visitors too of a sort) driven by knowledge he cannot shake, by feeling which cannot be eased. Such a seeker is terrorized most especially among what are referred to as *Peoples*, those with ritualized lives, a sense of place or duty; particularly among their monuments and scenery, he feels humbled and even dishonored. For these have an adamantine hardness; they are more like strangely distorting mirrors than objects; their inaccessibility reminds him that everything about his own culture reeks with motive and reason. Its faiths and concepts are a mere means of holding fast to a world which through science has become a kind of *perpetuum mobile* swimming in seas beyond the net of Eros as do now our distant and unseen constellations. Even matter, as the physicist insists, is, in itself, simply another guise for symbol. The tourist is swamped by his own historicity, his awareness that every strangeness in his culture can be defused, identified and catalogued under a multiplicity of systems—every act of his has been determined on its calculus of thought.

What can save this Tourist, this one who wants to mean but who has lost every prop of a faith or culture? Perhaps the question is ill-put and should be, what is meant here by *to save*? The world of our thoughts, the world of our World, is a mediation, and the desire to travel, the reason for the Tour, at least for those who by conscious effort have placed themselves outside the museums of received ideas, involves a bald-faced metaphysical contract which acknowledges this present state of affairs.

For what is clear is that travel, once envisioned as pilgrimage or aspiration toward a visionary or symbolic entity, no longer conforms to these ancient forms of spirituality. These older forms now seem tainted with limitation, with determinisms. It is, rather, as though the modern traveller catches the wafting odor of himself as he faces into the wind ahead. The tour, real or imagined, already smacks of failure, and the lucky voyager, like the religious aspirant of the Orient, will find he has made the journey he need not have taken. Thus, Benjamin travels to Russia to find: "More quickly than Moscow itself, one gets to know Berlin through Moscow." The only way to travel, he remarks, thereby indicting the metaphysics of the exercise before he begins, is by "having chosen your position before you came."

A priori or *a posteriori*, the result of travel is quite likely to result in foregone conclusions: written in the distant desert sands was your very name. Baudelaire recognized that his wanderers, even in their love of the quest itself, carried their own excess freight, their incredible propensity for psychic projection. One of his traveller-narrators realizes: "as if in a shroud/ my heart laid buried in this allegory."

Still, to come upon oneself, symbolically transfigured, is both a kind of life and a kind of death. Because we encounter the "new" (life), we also encounter our rigidities, our fixities of mind (death), and it is the mediation between the two that make transformation possible. As Elias Canetti puts it, the traveller "wants to know something about other alien people. The path through the jungle goes step by step, the number of daily miles is carefully recorded. All the forms in which one later discovers new things are prefigured in these." Every traveller or writer must come finally to a kind of death, and, superficially, travel would seem to be merely another way of dying painlessly—hence travel's inherent propensity for being falsely used.

Canetti seems to suggest that we may look at the act of writing as we do the act of travelling. Consider that writing, like travel, involves life and death and so is like a kind of travel or tour, but of a more exciting nature. Where do words have their births, their deaths, their short lives, except as they are buried in their use in art? How, for instance, does the line or poem appear, the dialogue or scene of a novel? The writer takes a trip, a trip into the white space of the page, he sets down letter, syllable, word, sentence, moves from one to the other, as though across an Antarctic waste, the intensity of the white background giving a figuration to the word. But we should not perceive this 'whiteness' as some purified space upon which the pristine minted word will be set down. The word does not suddenly acquire visibility in this white space, but rather, like a voyager, has crossed or been wrenched beyond a border, the old contexts in which it occurred. It travels with this baggage much as we do, and the page is merely the possibility of recognizing the plentitude of the word, and in a sense the materiality which is both friend and enemy of the writer.

The past, the 'community of memories' of which we are all constructed both out of our experience and out of our readings arrives also in similar fashion. Travel presents unfamiliarity—but not enough to render us speechless; rather the Other often suggests, as William Bronk refers to the Inca ruins of South America, an "algebra of cats"; the very uncertainty which arouses in us not silence but an astonishment impelled into speech or writing. One of the deepest and most unanswered of questions is why awe leads *ultimately* not to silence but to words. One reason, to borrow a term from Clifford Geertz, is that what we do not understand we will attempt to make grammatical. When we travel, to place or to page, we will try to imagine a syntax for ourselves, a way of being which is like the way a noun has its appropriate place within a sentence. In cultures close to our own we often achieve something akin to this. In Paris, for instance, one might feel like an italicized English word embedded in the French discourse. But it is questionable that the true traveller could find a perfect syntactical relation to the patterns around him or her, or that it would even be desirable. Without the edge of difference, why travel in the first place?

The word then, like the traveller's weight, does not so much stand out on the page but leaves a footprint. Its density is there for all to see, but only its travelling to the page, only its placement, its inscription has given it again its totality.

So we journey, and man—the cliché runs—is a symbol-making animal. This is but a half-truth, for as I see it, man is also a symbol-escaping animal, and to achieve this he has had to journey to the exterior of the symbol, to experience the boundary of its contours, to break with its borders. *Now the words constellated on the page, a tiny island in the icebound seas; Now the letter tops, a city's irregular skyline seen from a distance.* And since these words are stand-ins for myself in their temporal evolution, are they not a kind of knowledge of myself? Do I not, as I give over my own words, circumnambulate my very ruination?

Otherwise the writer is the victim of the symbol's limitations, enclosed in the prison of its dimensions. When Eliot perceives that the symbol is the way of relating to reality, is it not in this fashion that he means it? For if we are unable to transcend the symbol, to pass beyond its limits, then it seems evident that there is no art, no thought, no growth, only the movement of counters, the manipulation of already received images and ideas, the tidy mechanisms of an inhibited survival.

Precisely because the unknown is unknown we cannot aim at it. In every true instance of travel, we will shipwreck on our own perceptions. Like Columbus, we must discover America rather than India, we must travel with an eye for our own obliquity. I am reminded of the ever-creative nature of our endeavors by Wittgenstein's remark, which is in its way about the kind of travel I have been suggesting here: "In the actual use of expressions we make detours, we go by side roads. We see the straight highway before us, but of course we cannot use it, because it is permanently closed." So we travel, not to find Spain or ancient Greece or the mystical East but something that belongs to no one but ourselves. This the act of writing witnesses and confirms.

MICHAEL HELLER

ARLES

for Mateusz

Thousands of colourful lanterns dress the moonlight crowds in a clownish hue. The open doors and windows are full of music. The squares spin like carrousels. It seems as though I have stepped into the middle of a huge feast on my first night in Arles.

I had rented a room at the top of a hotel which faced the Musée Réattu in a street narrow and deep as a well. I could not sleep. It wasn't the voices, but rather the city's penetrating vibrations.

I walked the boulevards towards the Rhône. 'Oh, river, issuing from the Alps, which rolls along night and day, my desire is where nature leads you, where love leads me,' sang Petrarch. The Rhône is truly powerful, dark and heavy like a buffalo. A bright Provençal night, cool, though conspiring with a hidden heat.

I return to the centre following traces of voices and music. How can I describe a town that is not of stone but of flesh. It has a warm, moist skin and the pulse of a snared animal.

I drink Côte du Rhône at the Café de l'Alcazar. Only the colour reproductions above the bar remind me that this was Van Gogh's *Le café de nuit* and that he himself lived here in 1888, having arrived in Provence to seize a blue deeper than the sky and a yellow more dazzling than the sun. Do they remember him? Is there anyone alive who has seen him in the flesh?

The bartender informs me reluctantly that there is one *pauvre vieillard* who can recall Van Gogh. But he is not here at the moment; he usually comes in the morning and likes American cigarettes.

Thus, I started my sojourn not with the Greeks and Romans, but in the *fin de siècle*.

The following day I was shown the old man at the Café de l'Alcazar. He dozed over a glass of wine. Propped on a cane, his head rested on his clasped hands.

'I was told that you knew Van Gogh.'

'I did. Who are you? A student, a journalist?'

'Student.'

I see that I have blundered. The old man closes his eyes and loses interest. I reach for the American cigarettes. The bait is swallowed. The man inhales with relish, empties his glass and stares.

'You are interested in Van Gogh?'

'Very much.'

'Why?'

'He was a great painter.'

'So they say. I haven't seen any of his pictures.'

His bony finger taps the empty glass. I fill it obediently.

'Well then. Van Gogh. He is dead.'

'But you knew him.'

'No one knew him. He lived alone like a dog. People were afraid of him.'

'Why?'

'He ran around the fields with these huge canvases. Boys used to throw stones at him. I didn't. I was too small. Three or four.'

'So you didn't like him?'

'He was very funny. His hair was like a carrot.'

The old man burst out laughing. He laughs long, heartily and with satisfaction.

'He was a very funny man. *Il était drôle*. His hair was like a carrot. I remember it well. You could see it from a distance.' That is more or less the end of the little man's memories about the prophet.

I dined in a small restaurant at the Place de la République. The Provençal kitchen is magnificent even on a limited scale in third-rate places. First comes a tin tray with *hors d'oeuvres*: green and black olives, pickles, endives, and spicy potatoes. Then the delicious fish soup, a cousin of the queen of soups—the bouillabaisse of Marseilles, in simple words, a fish bouillon with garlic and spices. Sirloin fillet baked in pepper. Rice from the Camargue. Wine and cheese.

More of Van Gogh's reproductions on the wall: *Le Pont-levis, Les oliviers, Le facteur Roulin*. 'A good fellow,' wrote the painter, 'since he refused payment. We ate and drank together, which was more expensive . . . But that was nothing since he posed very well.'

The *patron* did not know the master, but he remembers a family story often told by his mother. One afternoon this crazy painter rushed into their vineyard shouting for them to buy a painting. They barely managed to shove him beyond the gate. 'He wanted only fifty francs,' the *patron* concludes with a deep melancholy.

During his stay in Arles and nearby St Rémy, Van Gogh completed hundreds of paintings and drawings. None remain in the city whose citizens petitioned the authorities to place the madman in an asylum. The document was published in the local newspaper and may be seen in the Arles Museum, to the eternal disgrace of its authors. The grandsons would easily excuse their grandfathers' cruelty, but not the fact that they let a fortune slip through their fingers.

Time to start a more regular sightseeing.

The fertile Rhône valley attracted colonizers from time immemorial. The first to come were the Greeks, who founded Marseilles in the sixth century B.C. From its strategic mercantile site in the Rhône delta, Arles began as a small trading post within the powerful Greek colony. Not surprisingly, few remains have survived.

The real growth of Arles and of the whole of Provence came in Roman times. The town was called Arelate and was conceived with real Roman panache and planning skills. Its rapid development began when Marseilles, allied with Pompey, rebelled against Julius Caesar. The city was stormed in 49 B.C. with the aid of ships built in the yards of Arelate.

New colonists came to Arles: the poor citizens of Latium and Campania, and the veterans of the VI Legion. Hence the official, rather long name of the city: *Colonia Julia Arelatensium Sextanorum*. Perfect roads, large aqueducts and bridges bound the conquered land into one administrative and political organism. After the cruelties of the conquest, the bounty of new civilization descended upon Provence.

The glory of the good Caesar Augustus is still alive on the banks of the Rhône, and people speak of him with as much affection as my Galician grandparents used to speak of Franz Joseph. The Caesar's beautiful head in the Arles collection of stone carvings is full of energy and gentleness. This sculpted

193

portrait presents the young ruler with a beard worn like a black mourning band, commemorating his adopted father, the divine Julius.

The pagan sculpture collection is modest. It holds no master-pieces, not even outstanding works like the Venus of Arles, a copy of Praxiteles' status found among the ruins of a theatre in the middle of the seventeenth century and offered to Louis XIV. Some heads, sarcophagi, fragments of bas-reliefs, two charming dancers in wind-blown, stony robes. The best sculptures harbour the Hellenic tradition, but many bear the stamp of a somewhat provincial, lumpish Gallo-Roman craft. Here, one has the oppor-tunity—not available in collections of masterpieces—of observing mediocre art, that semi-artistic handicraft, which, though void of genius, is deep-rooted and centuries later, will flower as Roman-esque sculpture.

The clock strikes noon. The keeper closes the collection, walks towards me, and in a conspiratorial whisper offers to show me something that is not yet available to the public, but should impress me more than all the sculptures on display. I expect a newly-discovered Venus. We descend the winding stairs to the cellars. The torch lights up a wide, vaulted, stone corridor split by a low portico. It looks like a casemate or an entrance to an underground temple.

In fact it is a Roman food-store: Arles was both a mercantile and a military settlement. The underground storage-room is impressive. To impress me further, the keeper offers information about the disposition of particular products. 'Here, where it is dry, they kept grain. In the middle, where the temperature is stable, casks of wine, cheese ripened down there.' I don't know how accurate this information is, but this simple man's enthusi-asm for the Roman economy makes me agree without objection. Now I know what excites the imagination of the descendants of the Gallic tribes. Not triumphal arches or emperors' heads but aqueducts and granaries.

'And don't forget to visit Barbegal,' says the keeper when we part. 'It's within walking distance of the city.'

On a slope—what appear to be the remains of huge steps lead-ing toward a non-existent temple of giants. Yet there is nothing sacred in the ruins, just an intricate watermill on eight levels with water forming an artificial waterfall which moved the paddle wheels. In spite of its ordinary function, the structure is considered one of the most interesting artefacts of Roman stone architecture.

The most monumental Roman remain is the amphitheatre.

It was built on a hill. Two floors of mighty arches with Doric pilasters at the bottom and Corinthian columns at the top. A bare construction of titanic boulders. No trace of 'lightness or charm', as a naïve admirer of the Romans wrote. A place suitable for gladiators and amateurs with strong emotions.

I am shown around by an invalid who lost his leg in the First World War. It is late autumn and tourists are scarce. He has just closed his ticket office and wants to talk to someone.

'The old days were better. I lost my leg on the fields of Champagne, and what's my compensation? A miserable job. Under the Romans I would have had a house of my own, and a vineyard, a piece of land and free tickets to the circus.'

'But in this circus beasts tore people apart.' I try to spoil his pastoral image.

'Maybe somewhere else, but not in Arles. All sorts of professors came here and didn't find a single human bone. Not a bone.'

All right, all right then. Sleep quietly, old veteran, who would lightly trade Foch for Julius Caesar and de Gaulle for Augustus. I did not expect that the Romans, who for me are 'flat like a flower in a book', could still command such vivid human emotions.

The amphitheatre's walls were so thick that during the barbarian raids the construction was turned into a fortress. Inside, streets were laid, with a church and some two hundred houses. This strange hybrid remained till the seventeenth century. Now the houses have vanished without a trace; the immense oval of the arena is covered with yellow sand. On this sand, in dazzling sunlight, I watched a bullfight. Famous Antonio Ordoñez 'worked' with the bull in a cowardly and graceless manner. Thirty thousand spectators, the incorruptible judge of caesars and games, yelled long, avidly, with contempt.

The site of the muses, the nearby ancient theatre is smaller, more private and 'Greek'. The sense of antiquity is not shattered, but reinforced by St Trophime's bell-tower in the vicinity. The theatre is a mournful ruin, with two protruding Corinthian columns, described by poets as embodying an ineffable purity.

Our forefathers were far less inclined than we to set up museums. They did not change old objects into 'items' enclosed in glass cases. They used them for new constructions, literally re-forging the past into the present. Thus a visit to a city like Arles, where epochs and stones intermingle, is more instructive than the cold didacticism of an orderly collection. Nothing can tell us more about the duration of human artefacts and the dialogue of civilizations than the sudden encounter with a Renaissance house, unacknowledged by guide-books, built on Roman foundations with Romanesque sculpture above its portal.

For centuries the ancient theatre was treated nonchalantly as a quarry of ready-made architectural elements. It was also a battlefield for the old and new creeds; a fanatical deacon brought a crowd of believers to destroy this testimony of ancient beauty.

In Arles, the period of Roman glory lasted only three centuries. In A.D. 308 Constantine the Great arrived with his court. What an ennoblement of the ancient Greek trading-post! A large palace was built for the emperor. Only the baths have survived. They were supplied with water from mountain springs seventy kilometres away.

A century later Emperor Honorius describes Arles as follows: 'This place is so conveniently situated, its trade is so animated, and the travellers who stop here so numerous, that it is easier to exchange the products from all parts of the world here than anywhere else. Whatever the opulent East has to offer, or fragrant Arabia, Assyria or Africa, inviting Spain or fertile Gaul, you can find here in abundance, as if they were local products.' Less than a century later, the Visigoths had conquered Arles and Marseilles.

Yet it was not a sudden descending of night, at least not for Arles which remained a stronghold of the non-existent empire. The Roman walls and columns withstood the pressure of time. There were games in the circus and performances in the theatre till Merovingian times. Untroubled by rubble, the fountain still played in the Forum. The apogee of barbarism came in the seventh and eighth centuries.

The rule of the Roman provincial governors was substituted by that of the bishops and archbishops (a natural rather than a legal succession) called *defensores civitatis* by grateful citizens. One should not be surprised that in these times of turmoil, art was no longer an activity of first importance. Roman temples became the sanctuaries of a new creed. The Mother of Christ moved into Diana's house.

Nevertheless, objects of considerable aesthetic value have survived from the period of invasions. They possess a certain symbolic character: they are the tombs.

They occupy a huge necropolis called Alyscamps (a corruption of *elissi campi*—Elysian Fields) reaching back to ancient times, an immense salon of death. The universal fame of this legendary place—it was claimed that Roland and the twelve peers of Roncevaux were buried there—gave rise to a rather macabre custom. The coffins of those who declared a wish to be buried in Alyscamps were entrusted to the waves of the Rhône. A special undertakers' guild fished them out when they reached Arles, charging the so-called *droit de mortellage* for their services.

From the time of the Renaissance, Alyscamps was a real storehouse of bas-reliefs which were frequently stolen in order to decorate palace and temple portals. Charles IX, the rapacious ruler, ordered a barge to be loaded with such a quantity of these priceless treasures that the barge sank in the Rhône near Pont Saint-Esprit.

What remained forms part of the collection of Christian art displayed in an old church. The simplicity and beauty of the old sculptures contrast unpleasantly with the bombastic Jesuit baroque interior.

Were it not for the biblical themes and Christian symbols, one could think that they are bas-reliefs from the late Roman era. *The Crossing of the Red Sea* (now in the cathedral) could easily be placed on a triumphal arch praising the heroism of Roman legions. The ancient tradition is vital till the end of the fifth century. It is then replaced by geometric ornaments, stylized leaves. Art begins anew with an alphabet of forms.

Only a small part of the once immense Alyscamps has survived. Twelve funeral shrines have turned into rubble. The remains of the stone sepulchres seem to float along an avenue lined with old poplars toward the church of Saint-Honorat, built in Provencal style with a dome and octagonal spire and ornamental windows in which fire once blazed. The dead drifted toward its glare like sailors toward a lighthouse.

Dans Arles où sont les Aliscams
Quand l'ombre est rouge sous les roses
Et clair le temps,

Prends garde à la douceur des choses,

The poet completely misses the mood of the play—where it is impossible to detect any sweetness. This collection of old stones and trees is austere and full of pathos, like a volume of history turned into marble.

It is curious that Provence, a country with both a distinct geographical physiognomy and a distinct civilization, did not create a strong political organism which would have aided its survival as a sovereign state. The rule of the Provençal dukes lasted five centuries (from the tenth to the fifteenth centuries) yet it was constantly interrupted by foreign interventions: by the kings of France, German emperors, and the dukes of Barcelona, Burgundy and Toulouse. This 'eternal preface' (not only to Italy but also to Spain) shared the fate of all lands lying on the cross-roads. It was too weak to resist its neighbours. In addition, the hot temperament and anarchistic spirit of the Provençal people discouraged attempts at unification.

Arles was well-equipped in both the material and spiritual domains to become the capital of Provence. The city council was relatively strong and the voice of the local archbishops could be heard far beyond its walls. Numerous ecumenical councils were held here and Arles was called the 'Gallic Rome'. The crusades stimulated trade and intellectual life. When Frederick Barbarossa was crowned in 1178, in St Trophîme's Cathedral in Arles, it seemed that the illustrious epoch of the Augusti and of Constantine would return.

If I say that this cathedral—counted among the great treasures of European architecture—is proof of Arles's glorious past, this might evoke an image of a huge edifice dripping with ornaments. In fact, this church, dressed in a cassock of grey stone, squeezed within a row of houses, is so modest that but for the sculpted portal one could pass without noticing it. It is not a Gothic cathedral that slices the horizon like lightning and dominates its surroundings, but a building whose greatness resides in its proportions—rooted to the ground, squat but not heavy. The Romanesque style, particularly the Provençal Romanesque, is the true daughter of antiquity. It trusts geometry, simple numerical rule, the wisdom of the square, balance and weight. No juggling with stone, only a sober, logical use of the material. One receives aesthetic satisfaction from the fact that all the elements are visible, uncovered to the spectator's eyes so that he can clearly recreate for himself the process of construction—dismantle and assemble in his imagination stone after stone, volume after volume—something that possesses such a convincing and overwhelming unity.

The portal is richly sculpted but the whole composition is controlled by the architect's hand. Bas-reliefs emerge like whirlpools in a big river, but do not lose touch with the main current.

Above the main entrance, an oval aureole encircles a Christ in majesty, with a thick, semi-circular braid of angels above him. A frieze with the Apostles. To the right—a procession of the saved. To the left—the dense, stout crowd of the damned. Between the columns resting on the backs of lions—the saints like uplifted tombstones. The entire composition inspired by Graeco-Roman and early-Christian sculpture.

Among the Old and New Testament scenes, we discover—not without surprise—Hercules. What is this Greek hero doing on a Romanesque portal? Killing the Nemean lion. Yet it is not a misplaced page from mythology.

The Middle Ages knew no rigid division of epochs. Human history was a well-knit texture, a tapestry. The heroes of old returned in images and legends to serve the new creed. Untiring Hercules combats sin embodied in the Nemean lion.

The cathedral's interior is a harbour of peace. The portal was a song of hope and fear; it led into a vestibule of eternal silence. The central nave and the side naves are narrow, which gives an illusion of height, but not of vertical lines flying into infinity. The vault is a full arch, like a rainbow above a landscape. Day penetrates through small windows in the thick wall, but the cathedral is not gloomy. It possesses an inner light, seemingly independent of any exterior source.

Abutting the cathedral there is a monastery with a central courtyard. A small boxwood garden, like a pond, surrounded by a cloister. It was built during the twelfth and fourteenth centuries, thus it is half Romanesque and half Gothic. Yet the Romanesque frame is so strong that at first one does not notice the mixture of styles.

Above the delicately drawn arcades rise the massive walls of the cathedral and the graded roof of the monastery. According to all rules such surroundings should smother the monastery courtyard, deprive it of air, change it into a stone-faced well. And it is incomprehensible how the masters of living stone could transform this limited space into a garden full of delicate lightness and charm.

The sculptures decorating the cloister are of varying artistic value, but at least a few are true masterpieces: especially St Stephen, the first patron of the cathedral; Gamaliel, the finder of his relics; and St Trophîme. The Greek apostle with a beautiful, flat face surrounded by a cascade of hair has an open mouth and huge, wise eyes which sink into one's memory for ever.

Arles was the capital of Provence till the end of the twelfth century. St Trophîme's Cathedral is the last edifice of the epoch of glory. Later, the political centre shifted to Aix; and Marseilles came to dominate economically its old rival. Since that time, Arles has been a quiet country town. A humid wind from the sea blows over it and the Camargue, the soaked Rhône delta where herds of wild horses and bullocks graze. A scorching wave from the Alpilles brings the scent of lavender, heat and almonds.

There are no grand events. The emperor no longer comes. But the calendar is full of holidays, feasts and bullfights. On such occasions Arles is reborn. The Boulevard des Lices seethes with visitors.

On my last day in Arles, I went to pay tribute to Mistral.

The Provençals remember him with the same keen sentiments as the good King René, the Andegavenian Duke, the Count of Provence—the last ruler to defend their independence. He was a typical member of the Mediterranean race. He liked and patronized music, painting and spectacles. He wrote poems and was a gifted jurist; mathematics and geology were also among his passions. Though historians cite his lack of political and military talents, legend does not bother with such trifles. The people of Provence will remember that *le bon roi* René introduced a new kind of grape—the muscat.

Mistral was the son of a peasant; his rule over Provence was truly regal. Moreover, he restored it to life. The poet's father read only two books: the New Testament and *Don Quixote*. One needed the faith of a knight-errant to exhume the great poetry of the troubadours stifled for seven centuries—and to do it in a language ousted from schools and reduced to the level of folk dialect.

The beginnings of the Provençal revival were modest. '*Félibrige*', an association founded by seven young poets in 1854, despite its lofty aims could have been easily transformed into a merry company of glass and gill worshippers, but for the genius and diligence of Frédéric Mistral, the *félibre* with the 'charming glance'.

His first long poem *Mirèio*, published in 1859, was received with enthusiasm not only by his friends but also by the highest literary authorities in Paris. This event decided the poet's career and the fate of the movement. Mistral's entry into literature was unusual. In the age of declining romanticism, there emerges a poet that is the embodiment of romantic ideals: a spontaneous folk singer writing in the tongue of the most perfect medieval lyrics. If he had not existed, he would have been invented, like Ossian.

Its very spontaneity, lightness and natural charm guarantee the lasting value of *Mirèio*. 'I have conceived a love affair between two children of Provençal nature, different in their social status, and then entrusted this tale to the winds and surprises of life. . .'. The poem could be called a folk *Pan Tadeusz*, a rich presentation of works and days, beliefs, habits and legends of the Provençal countryside. The critics' enthusiasm was so great, that for the sake of comparison Homer, Hesiod, Theocritus and Virgil were dragged down from the Pantheon.

The Provençal Virgil did not confine himself to poems and dramas. He edited *The Provençal Calendar*, a journal that outlived its creator; he worked on the systematization of Provençal spelling and compiled a work which today would require a team of specialists. Two thick volumes in quarto (more than two thousand pages) are entitled *Lou Tresor dòu Félibrige ou Dictionnaire provençal-français*. It is by no means an ordinary dictionary, but a real Provençal encyclopedia containing—apart from its impressive grammatical and lexical material, historical notes, descriptions of habits, beliefs and institutions, as well as a collection of riddles and proverbs.

Mistral was not only an outstanding poet, but also a vigorous organizer. His dedication transformed *'Félibrige'* from a company of merry banqueters into an organization which fought for the preservation of language, freedom and national dignity of the Provençal. This cultural manifestation gradually changed into a semi-political movement, though there have been attempts to blur the contours of this confrontation.

In 1904 Mistral, the heir of the troubadours, received the highest literary award, though not from the hands of a beautiful châtelaine, but through the bequest of the inventor of dynamite. With the Nobel Prize he founded an ethnographic museum devoted to Provence, which is still housed in the Hôtel Castellane-Laval, a Renaissance palace in Arles—the favourite city of the author of *Mirèio*. Recalling his early days, he says: 'In those naïve days I did not dream of Paris. If only Arles, which dominated my perspective like Virgil's Mantua, would take my poetry for its own.'

The Place du Forum, despite his name, is small, silent, with a cluster of trees in the middle. Two Corinthian columns and fragments of an architrave are built into the ugly wall of a tenement—evidence of a better past.

Mistral's monument stands in the shadow of plane trees, a very accurate representation of the poet: a broad-brimmed hat (as if sculpted especially for pigeons), beautiful beard, waist-coat buttons, even shoe-laces. The celebrated model participated in the unveiling ceremony by reciting the first stanzas of *Mirèio*, instead of a speech.

In old age fate granted him a peaceful death on the eve of a great massacre. At the end of his life, he was a living monument receiving homage, like Goethe in Weimar, not only from poets and snobs, but even from the President of the Republic.

His death proved his true worth to *'Félibrige'*. The organization began to wither, turn provincial and disintegrate. Though meetings are still held, authors write, and magazines are issued, they are but a distant echo of the enthusiasm and momentum of the first *félibres*. Provence is no longer the exotic country of the Romantics. Publishers in Paris do not wait for a new Mistral. Was he the last of the troubadours?

> And no one knows
> Through what wild countries
> His wandering rose returns.

ZBIGNIEW HERBERT
Translated
by Michael March
and Jaroslaw Anders

LETTER ON TRAVEL

Travel is a complicated subject because people do it in the exuberance of a honeymoon or from the devastation of divorce; to sun themselves or hike museum corridors; to live well as "the best revenge" (I've often wondered what the revenge was supposed to be for, in the dictum that "living well is the best revenge," a sold-out life?), or to try to set off starbursts in an imagination that has flagged. Some people wish to go and stand on the edge of the known world in the Arctic or the Amazon. Others choose to visit British cathedral towns and the Louvre and Parthenon.

With a passport and a credit card one can transport oneself in a day or so from New York City not only to a shooting war in Beirut, Nicaragua or the Afghan-Pakistan zone of horror, but to numerous places in Africa where famine is now building toward a human catastrophe unknown in peacetime on a comparable scale since the Black Death plague of six hundred years ago. This sort of telescoping of experience is of course new to the world, but so is the fact that most destinations one may be heading for will have already been shown in precis form on TV.

Real travel in itself is often a matter of life and death—or at least I've thought so. One makes instant alliances on the spot to stave the latter off. I generally arrive by air, in the modern manner, but without plans or reservations and usually after dark in a city like Dar es Salaam or Cairo or Khartoum, to see what happens and lend my first impressions an old-fashioned immediacy. Then I go on by bus or truck or train. In Eskimo villages at 40-below I have simply put myself at the mercy of the residents: *help me or I'll die*. A selfish but effective method of learning how they live.

There is a voluntarism to risks like this; but most travel, and all travel by travel writers, has in the past been voluntary. Henry Stanley, Afred Russel Wallace, Charles M. Doughty. Nothing ventured, nothing gained. There should be a bit of the author's blood in the ink of a travel book, indeed. At the least, travel *ages* you—seeing starvation in Sicily twenty-five years ago or in Eritrea today. On the Greek island of Samos the villagers like to tell of a middle-aged Englishman who danced past midnight at a local moonlit festival, saying, "It's so beautiful I could die here." And in the wee hours he did. They like to point out his grave.

EDWARD HOAGLAND

A TRIP

Our tickets
won't be honored
on this line?

But we've paid
full fares—
Look, we've brought

our lunches, packed
in paper bags
—And who are these

who take our places
singing, in the long
steel cone?

At the countdown
we stand
numbed

as castaways
on Turtle
Rock who watch

their frigate's sails
shrink to specks,
then nothing

where the sea
becomes the infinite
unfeatured blue.

THE CITY OF SATISFACTIONS

As I was travelling toward the city of satisfactions
On my employment, seeking the treasure of pleasure,
Laved in the superdome observation car by Muzak
Soothed by the cool conditioned and reconditioned air,
Sealed in from the smell of the heat and the spines
Of the sere mesquite and the seared windblast of the sand,
It was conjunction of a want of juicy fruit
And the train's slowdown and stopping at a depot
Not listed on the schedule, unnamed by platform sign,
That made me step down on the siding
With some change in hand. The newsstand, on inspection,
Proved a shed of greyed boards shading
A litter of stale rags.
Turning back, I blanched at the Silent Streak: a wink
Of the sun's reflection caught its rear-view window
Far down the desert track. I grabbed the crossbar
And the handcar clattered. Up and down
It pumped so fast I hardly could grab hold it,
His regal head held proud despite the bending
Knees, back-knees, back-knees, back-knees propelling.
His eyes bulged beadier than a desert toad's eyes.
His huge hands shrank upon the handlebar,
His mighty shoulders shrivelled and his skin grew
Wrinkled while I watched the while we reeled
Over the mesquite till the train grew larger
And pumping knees, back-knees, we stood still and
Down on us the train bore,
The furious tipping of the levers unabated
Wrenched my sweating eyes and aching armpits,
He leapt on long webbed feet into the drainage
Dryditch and the car swung longside on a siding
Slowing down beside the Pullman diner
Where the napkined waiter held a tray of glasses.
The gamehen steamed crisp-crust behind the glass.
I let go of the tricycle and pulled my askew necktie,
Pushed through the diner door, a disused streetcar,

A Danish half devoured by flies beneath specked glass,
Dirty cups on the counter,
A menu, torn, too coffeestained for choices, told
In a map of rings my cryptic eyes unspelled
Of something worth the digging for right near by
Here just out beyond the two-door shed.
The tracks were gone now but I found a shovel,
Made one, that is, from a rusting oildrum cover,
A scrap of baling wire, a broken crutch,
And down I heaved on the giving earth and rockshards
And a frog drygasped once from a distant gulley
And up I spewed the debris in a range
Of peaks I sank beneath and sweated under till
One lunge sounded the clunk of iron on brass
And furious scratch and pawing of the dryrock
Uncovered the graven chest and the pile of earth downslid
While under a lowering sky, sweatwet, I grasped and wrestled
The huge chest, lunged and jerked and fought it upward
Till it toppled sideways on the sand. I smashed it
Open, and it held a barred box. My nails broke
On the bars that wouldn't open. I smashed it
Open and it held a locked box. I ripped my knuckles
But couldn't wrest that lock off till I smashed it
Open and it held a small box worked
In delicate filigree of silver with
A cunning keyhole. But there was no key.
I pried it, ripped my fingers underneath it
But couldn't get it open till I smashed it
Open and it held a little casket
Sealed tight with twisted wires or vines of shining
Thread. I bit and tugged and twisted, cracked my teeth
But couldn't loose the knot. I smashed it
Open and the top came off, revealing
A tiny casket made of jade. It had
No top, no seam, no turnkey. Thimblesmall
It winked unmoving near the skinbreak
Where steakjuice pulsed and oozed. I thought aroma
Sifted, thinning till the dark horizon
Seemed, and then no longer seemed, a trifle

Sweetened. I knelt before
A piece of desert stone. When I have fitted
That stone into its casket, and replaced
The lid and set that casket in its box,
Fitted the broken top and set that box within
The box it came in and bent back the bars
And put it in the chest, the chest back in the hole,
The peaks around the pit-edge piled back in the pit,
Replaced the baling wire and crutch and oildrum cover
And pushed back through the diner, will the train
Sealed in from the smell of heat and mesquite
Envelop me in Muzak while it swooshes
Past bleak sidings such as I wait on
Nonstop toward the city of satisfactions roaring?
If I could only make this broken top
Fit snug back on this casket

DANIEL HOFFMAN

EXPRESS

I would make a crown
Of all the cities I have known

London	Madrid	Paris
Rome	Naples	Zurich

Locomotives covered with seaweed
whistle through the plains

I HAVE FOUND NO ONE HERE

I would make a necklace
From all the rivers I have crossed

The Amazon	The Seine
The Thames	The Rhine

A hundred brilliant ships
That have closed their wings

And my orphaned sailor's song
Bidding the shore farewell

To breathe the perfume of Mount Rose
To braid the flowing hair of Mont Blanc
And then on top Mount Summit
To light the last cigar
In the dying sun

A whistle splits the air

It's not a waterfall

ONWARD

Hunchbacked Appennines
         leave for the desert

The stars of the oasis
Will give us honey from their dates

On the mountain
The wind makes the rigging creak
And all the conquered peaks

The volcanoes fully charged
Will lift anchor

      THEY'LL BE WAITING FOR ME THERE

Bon voyage   *SO LONG*

The earth ends
A little further on

Rivers pass beneath the boats
        Life must pass

          VICENTE HUIDOBRO
          Translated
          by David Guss

TWO FROM *COMES*

88.

(The Neurosurgeon's Report, scarcely legible in his notebook:)

Cutting through the cortex
we came first to a region of outrageous women
vying for a sort of Universal Prurient Attention
or audience fictive only in that place.
Past their seductive excesses
we reached a weird little horny process   (The Condyle of
                                                                           Boedromion)

with bridges at either end.
Mockers stood on the spans
and spat down on a mournful procession
of simpler molecules. Mostly water.   (H_3O)
It was evening. When we got to the wedding
the rooms were all empty, painted
raspberry and pistachio; there the marriage feast
had enacted itself with no one looking.
Silvergilt cups tossed into corners.
Nuts all over the floor.
The lovers—bride now and her bridegume—
were still awake in the thalamus.
We entered concealed behind the bright
glint of sunlight on our scalpels they
took for some ordinary sun
She lay on her side and he watched her,
at times reaching out to check what he beheld
with a slower and lower sensory
that looked like a hand. Is he blind?
we wondered, so twisted our knives
so the gleam would strike his eyes.
They were healthy but empty
of every sensation.
                              Through them we saw
the long way we ourselves had come,
all the way across the huge wheatfield

where, before even morning, all
our researches had begun.
Then we left the lovers
to their slow preliminaries
(sad or glad the way
love's always getting
ready for something)
and opened the trapdoor
to the hypothalamus.
There we came upon a lugubrious machine
churring in frantic orderliness.
As far as we could determine in the poor light,
its output became its input—
it thought to control the world
but fooled only itself.
We left it eagerly by a tunnel
out into the great Rotunda
far below the skylight
from which sifted down slow as snow
great chunks of crystal,
garnet and emerald and sapphire,
perfect cubes of most common salt.

(From the Guidebook and Plan of Noöpol)

". . . palaeo-acoustics and archaeo-acoustics. The latter is on consideration at the Bruckner Pavilion (turn left from the Queen's Rose Garden). Early performances of his spacious symphonies have been recovered from the palimpsestical air of old Central European cities. The science is based on the discovery that music permanently realigns molecular patterns in the space where it is heard. These patternings, subject to their own 'aeonic decay' or half-life elapse, are recoverable, using the subtle philosophical instruments on loan from the Collegium Parvum. Palaeo-acoustics, on the other hand, succeeds in constituting for the very first time unperformed, even uncomposed, music, using for its source of data retrieval the comparable but far weaker traces of molecular disarray in air, personal effects, wood, rock and bone formed by formal or melodic thinking.

The first great triumph of the archaeo-acoustic method was the reconstruction and stereo *enregistrement* of the performance of *Parsifal* given at Bayreuth in 1934 under the baton of Richard Strauss, with Helge Roswaenge at the peak of his powers in the title role. The palaeo-acoustic technique produced even more brilliant results when a team of palaeo-acousticians recovered the last, lost, contrapunctus from the *Art of Fugue* by using holograms of the Thomas-kirche and a teaspoonful of earth from a parking lot built over what neo-physiological and resurrectionist research revealed to be the grave of Sebastian Bach's second wife."

ROBERT KELLY

WHILE WATCHING THE
BALLET FOLCLORICO NACIONAL DE MEXICO

I

A black mat taped across the free-throw line
muffles their steps,
the feathers and flowers are crêpe,
and when the dancers whirl, step,
clatter their boot heels, toe tap,
or slap the strings of their over-sized guitars,
polite applause
patters like falling rain. The thud of wet tennis balls
is all their feet can hammer from the matted floor.

II

Just so, just so.

        In Montezuma's dream,
his shadow swept a scythe across the ground,
and the Aztecs fell in windrows, as beneath
his black man-high wing-span
their bodies passed—

        until Cortez and Spain,
blood, gold, and all his dream forewarned
had come to pass. Preserved now in tapping feet,
the nightmare's simply called "The Feather Dance."

III

Parrot and peacock,

        toucan, *Quetzel*, macaw—
all fade to colored ribbons, wadded rags,
and *papier mâché*, as, whirling their swords,
the *mestizo* dancers side-step history,
slapping their thighs, and clapping blades and spurs,
until a dance stepped by conquistadores
is lost in the spin, twirl, strike, and shout;
redubbed "The Spurs," its Christians and Infidels
were so much plumage to wide native eyes—

its strut and pomp of brass and drums and pipes,
birds chittering in branches or
                              a hubbub of peacocks.

IV

And other strange transplantings: Scottish jigs,
Mazurkas, Polkas, but for the program notes,
would seem like jungle flowers, they're so transformed.
The dancers spin, and as their measures change,
the motley's gathered into one homespun
where folk are stitched to folk—their artless art
making the world a common stamping ground,
or a dark stage where distinctions are stamped out.

Now a lone dancer, wearing a stuffed deer's head
enters the spotlight. His right forepaw raised,
he mimics the high step and half-cocked ears
of wildness, as it whiffs the scent of man.
Another dancer stalks him, step for step,
till the drama's played out to its foregone end.

But for a moment we are breathless—
                              in the dark,
teased past the flickering shadows by bright lines
of bison and elk and staggering elephant,
which, pierced by phantom arrows, fall and die
forever, in a deathless plenitude;
where, after its throes, each victim walks again—
mammoth with man, and elk, and sabertooth.

                              PAUL LAKE

SOME OTHER WHERE

"Tut, I have lost myself; I am not here;
This is not Romeo, he's some other where."

Even the most stony heart of a 29-year-old woman who has
passed her time for suicide
feels lonely, lost and too bourgeois at the sight of
Juliet's balcony; at the soaring, crumbled facade
of the home that they call Romeo's.
I buy a postcard. My neck cranks up
like a rusty crane. Wet leaves tumble down a pink wall.

No woman in her right mind visits Verona with her in-laws.
They balk at the admission price:
"Oh, what's to see? An empty house? Maybe a bed?"

Sucker for formula watercolors of the Canal of Sighs,
for plaster pietàs (eight days in a rented Fiat,
we've ripped through Italy like Hitler through Poland),
my husband's mother suddenly becomes a scholar:

"I think he made the whole thing up."

But they killed themselves!,
(or he said they did—it's just the same)
at the highest heights of love;
never grew together,
to bicker and mumble down these most beautiful streets,
of roughage, callouses and
"Michelin says you can see the whole city in an hour and a half."

Oh, where is Romeo?
Ken, resting back at the pensione, with a slight fever.
Maybe diarrhea.

JAN HELLER LEVI

LUNCH AFTER RUINS

The arcade of the ropemaker's cave
Dripped and echoed:
Green moss, pink quartz,
Shallow pool of endless rings.
Then a lemon touched my shadow
And cool steps carried my feet
Back to the streets
Of Siracusa.

I stopped her with *Ho fame* —
The guidebook's phrase for hunger.
She pointed, *Sinistra* —
And I followed: not a direction
But the veil over her eyes,
The black dress,
The soothing pace
Of vowels after stones.

On the arm
Of my momentary mother,
I entered the trattoria
And ate bright fish
Just parted from the sea.

PHYLLIS LEVIN

HARBOR MUSIC

Near the old fishing boats dipping
in oily swells by the worn, wooden pier,
no need eavesdropping to hear

what those blue-haired ladies are saying, dipping
rhythmically and bobbing like oars among shrimp
cocktails cupped in their faltering feminine hands. . .

Though the air has no petals now
and only the leaf-tips on the trees show
amber—"As far as autumn

gets around here"—, like petals on the air
the sea-breeze brings to ear,
"What do you like in bed,

tea or coffee?"—Still such choices left
drifting above running music and the heft-
y tug's wake growing still

powerful
with ever more power to
still the many voices noise uses

to mask the seasons'
wearing down and our own
giving in before the music

runs out; motors, street-hawkers, The Human
Juke Box; while around the ankles of a thin Asian
laying out a feast for them, a crowd of stray

mewing pier cats—
their sinewy muscles under sleep flowing
black-brown coats sprung from tunnels and sunken

embankments—have flown
toward roast chicken, a bouquet of oriental cuisine
spread on the battered hood of his pickup truck. From where—

unsmiling to smiling passersby—has he come? himself
thinning and near
to being cancelled, gaunt chef-to-go

on a housecall to his waterfront flock before stepping back
or forth into shadows that take
all in like foliage

to be let go. Is this
'Frisco or Lagos? And who
is he? No Buddha,

but lean as that other: ageless Gold Coast
guide in a creased fedora, Big John, whose heat-maddened
kitties we were then, more than

twenty years ago, drunken deckhands he led
past moon-lit natives wrapped in shrouds,
asleep, or dead mouths open,

gurgling in a ditch. To highlife
he led us, to shantytown,
the dank, earthen beds of scarred-cheeked women,

where love, the darkest
continent, taking us in, nearly blacked us
out. The voyage

had come to that.
Now with you under the shadow
of this retaining wall, is it the wraith-like spirit

again of harbors come to let us go? This time,
perhaps, into sunshine purple-rayed
as the aster you pick in the grass and say, "See

how more vividly than there,
among the many from which it came, here
we notice it against this green. . . . This

is the secret of poetry; the mystery
of the real and our being
here, which is not nothing." And though less than

midway to one's end each movement comes
to be carefully measured
by the effort needed, as are

not ready for it; if we were, it wouldn't be
now, it would be
over. . . . And we move on

to all there is
of all there will be: the silk-corded
sunlight stretching from its source;

brilliance undiminished
against faded harbor sheds,
the dun-colored length of the bullet-

nosed, fish-gilled sub's hull on view
at $2 a head by the foot of the pier
from where, turning back, it seems all harbors

look alike, alien even to such eyes
native for now as our's,
my Kittay, your Mary-Ann.

JACK MARSHALL

THE PALACE DWARF

The Ducal Palace, Mantua

The Ladder of Paradise would lead, this time,
    To the Apartment of the Dwarfs, the steps
        So short the rise was gradual as an afterlife.
    The French looked at pictures in their guidebooks
        As it was described. The Germans whispered
Loudly to each other. I watched the dwarf

Climb the stairs. I had spotted him the day before,
    Flat on a wall by the Mincio, reading *Emma*.
        That was put aside, some scenes too clogged
    With allusion, like the river with its frisbees,
        Detergent jugs, weeds in cellophane barettes.
But here he was again. No gainsaying the insistent,

Good and evil alike. Which did he seem, in sunglasses,
    A studded motorcycle jacket, smudge of stubble,
        Tatooed crown of thorns? His baby-head
    Bulged with its one secret, how to turn anyone's
        Gold back into straw, this whole palace—
Ticket-booth, fresco, tourist group, the long galleries

Overthrown with history—into a dropcloth, a slatting
    Canvas yanked aside from plaster-frame ambition,
        The heart made small with scorn of littleness.
    Did he feel at home here, where only he could
        Fit? But who ever does? Head bowed now
In self-defense, I followed him up the tilting

Scale, from the chapel, its breadbox altar and gnarled
    Crucified savior, in death near lifesized for him,
        Back to the bedrooms and the favorite's gilded
    Manger. Not a word, not a wink. He took it all in,
        Or all but what was missing, any window view
That gave out on "the former owner's" contradictions,

A garden's logic of originality, the box-hedged
   Bets, the raging winged cypresses, the royal
      Children playing with their head-on-a-stick,
   The jester's marotte, over whose cap they'd look
      Back, up at the Apartment, that skewed cortex
Through which I wormed behind him. How close

It had suddenly become, when as if into the daylight
   That jabs a shut eye from between the curtains
      Of his dream, we were led into the next room,
   Where guardian archers had once been posted,
      Their crossbows ready for the unseen nod,
Their forty horses still stalled in paint above.

Each niche turned a knotted tail impatiently.
   Instinct looks up. But where one expected
      Allegory, the simple bearings that tell us
   Where and how tall we ought to stand—some titan
      Routing the pygmy appetites, some child
Humbling kings to their senses—the ceiling's frame

Of reference was empty—the missing window at last?—
   Clouds bearing nothing. And nothing was what
      We were certain of. We looked around
   For the dwarf, the moral of these events.
      He was waddling out of a far door, as if
He knew where next we all would want to be.

          J. D. McCLATCHY

FOR CÉSAR VALLEJO

In Zivogosce, here, Vallejo,
                    I read you,
in a country you didn't know,
                         far from
your birthplace,
              closer
to my own possibly Slavic forbears,
                          so they say
"Dobre," as the Russians do, for "good,"
                              "sedyitsi"
                              for "sit down"

              In a café
among German tourists, I sit reading you
among them, it may be, the relatives
of those who bombarded Spain
from the air, unprecedented then, in Europe, 1937
                         & I, Jewish,
                         with a grief
that never can be healed
                    for my dead,
                    my tortured
people,   find myself
savoring their laughter,
                      their high spirits
                      & the eyes,
wondering, of their young children,
                      forgiving them.
                      Should you, César Vallejo,
to whom life dealt so many
terrible blows, continuously,
                         (I, too, know something
                         of those "golpes")
                         would you
forgive them?
                    For you these stony mountains

224

might recall the upper Andes,
        the cypress-trees, like spires,
        pointing remembrance:
        If you could see them
you would give utterance to
that darkness,
        your pain lifted
into clarity,
        darkness
made clear,
        your grief become
the blackness
of a diamond,
        its transparency.

Zivogosce,
Yugoslavia, 1983

HILDA MORLEY

LENIN, GORKY AND I

1

That winter when Lenin, Gorky and I
took the ferry from Naples to Capri,
nobody looked twice
at the three men having a lemon ice
in Russian wool suits hard as boards.
Behind us, a forgetful green sea,
and the Russian snows storming the winter palace.
We descended, three men a bit odd,
insisting on carrying our own suitcases
heavy with books: Marx, Hegel, Spinoza.
We took the funicular
up the cliffs of oleander and mimosa,
—yet through the fumes of our cheap cigars
we observed how many travelers had come
to Capri with a beauty. Lenin to Gorky,
—"In Moscow they'd kill on the streets for the girl
who showed me my room."
Within an hour of our arrival
we were sitting in the piazza drinking fizz,
longing for the girls strolling by:
a mother, a sister, a daughter.
You could smell an ageless lilac in their hair.
His shirt wide open, and not looking exactly Swiss,
Lenin commented a kind of lullaby:
"Love should be like drinking a glass of water. . . .
You can tell how good a Bolshevik she is
by how clean she keeps her underwear."

2

It was then I split with the Communist Party.
Gorky welcomed the arrival of an old flame
from Cracow. Lenin bought white linen trousers
but would not risk the Russian Revolution
for what he called "a little Italian marmalade."
It was I who became the ridiculous figure,

hung up in the piazza like a pot of geraniums,
not able to do without the touch, taste, and smells
of women from those islands in the harbor of Naples.

TRAVELS

1

Once I took a yellow cab up Jew Mountain
to a Golgotha of telephone poles,
I saw a horizon of lovers
suffering a hundred different deaths
I saw time as the mother in the lap of her mother,
kiss, give suck as women do in the beginning,
—their hands made the wetness they touched.
I had them both and a Magdalene.

Three Marys, oh what confusion!
I went into time and women like entering a cathedral
—they kept telling me what to do.
Above me, higher than the darkness,
stained glass windows told another story.
Returning, I waded across a river
a child stuck in my belt,
one on my shoulder.

What have women taught me
after all that lovemaking, that bathing,
—my beautiful teachers, how to read, dress and keep clean,
it is time to take on the inconveniences,
time to make and repair,
ways: kindness and deception,
ways to go to funerals and weddings,
—toujours la tendresse.

2

It's a spring day near the Atlantic,—
the sky as blue as her eyes,
time undresses before me,
moves like a girl
lifting her dress over her head.

Now the quarrel really begins:
I tell her I have no complaints so far,
I'm not really speaking for myself,
—that I don't want her to go.
I've seen the suffering she causes her lovers,
their utter humiliation.
Yes, old men and young boys,
old women and young girls.

Naked, she takes a mouth full of wine,
—smiling her wicked rose-petal smile,
her eyes an endless intelligent blue,
she leans over me, and from above
pushes the wine into my mouth,
—then puts her hands to my lips
as if to tell me
I was saying the wrong thing.

HOMING

On a bright winter morning
flights of honking geese
seem a single being,
—when my kind comes into such formation
I watch for firing squads.
I never saw a line of praying figures take flight.
On an Egyptian relief I've seen
heads of prisoners facing the same direction,
tied together by a single rope
twisted around each neck
as if they were one prisoner.

I reach for a hand nearby.
An old dream makes me cautious:
as an infant, howling and pissing across the sky,
I was abducted by an eagle,
I remember the smell of carrion on its breath,
I was fed by and kissed the great beak . . .
Now a ridiculous, joyous bird
rises out of my breast,
joins the flock, a spot on the horizon.
I am left on earth with my kind.
They tie us throat to throat down here,
unspoken, unspeakable.
Again the honking passes over my roof.
A great informing spirit kneels overhead,
gives the mind a little power over oblivion.

STANLEY MOSS

TREE OF AN EMIGRE

Still like a traveler, he sifts through the land, getting to know the trees first. What's this, what's that—pine? eucalyptus?—in the language of infant fingers.

He lives on a block. His neighbor the young American once traveled to Russia on business. When he got home he said to the Russian émigré, "your trees are like our trees, your winters not much different." The old man had spent years in the tundra, years abroad. His tongue was so thick with bark he couldn't answer. Vinnitsa. Vladivostock. He lives outside now. He's getting wet.

Deep in the lung of tree, he lets the rain in. His children get dizzy running around him. They sink in his shade, in the crisp apple umbra of flesh. Birds land. The man's arms warble. Tree of his loneliness, tree of his loveliness. Tree, tree, tree.

ANN NEELON

Standing in the doorway of his radio room Einert Sohms, in a curiously surprised voice said, "I've been talking to Willie Savoie. He's about to land. I'd go out to the plane if I was you."

I had been helping in the store, sweeping up, unpacking boxes of Brunswick Canadian sardines. The cans had labels depicting a troller on misty waters. Sardines packed in soya oil, mustard, tomato sauce. There were King Oscar sardines; their label read *By Special Royal Permission*. There were Norwegian Crown Prince sardines packed in sardine and olive oil.

I went out on the porch. Savoie's plane was just wheeling around at the end of the strip. Then its propeller blurred to a coughing halt. My mother and cousin Charlotte crouched out and arranged themselves a moment in the wind. The afternoon was gusty; on the horizon clouds were both being whipped up and flattened out. As Willie Savoie, a short, wiry man walked by me he nodded, "How have you been?"

"I see you landed on the strip, not the lake."

"I brought them in from Thompson. Changed there from floats to wheels. They were on their way to Toronto. They changed their minds at the last minute, and I brought them back here."

Willie Savoie went into the store. I saw that he was opening and closing both his fists; it made me think he had been gripping tight the wheel, buffeted as his plane must have been by the wind.

A bit dumfounded at seeing my mother and Charlotte I walked toward them. Stopping, I took in my mother's appearance. She had on a long, dark green raincoat, the cuffs of her black dungarees were showing above black galoshes. It had been raining at Nelson House. She looked tired, sallow—; the rumpled raincoat struck me as odd since in her dress she was usually so fastidious.

They had always met *my* plane. Now things were reversed. Seeing them in Quill in itself made everything seem out of character.

My mother noted my concern. "I haven't been sleeping well of late," she said, referring just to the tiredness of her face. She held her arms out to me. As my mother and I embraced, Charlotte hugged my back. The cold rain on their plastic coats soaked into my shirt.

Charlotte drew back, looking at the ground. I think she was trying to harden up for our leave-taking.

"I didn't expect you," I said, my voice too raised as if the plane was still cranking down. "Didn't expect to see you *here.*"

"Your father didn't come home this spring," my mother said.

"Or summer," Charlotte added. She tugged at the tie-string of her raincoat. It felt as if I already missed her, that I was memorizing her face. She was twelve, and for the first time I could imagine her as a young woman. Even in the five months since I had last seen her she seemed *older*, her features more settled. Her fine, black hair was braided up on each side, held by red, plastic combs. Her nails though were terribly bitten. During these decidedly shakey moments she held a stubborn grace.

"I doubt he's coming back at all," said my mother. "I'm not waiting it out. Not this time. Not again." She paused and rung her hands. "He'll never get on the Ark."

Charlotte's expression relayed to me, *it's gotten worse*; she scuffed the ground with her heel.

"We're going to Toronto," my mother said. "We'll stay in a hotel. Then we'll find a house or apartment. My family in Vancouver's been helping out. I've been writing to them. If you don't want to come with us now, there's another plane in a month. Well, you know that. It's liable to be the last reliable one until spring."

Now she was resigned to my staying in Quill.

"I've brought some money. And your medicine. Here."

I took a small package from her.

"I'll write you our new address."

"Mother, don't you want to look around? You've wanted to visit here. At least meet Sam and Hettie."

"I had best not. It's best I don't"

Charlotte turned away. She said angrily, "He's not coming with us." Her own confusion about leaving the north must have been enormous.

"I'll see you soon, I promise," I said.

Charlotte looked entirely unforgiving.

My mother, her resilience waning, bit at her lip. She placed her hands over her face and lightly sobbed. Charlotte threw the hood of her raincoat up over her head and walked to the plane, then crouched near the tires. Willie Savoie had returned from his coffee. He was latching shut the freight hatch. I could smell propeller oil. He hoisted a sack of mail—it would be an unscheduled delivery—into the storage compartment, folded back down the cramped passenger seats. He climbed into the cockpit and started up the engine.

My mother wrapped her arms tightly around me.

"It'll be fine," I said.

"It might or might not be."

They got into the plane. My mother and I waved through the small, oval window. It reminded me of a family portrait in Sam's encyclopedia, except now it was just a mother and niece. The plane taxied forward and nosed up toward the south.

*

That night I kept to my room, trying to make decisions. That makes it sound too much as though I had some control over my thinking when the opposite was true. More, I recall that fragments of memory, past conversations flew past, struggling in some way to cohere, to form a conclusion—about what? My father. This had occurred before. My mother and cousin's morning departure had brought it on again. The irony this time was, through a sleepless night, that their new absence was replaced by my father's old absence. I knew I would see my mother and cousin again, but my father I was not so sure about. And so I grew obsessed, if obsession is what my equally fracturing bitterness and longing was, if that is what the collision of memories sat me up in bed with:

There was my father's incessant study of *The Dictionary Of Musical Instruments*. There were the Cree men in Quill speaking about odd music drifting from the hermit's chimney. There was my father's inability to convince me—my mother, too, and later my cousin—that he was always where he had said he was, out mapping. At home we had never spoken of this aloud, but unspoken it was a shared doubt.

234

It was true he had given us money. I had seen government checks. He had to have earned it somehow. It was true there were rolled up maps and surveying equipment in the shed at Paduola Lake. Yet even taken individually as evidence on his behalf, these things did not change the basic, persistent feeling that little my father said was *wholly* true. In the end there was the painful revelation that I now believed irreversibly yet could not entirely fathom. I had no doubt that my father was Quill's hermit. And once I had decided this, the momentum of the entire night's thinking, around dawn, carried me to a larger sense of things: my fear of seeing my father felt equal to my fear of never seeing him again.

Had Hettie and Sam known all along? Had Pelly known? I could not believe he would not have told me. I did not want to believe it.

Early in the morning I washed my face in the sink and walked out to Sam's shed. He was already at work on a new decoy. With a pen knife he raised a mallard's eye by notching a small moat, then smoothing down the wood around it. In even strokes he planed the duck's slightly upcurved back. Taking up the knife again he marked the borders between its wing feathers and underside.

Sensing I was there for more than watching, he looked over. "That must've been a hard thing," he said, "seeing your mother and cousin off that way."

"I figured out he's the hermit, Sam."

Sam saw it was useless to ask me how I had come to such a conclusion.

"I'm going out after him," I said.

"Say you find him. It's your intention to what, teach him a lesson?"

"How do you mean?"

"Showing him your face. Just saying here I am, explain yourself. You figure it'll go like that, that some shame will wash over him and everything will be out in the open?"

"I'm no fool, Sam. Maybe hearing him lie one last time will do the trick. It's better than nothing."

"I'd argue with that."

"Well, don't. My mother could hardly talk."

235

"Oh, so that's it. That's what you'll tell him. You think *that* will cut to the bone? I sincerely doubt it. Did it ever occur to you there might be something you don't *want* to know?"

"For instance?"

"Why not just let me take you down to Winnipeg. From there I'll put you on a train to Toronto."

"How'd you know they were going there?"

"Willie Savoie said it."

"Maybe I'll go later."

"We could leave today. We'll just go."

"For instance, what wouldn't I want to know?"

"I'll say it this way. You can feel abandoned more than once by the same person. It happens all sorts of ways, all through a life. Time heals what it heals and makes the rest worst, just because it's gone on longer. Can you see what I mean? It's not just what's the truth, but how it finally settles in your mind."

"He stopped talking; the expression on my face must have been rejecting everything he was trying to say. He just stopped. "Better go over and explain to Hettie then," he said.

In the kitchen Hettie was preparing a squirrel. She skinned it, then removed the scent glands from the forelegs. She washed it all off in a bucket. She cut the squirrel into smaller pieces. She opened a package of salt, rubbed each piece with it, then dredged the pieces in flour. She cut up some bacon she had bought in Sohm's store and started to fry it.

"Hettie, I'm going to try and find him. Don't tell me you don't know who I mean."

"Sam told you?"

"I figured it."

"Did Sam say go?"

"He didn't say one way of the other."

"I say go but take Sam with."

"No."

"If you find him Sam can leave the two of you alone."

"No."

I started to pack a few things; a blanket, fishing rod, hooks, a jar of honey, tea, some bread, a small tin pot, shirts, a jacket, a thin goosedown quilt. I wrapped up the food, stuffed everything

236

into an old railroad pack of Sam's which could be slung over my shoulder. "What you got there's little good for more than a couple days," said Hettie. I did not listen. She just watched. Sam had stayed out in his shed. I was racing around the house, gathering up things like a thief. Hettie and I exchanged few words, nothing about what was going on in front of her, nothing that made sense. I felt my stomach turning, then tighten. I could not look at her. Deep down the idea of looking for my father struck me dumb, at best it was an abstract notion. In some sense I knew it would have been best to go to Winnipeg, then on to Toronto, just to get out. My father's absences had muddied so many lines of thinking, knowing he was the hermit only cleared one of them up. *Hermit* was a ludicrous, intangible word. It meant nothing. The problem was that now hermit and father were synonymous. Yet both words equalled less than either. It was all I had to work with though. Words with the weight of thin air.

Then I simply set out. Discordent with the woods, half blinded by my intent, I hardly looked around. I more or less meandered north. Then, calming a little, I slowed my pace. It is difficult to remember the distance I covered, perhaps two or three miles. I saw a tributary creek with light streaming down into it from the spruces. It threaded into a wider stream, itself half in shadow. Occasionally a raven called out, in that peculiar *kak-kak* voice which seemed to pry open hinges in the high air, letting even more of the sky loose. Walking out into an open field I was warmed by the late October sun, but shortly it was cold again in the spruce shadows. That was the lay of the land, stands of trees, soft muskeg, fields of coarse grass, stretches of marsh to walk around.

I walked through most of that day. I saw no cabins, no trapper's shacks. I had slowed, speeded up, stopped three or four times to rest, was dismayed at my own fear yet strangely enough encouraged by the probability that I would not locate my father— I could not see turning back.

Around dusk I set the railroad pack down by a small lake. I whittled kindling, made a small fire, arranged additional wood nearby. I took out a few items from the pack, then hung it from a low branch. These were things not of any great expertise, only what I had picked up from watching, from going on short journeys with Sam and Pelly not too far from Quill. Looking out across the lake I could see where night had already arrived, darkening pockets of green. I made tea, ate some bread with honey. Laying down on the blanket I pulled the quilt over me; I was lost to exhaustion.

Heavy-lidded, curled on my side I woke. It had gotten colder than I had expected during the night, and I had pulled the quilt up over my head. Everywhere at eye level dew was on the wicks of the grass blades. There was a chill wind off the lake.

"Well look who's here!"

The voice arrived, it seemed from both the well of sleep and an invisible face calling down into it. I did not turn to look. I just closed my eyes, trying to echo the voice in my mind so I might recognize it.

"Life's certainly give and take," the voice said. "I mean, you were never one to venture out on your own. Let's have a look at you."

I rolled over to look at my father. He was thinner than when I had last seen him nearly a year earlier, almost gaunt. He had on a slate-color greatcoat I had not seen before. He pointed to a twitch on his cheek. "This arrived about a year ago," he said, "it hops around my face like a sparrow in a bush." His hair was longer, matted down in back with some kind of grease. As I stared at him he started to grab at a fly in the air; it was an antic totally incongruent with the moment. Catching the fly he pretended to swallow it.

"I used to do that when you were a boy," he said. "Broke you up laughing every time."

"No you didn't."

"You don't remember."

We looked at each other.

"I figured it out," I said.

"You didn't figure anything out."

"Lie number one—"

"Wait a minute. Hold on."

"I'm out making maps."

"True. That was partly true."

"Here and now partly true's a lie."

"None-the-less, partly true is what it is."

238

He rocked slightly on his heels, his hands in the greatcoat pockets.

"How's your mother?"

I waited, saying nothing.

"I saw the plane leaving. Backward in its route. Must've been a reason for that, don't you think?"

"You figure it."

"So, they've finally gone," he said. "I knew she'd eventually do that. Go on to Vancouver. Stay with her sister."

"I guess that's so then."

"Unless you know differently."

"Even if I did you'd turn it into what you want to believe. Then you'd tell *that* back to me like a truth."

". . . or maybe Toronto," he said, ignoring me, rubbing his chin absent-mindedly. "She had a curiosity about living there again. And I bet her curiosity's about all she took with her, except for Charlotte of course."

For a crazy instant just then I saw the house at Paduola Lake filled with snow, the table, beds, couch, wash basins, phonograph, only their outlines visible. A fox sat on the kitchen table panting, its tongue out. I had to shake my head to get rid of the image. He saw that I was not about to answer. He kept glancing nervously at the distance, then the ground, detouring across my face every so often.

"Well," he said, "I suppose it's all too complicated to explain."

"That's your problem."

"Must've been yours a little, or you wouldn't be out here."

I said nothing.

"Look," he said, "certain decisions I've made haven't done too well by me."

"Not by a few other people I can name either."

I studied his face.

"Where do you *live*?" I said. "I mean *exactly*."

"I thought you had things figured out."

"I'm looking at you aren't I? The exact location I didn't...."

"Know what?" he interrupted. "I'm considering going right into that lake there, up to my neck. It's getting to be a hot son-of-a-bitch day all of a sudden."

I was still cold. I had the quilt wrapped around me.

"What month is it anyway?" he said.

"End of October," I said, immediately realizing I had just collaborated with some scheme. Perhaps I had been under his influence ever since I turned to look at him, gradually losing my resentment, building it up again, back and forth, being puppeteered.

"October! God damn. It's hotter than I can remember it being in October in a long time." He paused. "I can't swim. You probably didn't know that."

"You didn't ever bother to tell me. Where'd you get the coat?"

"This?" He looked at the coat. "This coat I got from a railroad worker, near Churchill." He winced. "Well, I'm about to go into the lake."

He took off his shoes, threw his socks aside, put his shoes back on. Then he stepped into the water. "I'm not even going to take off this fine coat I got in Halifax," he said. He gritted his teeth and waded in deeper. Up to his waist now, he said, "Jesus, I'll never walk again! This water is merciless. What fun!" The lake rimmed his neck. Then, with an almost bemused look of panic he went under. The greatcoat flared out like a giant, dark lily pad he had sunk through. His arms flailed under the coat.

I stood at the edge of the lake, torn between thinking he was either faking the whole thing or else it was a cruel joke gone awry. It did not occur to me that he wanted me to witness him drown. Or that he wanted to see if I cared enough to do something. His head bobbed up. He spouted water. I shouted, "Stop waving your arms like that! Just tread water! Get out of that coat! Let your legs go empty!" I was throwing barely coherent, useless instructions at the top of my voice. He went under again. When he came up he made the oddest sound I had ever heard a person make, something between an hysterical donkey-bray and a wailing child.

"Calm down! Get toward shore!"

I hate to admit it but up to the moment he managed to grab hold of the branch I had held out for him, all trust was still eclipsed. I kept thinking, *He's fooling. He's planned this.* Sprawled now on his back on the bank, he clutched his throat, choking out water, his face congested as a plum. He groaned and rolled once, then turned toward me. "Go," he gasped. "Go back, just go." He took a feeble swing at me with his fist. It widely missed but scared me, and I fled.

But I did not return to Quill just yet. I had run a ways then stopped to catch my breath. I did not want us both to be choking, even on different elements. Sitting down I decided to wait a while, then go back and retrieve my things and see if he was still there. I must have sat for a good two hours. Then I started back.

He was gone. The wet grass was tamped down where he had lain gasping. All my things were there. I took the pack down from the branch. I gathered up the rest. I hastily chewed down some bread. With little thinking I said to myself, *I'll give it a day or two more.* How far could he have gotten? He had caught me by surprise. He had steered the conversation, if even it deserved to be called that. I did not want that to happen again. I was prepared to lie, although as a liar he would no doubt see through it. I would say that I was going to Vancouver.

I walked slowly. Roughly midday I happened upon a stream widened to a pond by a beaver dam. The various currents played different light off the surface. I admired the intricate weave of mud and sticks and decided to rest there and inspect the dam. When I stood on the shore as close to the water as I could without stepping in, I noticed an unusual shape protruding from the dam, a smooth piece of wood, wrist-thick and tucked over at its end like a fist, with a few wires spiralling outward. I waded in. I climbed onto the dam. The chewed, tapered branches shifted a little but the architecture held. I sat next to the top section of a cello. I recognized what it was from the dictionary. It had been splintered, tooth-notched, obviously dragged from somewhere close by. I splashed out and sat on the bank, facing away from the dam. I took off my boots and socks, placing them in the sun to dry. *C for Cello, Columbian lute, coronet* —: in my mind I heard my father saying the names, showing me the illustrations. I sat a long time, trying not to think. I stood up, put on my socks and boots. Then I found the beaver's tail-drag path. Following it through some scrub I had walked only a short distance when I came upon the cabin. The door was propped open with a bassoon stuck in the ground. The rest of the cello lay scattered in pieces.

I could hear the fire, see the chimney smoke. I walked to the door, hesitating before looking in. Maps, some in cardboard tubes, leaned against the walls. There was a cot, a few blankets on it, a writing desk, an axe. An iron pot, the soup ladle still sticking out of it handle-down, was like an upturned bell hung in the fireplace. A clarinet, oboe and violin crackled in the fire, heating the soup. I saw silver keys glowing. Hung on the wall were a coronet, triangle, trombone. An accordion was fanned out on the floor. There was no French horn, the instrument my father had played as a young man; had there been? Did he take it? What could all this tell if I knew how to read it? How had my father obtained these? Over how many years, in what places? No doubt I would never know. What was the purpose, to acquire the entire dictionary's worth? To me, amidst the havoc of these sprawled, broken instruments even *that* seemed possible.

I decided, perhaps stupidly but knowing I had to rest, to stay one night in the cabin. I doused the fire. Having wrapped my hands in two shirts I took the oboe and clarinet out of the ashes. The violin was all but beyond recognition.

Then I went out to search for other instruments and found lutes, reed instruments, some I did not recognize, scattered in the woods. I searched for an hour or so.

At dusk I brought inside the remainder of the cello along with a few pieces of wood I had collected, and built up the fire again. I sat on the cot, taking up one instrument after the other, trying to play them. This was ridiculous. I could barely manage slurred notes. The sounds were rasps, awful shrieks, sputterings. I wondered if any Cree people were listening. I built up the fire more. I slept on the cot.

In the morning, carrying a bassoon split half way down its length and tied across my pack, I began to walk home. I walked steadily and directly as I could and stopped only four or five times to rest. I made it to Quill just before dark. When I walked into the house Sam was just lifting the radio from the table to put it on its shelf.

"You look like hell," he said.

He took the railroad pack from me. The bassoon spilled onto the floor, cracking more.

"What is *that*?" Hettie said, gently kicking the bassoon.

I picked it up and placed it on the table.

"You're home from angry," she said.

"Yes, an angry place all right."

"Where?"

"It doesn't matter. A lake."

"Did you find him?" asked Sam.

I sat down. Hettie put a cup of coffee in front of me, and Sam poured whiskey into it, then swigged from the bottle.

"I'll say what happened"—suddenly I was worn to a frazzle, slumped, hardly able to size up the cup of coffee in front of me—"then you tell me if I did."

HOWARD NORMAN

FARM HOUSE, NIIGATA PREFECTURE

A chilly house by the river, just under the mountain. Near midnight, the rain falling for 24 hours now. On the record player a British composer is playing a hundred random chords on the piano: his rainfall in answer to what drums on the roof. Chord. Drop drop drop. Chord chord. Drop drop drop. Between the two rainfalls we are poised, silent, distant from everything: dirt road, sky shot with stars, muddy vegetable garden, cold tatami floor, two small tables, the clock chiming the hours, spiders and flies drooping in the cold, deep red pine doors.

*

Day and night, cousins and cousins of cousins pass through the house or settle down to long hours of beer and whiskey and cigarettes, talk and silence lifting and falling in easy rhythm, and then are gone and the room is empty. Today I met the man who lived here six years ago. About 55, bald head and unwrinkled brow, walking on crutches following a motorcycle accident. He showed me his poems, of which I could read no more than "mountain," "flower," "evening," could admire only the texture of the paper, the flow of the handwriting, the elegance of the binding: and the lines of his face, wondering if his poetry had that much character. He explained his ideas about poetry; I could not follow. My friend was called in to translate: "The fallen leaves gave him inspiration . . . to him they are not dead, they become part of the ground and so rise again as new flowers in spring. . . in the same way people do not die . . . they become, what is the word, a spirit?"

*

Landscape of streams and furrows. The paths wind up around them, and where the path ends you jump down or duck under brambles, find the thin strips of dry land edging the paddies, stumble along the cliff edge. Two boys about nine years old were guiding me. "Over there" (pointing through the woods to the lower road running parallel to us) "is the charcoal burner's hut. He lives there sometimes. But I don't think he's there now." "I saw him last October when I went walking on the mountain." "He was there in October. But he's gone now. He comes and goes."

*

The hut, crudely but solidly made, is right where the trail bends. The charcoal burner, a dark old man, hunched over, emerged from behind it one October evening, barely visible. It was dusk and the smoke from the fire hid his face. Now, months later, I'm twenty yards away, looking at the empty hut and the pile of ashes.

*

Space is never straight. Paths go in all directions, above and under. The steps to the shrine culminate in a shaded clearing on a hilltop, concealed by trees. Snakes glide among the dusty gravestones. The boys start whispering about ghosts. Apparently the place is full of them.

*

The family is spread among the mountain towns, among the roads and fields everywhere intersected by streams. No way to know whether it begins or ends, or to tell when you reach the edge of it. The family recedes, blends with the bark and mushrooms and wild purple flowers spring up under the rock ledge and the boulders with the water sweeping over them, just downstream from the power plant. Near there, under a wooden lean-to, the forest rangers are drinking sake, gathered around the fire singing, just like boy scouts. The rain has begun to let up. A thick mist still hangs over the peaks. Further down the slope it clears in spots to let through patches of green and black, a round rock the size of a house, fragments of a thin curving path. A plump woman and a bent old man walk gathering herbs. Young boys crawl in the thickets talking about snakes and spiders. The sound of rushing water is everywhere, echoing as if the circle of mountains were a giant amplifier.

*

The weathered houses wedged in to fit the sloping of the mountain seem as tiny and resilient an outgrowth as the roots and flowers which presently will be eaten under their roofs, cooked over the fire which smolders continually in the center of the room. One cousin, after driving an ambulance all day, is approaching the house now, across the bridge, listening to high cracked female voices singing local songs on the car radio. Another cousin has just finished presiding over a propitiary Shinto rite commissioned by the builders of a new golf course. Taking off the white robe he changes into a three-piece suit, tucks a gift-wrapped bottle of whiskey under his arm. The light dimly visible from the foggy riverbank is the third cousin lighting the fire, boiling up water in the heavy black kettle, steeping butterbur and dog's-tooth-violet in soy sauce, while Miles Davis and John Coltrane trade choruses on the stereo.

GEOFFREY O'BRIEN

PADUA

Inside the Basilica of Saint Anthony they're celebrating a mass for Aldo Moro, murdered two years ago by the Red Brigades, his body jammed in the trunk of an abandoned car in Rome. The first mass I've ever been near—the fascination of the chanting and incense.

Lightning from a storm gathering all day knocks out the electricity, but the mass continues, lit only by its candles. T. directs my eyes up toward the huge, central dome—how the gold background of the Byzantine mosaics isn't simply gaudy but catches and reflects the half-light of candles that gleams back down through the shadowy vastness.

In the basilica's Treasury we see a large case full of saints' relics, including Saint Anthony's "incorruptible tongue." Once he came to preach at Rimini but was locked out of the city by its tyrant and so preached to the fish along the shore and they listened with great interest. The tongue itself is difficult to locate in its elaborate chalice of crystal and gold; it looks like a tiny piece of lava, charred and porous.

*

In the space of ten minutes we look at two statues by Donatello. They couldn't be more different, or more disturbing in their differences. On the high altar, a sensual Christ on the Cross that reminds me Donatello was the first Renaissance sculptor to go back to the "ancients," to bring over from the Greeks and Romans the grace and nakedness of the human body.

In the piazza outside, his statue of the Venetian mercenary captain known as Gattamelata, "Pussycat," because of the ruthless, agile way he pounced on his enemies. This grim and rigid man on his huge bronze horse makes me want to think of the statues as two rivers flowing apart, separating forever: a river called History, whose water is only brute force, and a river called Beauty, whose source is sexual grace.

*

Next week in Florence, we rendezvous with a friend who lives and works in Tuscany; he's just finished a novel about terrorism. He knows a lot and wants to talk about it.

After dinner I say how fond I am of Padua's quietness and arcaded streets; he tells us that it's one of the most violent of Italian cities. Its university, whose shaded walks Petrarch and Boccaccio strolled, hasn't been open an entire semester in years. The preferred mode of brutality in Padua is for a group of young thugs to step out of the shadowy arcades and bludgeon a professor to death with bicycle chains. What makes Paduan violence distinctive, he insists, is that victims are both right and left wing. I see a naked human like Donatello's Christ: two wings are being torn from his body.

*

Now, home in Virginia, I find myself mulling over certain vivid details of that calm day in Padua:

It's dusk. We're on our way back from the basilica to our hotel when we realize how cold it is, much colder than we were told Italy would be in May. T. isn't dressed warmly enough, so we search the shops for a sweater, finally find one in a place called "Jeans West." It's one of a chain of trendy boutiques; its logo stenciled below its name in a long line across the large, plate glass window: an American cowboy on a galloping horse. It makes me think of the statue of Gattamelata, but it isn't solid and heavy; the horse races at a precipitous gallop, all four hooves off the ground.

The store's theme is American, from name to logo to style of clothes, but everything for sale is designed and made in Italy. One wall is jeans; the second, sweaters; the third, mirrors. The jeans and sweaters are all in solid colors arranged on shelves so they form verticals of yellow, orange, red, purple, blue, and green. At first the shop seems cheerful, then merely intense, finally claustrophobic: as if a rainbow had been crammed into a box.

The feel of that shop reminds me of the photo of Aldo Moro's body crushed into the small space of a Fiat's trunk. I realize that History is the only river, that the two of us hope to swim across its swift current. Like everyone else though, we're knocked about and clawed at by bodies and logs. Sometimes we're pulled under by the swirling water. When we come up, we gasp for breath.

CHATEAUBRIAND ON THE NIAGARA FRONTIER, 179–

He could be just one more erstwhile aristocrat lightfooting it from the guillotine who's crossed the Atlantic to research Rousseau's wonders of nature at first hand. And he is, but tonight, writing in his travel journal, he'll make his own contribution: the invention of the literary beauty of moonlight. It's a concept destined to fascinate and console the melancholic children and love-starved wives of the bourgeoisie he loathes.

It happens because he can't stand the smell of the frontier inn where he's stopped for the night: an earth floored room with a fire in the middle. Everyone lies crowded together with their feet near the embers, their bodies radiating out, Indian and trapper alike. In a dream he can't share they become greasy spokes of a great, breathing wheel that rolls along a rutted trail deeper into the new world.

AMOR AS A GOD OF DEATH
ON ROMAN STONE COFFINS

1

All those sarcophagi
carved with hieros gamos—
a gamey exchange
between gods and mortals
that involves no clothes
and no holds barred.
                              There's
Leda with her swan,
and Zeus is fondling
Ganymede. . . what this has
to do with death
only the Romans knew—something
about: "If you really love
me, you'll take me with you. . ."
which in this case meant
Mt. Olympus. I've seen
that peak in photographs;
it isn't Everest, but
it's way above the treeline
and you'd freeze without your clothes.

2

I hate it when they wind those funerary
snakes about the female shape, or
take the torch of Venus and hold
it upside down. I say
it's morbid to confuse the mysteries
of sex and death. What's more,
if we don't keep them distinct
we'll never be able to move
unafraid among the objects of light
or learn to speak that single, simple
word that's lifted to lips
like a goblet of mysterious crystal.
Our only hope's to sort them out,
to tease the shadow from the form.

VARIATION ON
"THE DISCOVERY AND
CONQUEST OF MEXICO"

Puttering along the coast
trading for gold— little
ornaments and such, but
dreaming of hoards
that must be inland
at the capital.
                    Credulous
and greedy, just like me—
I think there's something
at the heart of poetry—
some fabulous palace
whose walks gleam
and when I stroll them
I'll be mistaken for a god.
But the Emperor keeps sending
armed envoys with small tokens
of friendship and the same
stern message: "Don't come."

My ship's hold is full
of earrings and trinkets
that, melted down and shared
among the crew, might still
amount to treasure. Yet
I can't quit this shore,
break this spell.
                    Each day
I rise with the dreamed
summons still in my head,
then hoist anchor, navigate
further down the coast
putting in at every cove

or stream among the mangroves
to find the fishers' shacks
and villages where I'll squat
in heat and dust, haggling for baubles.

GREGORY ORR

from *JOURNAL FROM THE RUE*

I went to Paris that year in the fall and stayed, temporarily, at number 8, Rue du Val-de-Grâce, with Fanny, an old friend. She always put me in the same room, in which her daughters and, before that, she herself grew up. It was both familiar and frightening for me to be there, already aware of the city and its overstimulation. As a routine, I started work in the Library of the City of Paris on the critical edition of the French Romantic historian, Jules Michelet's book of natural history, *The Mountain* (1868). First I undertook to read most of the manuscript correspondence and found myself identifying with the tribe of associates around him—son and son-in-law from his first family, and "secretaries"— which left me angry at both him (his prolific facility) and the young woman he married, doting over her, late in his life. But my loyalties would shift, for his extraordinary diary, in which he noted menus and bowel movements as well as Her periods and moods, fascinated me as I began to keep a notebook of my own. I came also to understand how his wife, Athénaïs, must have felt. Fanny, who read on her daybed in the living room at night before sleeping and then in the morning, was kind yet resistant to my constant self-reflection, and I felt that it was time to find my own apartment, so that, ready, I was nonetheless anxious about the next step.

*

FIRST NIGHT, A NEW PLACE

The lamp switch in France hangs on a cord
by the bed and fills the hand like a small
plastic boat. The room plunges in dark,
for the shutters roll tight,
leaving no slit on the courtyard calm.
Black deeper than pigments of paint,
thicker than sailors imagine a cloudy night
at sea. Short notes in a log.
Before or after the turbulence? The mattress

curves in the right-hand corner where I try
to breathe. Unknowable years.

*

THE DREAM OF THAT NIGHT

With our suitcases, mother and I are led to a little
framehouse on a dock covered with tar, reeking
of oil. I look at the houses lining the shore
under a bone sky saying it's not so bad (horrified inside),
and when the next wave grows enormous, I doubt
we can outwit this one, running.

*

ST. MARTIN CANAL

The exhibitionist shaking his flaccid thing
as if to dry, struck me as young in his flight jacket.
I muttered *fou* and whirled around, while he took off,
then still trembling I climbed onto the bright bus,
tracing the shadow as it vanished up the street.

The motorcycle lay where the driver
kneeled by the body, holding his helmet in one hand
and her hand in the other, for it must have been a she,
though I could not, from the bus, make out more
than the soles of her shoes and a heap of coat.

The couple leaning into each other on a cold night,
not a showcase couple, but pleasantly radiant,
their mouths close for secret speech: as I passed,
both sets of eyes, lurching on mine,
threw their bodies oddly off-balance.

254

I paused (in mind) to let the damp air
penetrate my face and think,
this would not be the sensation I would feel
in New Haven or New York, or Atlanta
where I was born.

St. Martin Canal. Nothing moves
but a taxi like us. The other cars are parked
at the water's edge as if without a thought.
The water must always lie flat, never unruly,
never bristling at the perfectly spaced bridges.

*

from the *Journal* of Jules Michelet

Friday, 15 November 1867, Paris

Her intestines are better. She read me her admirable chapter: the
aurora borealis marriage of magnetism and electricity, a lovely
piece on sleepless flowers, the polar forget-me-not, etc.

At dinner, Madame Dargaud and her sweet verse. Dry though.
Was judged severely by my dove (ferocity of the food? descending or mounting flux?). Alfred came to visit, kind of cold. In the
evening, Henri Martin. Discussed my wife, so changed for the
better after years of marriage. (I dreamed she was pregnant,
pressed me against her: of course it's yours, she said.) A nightmare: my son drowning.

Sunday, 17

Calmer (little b.m. at noon). The meatpatties easy to digest. My
toothache disappeared. I'm taking magnesia. I send the entire
first section of *The Mountain* to be printed in pages. I revise her
flowers. I don't go out. (I want to . . . but her bread-milk soup
and salad were heavy.) She drank some coffee. She visits Madame
Fagnier who is not so congenial. In the evening, Etienne. She
reads the second section of my book: criticizes.

*

During the winter, after I had moved into my own place at no. 13, rue Croulebarbe, I underwent the melancholia associated often enough with Paris after the excitement wears off. You fight the daily assault on your self-image, and there is no abating of grey skies and drizzle. Sometimes I obsessed about the man who had conveniently broken off with me before I left (my side of the story); sometimes I was drawn to the bizarre, but not hopeless, creatures I encountered on the street and in the park. Once, I tried to pawn a gift given to me by the old man in Normandy, until I realized that it represented myself. The most melodramatic—and so comical—moment, in which I came face to face with yet another look at my own terrifying littleness (smelling mortality), occurred at the library where I went every afternoon. By now I had read all the material surrounding Michelet's *The Mountain* and began to transcribe the manuscript itself, by a method which mimed the hesitations of the author's composition. I was condemned to copying, literally, another man's work, but not even the finished product, rather scraps, drafts. At the same time, I was cheered by the arrival of a second daughter to the woman, responsible for the critical edition of Michelet's *The Sea*, whom I had met while doing research in the provincial town, Clermont-Ferrand. (She gave her daughter my name.) It was with her one day that I came across (as Michelet himself must have, with a shiver) that single entry which his wife, otherwise silent, made in his diary.

But when spring came, I began to see the humorous absurdity of my discouragement, and to accept what I had known all along—that the walks and sensations, the solitude and especially new friends (who appeared in Orleans, wouldn't you know! at the end of my stay) formed a kind of history, which was already mythic: upon leaving the Valley-of-Grace, I was to confront life on the rue Croulebarbe (Street of the Cruel-Barb or the Collapsing-Beard) after which I emerged with a typically ironic calm.

*

Dining alone, he does not see me
examine the northern exposure of his face,
the passing abyss and the drifting years,
the way he chases the fold of his cloth,
and the crumbs, with his hand.

                              *

Transcribing the mss. (by the "dynamic method")

How can you talk about not liking your work
How can you talk about not liking
How can you turn on yourself
without embarrassing those closest
How can you speak the shameful refrain
against the scapegoat of the self
you hear yourself berating
and then regret, compounding shame?
Now you're a giant surveying an oak,
now you're (*illegible*)
whalesong of defeat on the broken disk
of your mother's back at night—
Is the anger Is the anger copying his waste
Is the anger copying her waste copying his waste
Is the anger copying her waste copying his waste
copying documents lost in the stack a waste in itself?
The long metamorphosis of anger you cannot touch—
This note was not published in the books:
"My wife adds much of herself to the aliment she eats,
giving sweetness to the daily alluvion of death,
the excrement of earth." They are right to repress
She was wrong to repress
We cannot be expected We are taught
to ignore (*delete*) the process
by which the pure discourse of light emerges
from the panic to which it reverts back under pressure.

                              *

20 April 1868, Monday

It's not my fault if your impression of the last few days is so unpleasant. I read your Diary that you left around. What did I see on each page? The clear, cold eye of the enemy. Everything is written there, scored in black and red, the attitude, the words, conversations, even the insides, but false. It is a veritable anatomy. If less interested in [*literally*] you [*meaning: your opinion*], even in my moments of discouragement, I wrote a counterpart to your journal, maybe I could be blamed at times, but I'm sure I would meet with sympathy.

[*Here follows the list of sacrifices, unfortunately skirting cliché because they are true, but I still (descending from Michelet or her?) felt obliged to cut them out*: "For twenty years, I lived in sacrifice. I married you when the trials of fortune began", *etc.*]

[*Cont.*] Being your wife in heart, in thought, I should have stayed more me, not effaced myself in front of your tastes, your will, your habits, so that the day would never come when the least observation on this point would be a subject of division between us.

You no longer count with me [strange fortuitous ambiguity? She could not possibly mean I no longer care for you—Freudian slip?—but appears to mean: you no longer count with me, number me in your plans.] —your destiny must be the fatal arrest of mine. Neither my so modest desires from before nor my youth, that has remained almost whole for not having been used [*Fr.: used up, worn away*], nothing is placed into your balance. Is that what I should expect from someone who loves?

There is finally this cruel word: no remedy? It sounds like a sentence. You know yourself that a remedy exists for everything. Nature takes over where the heart refuses. Without changing your life, without compromise, there was a way to prove to me that you were not closing yourself into an egotism that chills. You could authorize me to take a little air, freedom, diversions with those I choose. Here I am, *twice the age of maturity today*. Even if I stay young at heart, the world calls me old. Would that I gain at least the privilege of age!

[*She goes on to elaborate recent grievances, how he brooded when she wanted to go out with friends at Glion*—"a waste of time, you say, empty, vulgarity." *And yet she had corrected the proofs of the History of the French Revolution, and the doctors ordered him, as well as her, to take the mountain air.* . . .]

[*Concl.*] You tell me to have confidence at the very moment I see the unjust way you appreciate [*faux ami: appraise, judge*] my actions and thought. This only contributes, don't you agree?, a continual storm to the times of our sadness. I've had enough of their weight.

LINDA ORR

* * *

How life lulls us—how all
is revealed to the sleepless!
Can you sunder your grief
on the foundations of bridges?

Where the smoky semaphore
chased night off the tracks:
where the bridge of the Apocalypse
rocks the sighs of stars,
where beams, ribs, rails, and ties
gather in a shrieking avalanche,

where jostled bodies grasp
hands, break embraces,
chant and repeat
a tireless refrain,

where the dipstick thrusts
benzine into faces
clinging like soot
on the ends of dead cigars. . . .

It's a burning tulip,
wild begonia fire,
inhaled by the crowd
through cupped palms.

The delicate pistils
burn as if ashamed,
every fifth one—engineer,
student, "intelligensia."

I am not one of them.
I was sent by God to torment
myself, my family, everyone
whom it's a sin to torment.

Near Kiev—sand
and splattered tea
stick to hot foreheads,
in fever—by social class.

Near Kiev—sand
in multitudes, like boiling water,
like the freshly washed trace
of a compress, like dropsy. . .

The tall pines can't dilute
this puffing, soot, and heat—
and now the storm juts out
of the forest like an ax!

But the woodcutter, where is he?
How long will all this last?
Which road leads to the depot?

Passengers clamber aboard,
the bell rings, the whistle hoots,
and the smoke spawns
a desert of its own.

Bazaars, illuminations
of night's finery, fog,
and out of day's weeds
noon and a saw lament.

You stretch your legs, hear
sobbing in the sheds—
hens and mattress springs
clucking, coupling in the sun.

I am not one of them.
I was sent by God to torment
myself, my family, everyone
whom it's a sin to torment.

Coffee, cigarettes, kefir.
It takes so little
to make me burst into tears—
some flies on a windowpane will do.

The pig in horseradish
sends tears down my napkin,
blurring my field of vision
like yawning rye.

For me to burst into tears
it takes only the odor
of tobacco from an editor's door,
or the heat to fall down,

or the click click of an abacus
amidst office gossip,
or desperate clouds to blow out
their brains on cucumbers,

or for high noon to strike
through the gauze of sleep,
or empty tables to rattle
at the call of cafes,

or the shadow of a raspberry bush
cooling my sweating forehead,
where greenhouses glimmer,
where the white body of a clinic stands.

I am not one of them.
I was sent by God to torment
myself, my family, everyone
whom it's a sin to torment.

Can it be that this midday moment
in a southern province
is not wet, barefoot, or hungry,
but racked with ecstasy?

Does that sulky, superfluous,
railroad hobo, that leech,
spy an angel's embroidery
on neighboring cherry trees?

Suddenly noon turns blue
as a sea of dots, and stoops
like a boneless shadow
hurled upon tired shirts.

Can it be that those willows—
chased away by railroad ties—
hurl themselves in a giddy spasm
to be embraced by a miracle?

Will they come back at night,
breathe essence from a wing
and start to play the housewife
over the strife of towels?

Will they spot the hazel's shadow
on a stone foundation,
or trace the spent day
in smoldering dusk?

Why make distress persist,
sifting through trivia?
The watchman switches our memory,
and chases us off the tracks.

BORIS PASTERNAK
Translated
by Mark Rudman
with Bohdan Boychuk

Perhaps as a penance, though a far from onerous one, I followed
Oscar Milosz's trail to the Rigi-Kaltbad not far below the summit
of that mountain.

My sins had been those of transmission. Long ago I had
brashly made English versions of several of Milosz's poems,
including one of the metaphysical poems, when I had still been
largely blind to their author's full profile and mostly deaf to the
particular character of his abstract nouns. Much later I read
Czeslaw Milosz's confession that the French written by his older
relative was "nearly untranslatable" into Polish. And what, then,
about English? So perhaps I should have rowed with my uncal-
loused hands across the Vierwaldstadtersee from Luzern to
Vitznau, and then labored up to the tourist spa on foot. As it
was, I had only one day, and so took the large excursion boat and
then the cog railway to the Kiltbad, along with five heavily armed
troops in olive and sumac camouflage gear, through the haze of
a May morning.

It was in 1905 that Milosz first met his great friend Léon
Vogt, the Alsatian-born sculptor. In letters to Vogt Milosz looked
back on their days of conversation in this place as an "initiation."
Twenty years later he wrote to Vogt's widow that the course
which his work had followed had been anticipated by his procla-
mations of purpose during those early exchanges. Wagner, Nietzsche, and Goethe they both admired; and above Wagner and
Nietzsche's Luzern the lively enthusiast (Milosz) broadly sketched
for the reflective mocker (Vogt) his conviction that one day he
would be called to play a "rôle . . . dans la rénovation de la
métaphysique chrétienne." His high spirits in this high place
unfurled more than a bright pennant of fancy for Milosz. His
work weaves such a design. That fulfillment, along with Milosz's
exile, his service as a Lithuanian diplomat in Paris, and his resemblance as a visionary to Blake and Swedenborg, has been treated
several times in the prose of Czeslaw Milosz. Yet even with
such assistance, most readers of Oscar Milosz's words to Vogt's
widow probably would find them presumptuous or odd. Of
course, the question is not of most-and-many, but of one-by-one.

I was back to my choice of means: who now travels to Rigi-Kaltbad on foot?

Christian metaphysics: does one intuitively sense the provocation in that phrase, its linkage of adjective to noun? It is a highly unstable compound, or rather a rapidly changing isotope of one of the rare metals. Its alchemy also became, in Milosz's day, the preoccupation of Étienne Gilson. But Professor Gilson was able to conceive it only under the initial impact of Henri Bergson's metaphysical teaching; it was the lucid French Herakleitos who renovated his access to Aquinas and Bonaventura and Augustine. Milosz's embracing metaphysical term, *le Mouvement*, has Bergsonian sweep if not function. Yet such lines of affinity may not greatly intrigue the traveller for whom the Rigi remains passé, that focus of the English Grand Tour whose great hotels have melted into the mist. Accomodations! Metaphysical energies have not very notably, like the Queen of Sheba, made their way to the bridal suites of modern Christianity.

Alas, there was some chance that my little journey—neatly convenient, privately archival—had been motivated by reactionary impulses, in a disgusted flight from the pseudo-Shebas where I lived and worked. Within the same month in Zürich, I heard a woman praise a "workshop" ceremony staged in the Alps by an American "shaman," saw a velvet-black poster advertising the materialization of a bearded, sveltly curled "Rael" at the Hotel Carlton-Elite ("Die Ausserirdischen haben mich auf ihren Planeten mitgenommen," his black breast slung with a fist-sized medallion whose silver Star of David nestled inside its points the swastika), and was shown several pages by a preeminent American Catholic theologian, who invoked in a seamless litany Messrs. Tillich, Bonhoeffer, Kierkegaard, Marx, Nietzsche, and Jung, as if these gentlemen were nimble elders and pals in one great chorus, whose choragos was yoked into service through the phrase, "the freshness deep down things": yes, Father Hopkins. This false theology of red herrings packed with neither salt nor philosophy, like the psychologies whiffling and burbling through the tulgey wood, suggested that "Rael" was anything but extraterrestrial, and that his attendant curses had not fallen from the stars. That day I read no further.

265

Here as elsewhere, it was a hubbub not so much of cults (cultic coherence was lacking) as of incantations, each one improvised in somebody's back yard. Was I using Oscar Milosz as a silencer and counter-charm?

I remembered some serious walking during a day of rain down through the Val Bavona in the Tessin, among sparsely inhabited villages whose empty stone houses were used seasonally by cattle drovers as they moved up to the mountain pastures. "Freshness" in that valley had been not only salubrious but also practical; that is, when I stood near the waterfall shattering its column above the roofs of Foroglio, it was where lacquer-makers probably worked in the past, the fine spray clearing their heads of fumes and leaving their product clean.

Also in the Tessin was the doctor's house in Cavigliano, on which Dr. C. A. Meier noted the following inscription. It provides a caveat which I wanted to stretch over the general hubbub: *Noli esse stultus ne moriaris in tempore non tuo. Fingunt se cuncti medicos: idiota, sacerdos, judaeus, monachus, histrio, rasor, anus.* (Don't be stupid or you'll die before your time. They all pretend to be doctors: Joe Blow, priest, Jew, Monk, actor, barbar, hag.)

These reflections suggested to me that my reactions were sanitary rather more than aesthetic, and that Oscar Milosz had nothing to do with them. Whatever the pilgrimage to Luzern, with its yoke so easy, the burden was perhaps Milosz's own travel, his exile and his work—that is, travel in the Shaker sense, as travail, leading also in this case to a man's particular *travail.*

Idiota, sacerdos, histrio, rasor, anus. Mist which passes, cloud which reforms. And then there are the Christianities. When the Alexandrian Christian Valentinus (he did not call himself "a gnostic," and he relied on Paul's letters and John's Gospel before the Roman Church felt it safe to do so) became a candidate for the Bishopric of Rome, he was—*post hoc ergo propter hoc?*— "thrice-over thrown out of the Church" (Tertullian). In his Gospel of Truth he had written analogically about a walk in the mountains. It is as if there, he said, one heard one's name called and knew who one was, recognized where one had come from, and saw where one was to go. I suppose that Oscar Milosz of the

Rigi would not have anathematized the analogy. Indeed, he might even have stamped it "Empirically Valid."

Milosz initiated his friendship with Vogt in the billiard room "par un jour de brouillard et de mauvais temps peu propice à la promenade." Around the Kaltbad settlement at which I now peered, the cloud remained very white and very thick. To be sure, it was not a lonely place, but there was nobody to share a joke with above Nietzsche's lake, especially if it were the joke, still empirically valid, which Milosz's audience afforded him in the late 1920s. "Deux groupes gravitent déjà autour de moi," he wrote to Vogt's widow, "l'un ultra-catholique, l'autre athée, nietzschéen et anarchiste. Comme la Verité est une, la chose n'a rien qui nous puisse surprendre."

The soldiers lugged heavy equipment in packs and steel trunks off the old wooden railway car, began to reconnoitre a route, but then swiftly decamped into the dining room of a hotel sheathed in yellow asbestos sheeting: the "brick" of American expediency. The names of eight hotels hung posted at the station; none was the "Grand Hotel" at which Milosz and Vogt had met. When had it gone up in flames, or been sublimed into a more profitable "renovation"? It had burnt down, I was told, and was now replaced by the yellow asbestos box. The snow lay freshly laundered. I chose not to soil its folds by seeking out the Klösterli and the petit chateau. No steam lifted from the mountain-tucked sheets; no sins were to be remitted by pious traipsing. I worked my way on towards the summit.

The cloud, by then impenetrable, snugged itself around bevies of contented luncheoners at the Rigi-Kulm Hotel. A mountain tunnel which leads from the rail stop to a rock-shaft elevator, suggesting an impregnable command post, disgorges one at a choice of modern dining rooms. Once again, the whole structure has supplanted a grander prototype which had sat vacant for awhile, its vast sitting rooms quilted in red plush, its balcony floors rotted out by melting snows, until finally it had burned. Two flushed, white-haired old men in blue peasant dress rippled accordion music across the tables.

Entering from the mists, a figure whose arms and legs moved as if on strings, attended by an older man in a matching hiking outfit. The father spoke closely and patiently to the son, who displayed moods of panic and delight in rapid sequence, identifying most of the world's features by the two great sponsoring categories, *Mama!* and *Papa!* I smiled at myself for thinking of it, but there it was: on the way up from the Kaltbab of Milosz and Vogt, I had been idly reviewing a string of unequal male pairs, all of them alpine travellers—Wordsworth and his English companion trekking across the Simplon, imbibing the new wine of Revolution; then Hölderlin's pair in "Mnemosyne," Titan and wanderer; and finally the two Jews, Tall and Small, of Paul Celan's "Conversation in the Mountains." Oscar Milosz's pre-war symposium of two ("Nous étions trois, comme sont la Chair, l'Ame et l'Esprit") had predisposed me to tally these disjunctive male duos and even to expect another pair of wanderers to appear in the flesh and fill out the pattern. They had appeared; but then they almost immediately left, jerkily evanescing into the fog, their paired red knee-socks, and the rhythmic young left arm cocked like a butler's in service, pacing out the tempo of devotion and bondage. *Le mauvais temps* notwithstanding, it seems that they were to have their promenade, and that I was to lose my *trouvaille.*

Not quite, however. After drenching my legs on the mountain and jamming onto the two-car train with seventy others, I saw the children opposite me suddenly spring from their seats and the wandering pair just as quickly take them. Those excited, strange eyes, and the tensely cocked wrist beneath autonomous finger antennae, again framed his ecstatic and terrified invocations of the archetypal parents. In a moment I had become *Papa!* and the steep valleys, gulleying through lower skirts of the cloud, served as *Mama!* The father soothed him with frequent pats on forehead and neck; the Swiss passengers accepted the young man as they usually do all *Behinderte*, routinely and easily. But perhaps his gentle commotion nonetheless broke the reserve in one of them, a big fellow who began to show off to his wife and friends: "Da, da gehts der *Steam-Boat. The Steam-Boat is a-coming*, aus der Mississippi, ha! Und da gehen die *Sail-ing Boats.* Jaja, mit *Moby Dick!*" Of the two choristers in the car, it was clear to everyone which of them had drunk some beer and uncorked his normality. But for me there was also no question that the other, uncanny singer had convened a sitting of *la chair, l'âme, et l'esprit.*

The private imbalance to which Oscar Milosz's rôle finally drove him in his later years, an imbalance which Czeslaw Milosz records as coinciding with Oscar Milosz's greatest successes as a diplomat, was far more elusive, far less open to assessment, than the mobile opacity of the young man across from me, whose left hand duplicated that of a young Pharoah or Royal Overseer in the tomb paintings of Egypt, and whose eyes, wet with pained mirth, gazed steadily over our heads.

Milosz's *Epitre à Storge* (the proper name from the Greek for parental love) records a solar vision. Czeslaw Milosz ventures to compare that vision with episodes in the lives of Swedenborg and Pascal. I am sure that this is appropriate. Yet if I echo the claim it is only to bring out one of its implications: that such visions are nothing to chatter about, or to find "interesting." Easy access to the Rigi, which in a matter of minutes misleadingly can make any holder of a ticket the theoretic spectator of peaks, seas, Triebschens, and the prototypes of Valhala, is akin to our tours among what we think we read. Yet in either world a mountain retains its elevation. If the climb is rendered innocuous by one means, the mountain will reinstate its natural aristocracy by some other means, hidden from the eyes of Pizzaro.

To Vogt's widow Oscar Milosz wrote in several letters (November 1927 and December 1929) that he had accomplished the mission "des plus secrètes" to which his work had bent him, so that both he and his work had won "la gloire solaire dont ils sont dignes." Though I credit this claim in my own way, I cannot pretend to have followed Milosz all the way through *Ars Magna* and *Les Arcanes*. Does this mean that, like some of the foreign tourists sprinkled through our railway car in the clouds, I should have to blush, look away, or wish to flee? The facts of publication had let me eavesdrop on the following avowal to his friend's widow—"ma connaissance dépasse celle de Dante"—that is, had let me hear without perhaps hearing rightly, and certainly without being able to judge. Such is the part of decorum, between children and elders, in the commerce of parental love.

About the meaning which Oscar Milosz's work came to have for Czeslaw Milosz, the latter writes, "Had I not known tragedy, both private and public, and if most of my life had not been a struggle at the scream's edge, I too would have found nothing

269

there." In Oscar Milosz *la connaissance*, more than indicating "knowledge" or even a revealed "gnosis," denotes "perception," the kind of perception that emerges from great and prolonged suffering. Perhaps one may correspondingly lend emphasis to *le Mouvement* as the expression of a cosmic *Amour* which of its very nature sacrifices itself. And who, whatever their gifts, has looked for very long into that sun? The young man opposite—the boy in him and the ageless figure as well—bellowed *Papa!* to the vapor around us, while his father and fellow *Wandersmann* gentled neck and face and murmured familiar comfortings and commands. Watching those two while thinking of "la gloire solaire," I felt the escape of quadratic equations, the chimings and fadings of overtone series, the veering approach and flight of correspondences.

But the land was coming up faster, trees were acquiring branches, needles, sharp shadows. Back into mind swam the inexpensive reproduction at the Kunstmuseum, along with my desire to have it. If the boat landed before five o'clock, I could still have it indeed. Down there, they run those boats on schedule. Down there, when they write about Czeslaw Milosz's eschatological poem, "From the Rising of the Sun," and come to its dramatization of a vision of the underworld sun, they annotate it: "from Apuleius." When they happen to notice that Ezra Pound's seventeenth Canto ends with a similarly dramatized vision, they cross-index the annotation: "these people 'get up' their contacts with Persephone in a consistent fashion. Let us make homologies. Let us call them the literary *katabasis*." Very well, but first let us purchase our tickets at the *Schifflandung*. Surprise: among the men in blue uniforms, a young woman working the ropes at clews and moorings. Her face looks like a friend's, a professional scholar of Latin and Greek, who when uncertain about plunging further into those languages, dreamed that a huge sun rose over a tremendous canyon, to the sonorous, rhythmic chanting of the lines which begin *The Aeneid*. Thereafter, the career. But had Virgil, the master of *katabasis*, thereby finished with that person?

The young woman in blue unnoosed us from the creaking piles. Alone with my company, I was being drawn once more across the hospitable, unfathomable water. And so, very soon again, came the Benedictine church cocooned in green netting,

270

the painted wooden bridge roofed with the challenges of impudent, insistent Death, and the crowning, abandoned defensive wall with bannered towers.

JOHN PECK

THE AVIGNON TRAIN, AFTERNOON, SEPTEMBER

Their high season all seasons, in or
out of season the old & the adolescent
travel facing each other in cheap trains, to
where clockworkers on expense accounts must fly.
Riding the rails, we undo backpack
pockets or plump handbags for our lunch.

Three international European young
homing toward Holland from Kasmir
complain, "This train stops everywhere";
they're headed for Arles to watch men stick bulls;
they think that might he interesting.

The fresh white head of my opposite number
turns from them; she inverts her smile, nods,
remarks that the Avignon children she goes to see
give handsome returns on her interest in them.

The Dutch drink Cola poptop with their chips; I eat
a white-fleshed peach (I'm eating summer) and
envy madame her unvarying knife-cut;
salami & bread drop in classic rounds.

Prompt with Latin hosting courtesy,
once she learns I am a foreigner
we drink a wine, pale gold, drawn
from the grapes of her Burgundy acre;
she approves my raspberries, merely bought.

The young debate among themselves in Dutch. She
waits, then points, according to asterisks
on her up-to-date non-crack train-schedule,
to when they'll arrive, helps them endorse
their rucksacks, & smiles them out
into her big world. We, extravagant, take
our ease, stopping & starting everywhere,
off season, off hour, on our own.

MARIE PONSOT

You have never had a vacation. It might be better to say you never desired one. You have, desiring change, desiring to be changed, flown off to some exotic place, and spent whatever savings you had accrued over the course of a year on *travel*. You anticipate not ease, not daiquiris on a beach, but revelation.

A journey is not a vacation. And seeing the sights may not be as eventful as getting to them. Travelling is really a pilgrimage backward in time through our proximity in space. It has always been a primal desire. You had to know, since you were about twelve, that there was more to life than the city, the suburbs, the desert and the wilderness.

You go to experience not fullness (the grandeur of the past) but emptiness. Superfluity. To acquire, not souvenirs, but exhaustion. You go in order to exhaust yourself. To escape provincialism. And to know where each unfamiliar step went.

*

The mind, to ward off other anxieties, fixes on such things as what book to bring. Once selected, you are tempted to devour it in advance to make sure you like it because what would you do three or six thousand miles away from home, at eleven at night after twelve hours of wandering, of *seeing*, with no words, no story, no talisman to remind you of home, another order.

It's an old story, "to love that well which thou must leave ere long." Travel breaks you free of habit, and of the habit of performance or postponement. The knowledge that you're going to be leaving home heightens the time before you leave. You will finish projects that you're working on, (or bring them to a stopping point). You will see people you haven't made the time to see in the preceding months. (Mired in winter.) You will stop obsessing about other—inexorable—problems. (Money. What to do with your life.)

Escape: that is the subtext of the journey. And yet once we arrive elsewhere our longing for escape is swallowed up by the reality of that place which soon begins to exist as another place to escape from. The longing to escape civilization, our civilized weariness. The tragedy is that there's nowhere to escape to, not even, as did the Romantics, to Italy.

*

Remember Perugia? Its gentle, hazy, mesmerizing valleys where even the sheep clambered into caves in the afternoon and a man hand-mixed cement next to the madhouse named after these words from the *Paradiso*, "da porta sola."

Horizontal in spite of its height, Perugia transports the eye from spire to bell tower ringing the valley loud—over motorcycle growl and Citreon purr, caravans leapfrogging on the autostrada. We head out into the Perugian night, under stars blazing through the haze that flows through the valley Dante praised, wherein the just men are equally slaughtered and handed after-lives. . . . One way leads to the small chapel where Raphael painted his first fresco, the other straddles MTV, radios blaring American punk songs from windows and things American, tee shirts lettered "California Sports." And the rain came down from a cloudless (close to serene, albeit tilted) sky in the square where you were momentarily seated and they took the umbrella away from your table the moment the first drops fell, your camera disappeared and your copy of La Nazione was missing its Umbrian section....

*

Is antiquity anything more than a sham invented by modernity? St. Augustine was wise in his desire never to see the sea, thinking he could imagine it well enough from descriptions he had heard.

*

For Emily Dickinson as well, "To shut our eyes is to Travel."

*

Siena: It takes an hour of ceaseless circling to realize it is all stone, unnatural. The modern in the medieval: Basilicas stocked with SONY Walkmen and Seiko digital watches. No shadows on the sundial.

In Siena it is easy to find the spot where *it* travels by you (the world movie, the spectacle); as the guidebook says, "you can sit for hours watching the shadows" meander the Campo before vanishing—not so the people, the pigeons, or the palazzo, where Lorenzetti's battle still progresses with spears, torches, and horses, heightened by the hours' "rattling thunder." This restless searching, this curious seeking, what could you possibly hope to find (beyond the shadows in Carpaccio's *St. Jerome* where monks flee)? Something to eat? A crucifix? An unturned stone? Etruscan haybale?

You saw the stars last night, graced perhaps in that you looked at no artifacts or monuments, visited no sites— except the Campo whose shadows you watched crawl toward the center and disappear to the cooing of pigeons so like the woman's orgiastic moan echoing through our courtyard in Rome—Rome where Keats' grave rests in a shadow's coolness, placed there to rest for eternity after a mortal life without rest. Rest.

*

You're filled with the longing to escape: Desire revving up inside you wanting to move, wanting to be used. During bleak periods you have sustained yourself with the thought that come such and such a day you would be able to escape.

Escape: This is one response to intolerable conditions.

*

Tourism won't let you forget yourself. You are surrounded— more than ever—by your doubles. Camera packing, map scanning, guidebook bearing, post card writing, souvenir fingering, monument worshipping, foreign tongue speaking, guilefully guileless, relaxedly intent, lazily diligent. The passion to record each official site is the final sickness of this civilization which no longer trusts its own memory, or believes—believes? in the power of imagination to find what it needs.

Every time you take a picture you feel a pressure and a heaviness: is it necessary? You take mainly human scenes: an old woman and a young girl at an intersection, crossing Via Dante, whom you take to be grandmother and granddaughter, the old woman's arm resting gently on the young woman's shoulder as the traffic blares and rushes; a poster of two naked children hold- ing hands, words to the effect—will there be a future in the nuclear age when they radiate monkeys and cut mice to see how humans might survive after the blast? The traffic outruns the Tiber whose dark sandy banks suck feet to ankle . . . and a man's shoe washes up, circa 1930, laces in the shape of a nest, and larks flutter in the branches of the plane tree shading you.

*

Walking through mounds of graves and sarcophagi, among poppies, blazing on the hillsides, and a band of young German girls scrambling among the waist-high bricks. Frescoes of farmers. The continuity of human needs and desires. The structure of Ostica Antica in ruins is the same as most towns with its theaters, its senate, its Forum. Like a beehive. Myth has it Virgil was born there. Virgil, who wrote of Aeneas that "He came to Italy by destiny."

Looking at all these artifacts provokes thoughts about *form* — as in the sculptures by Bernini and Michelangelo where the origi- nal stone or waste marble is left and the figure emerges from that source.

The light casts abrupt shadows on the shy, hungry faces in restaurants. Smiles fractured, eyes walk off. They say: you will not be saved by art, or worry.

At the Rosati after a day's journey through the ruins to the ruins—splendidly revived!—a whole city!—where all you had to do was take two baths a day.

Rome: lovely to walk at night along the surging serpentine Tiber, under full moon, stars, or streetlights lighting up anything: a ruin, tomb, Citroen, cat, a couple embracing, some ragged body fishing from its banks—

The Colosseum empty. The city filled with gladiators. The city has become the arena.

*

The Protestant Cemetery—Keats' grave, without a name, just the epitaph "here lies the one whose name was writ in water," as requested—what a beautiful spot to be dead.

*

Everywhere you go, where there's a gate or a door—and hours posted—Chuiso, *Closed*. What is more notable about a ruin than its holes? Or a certain masterpiece in a museum other than that the museum is always closed? What we can't live without is the faith that there is something of value there, that Giorgione's *Tempest* is as good as it is said to be.

Only the churches and open-air ruins like the Baths of Caracalla and Ostia Antica are always there to welcome you under the shade of cypresses. And even the sound of construction, a tractor clearing paving stones, men hammering pipes to put up the bleachers for tonight's opera cannot disrupt the rest you feel.

The hike to Veio, an Etruscan site where green lizards remain perched over the waterfall, motionless while the torrent pours over them. In Veio, the walls are still warm from fires that went out over two thousand years ago.

St. Clemente, and the Mithraic Crypts, Cults, and Temples. Their image is the Hero as bullslayer, knife to throat, eyes to Apollo, O! Posters all around for Bob Dylan and Santana at Roma-Paleur. Masaccio assisted Massollini at St. Clemente.

*

Saw Moretti's *Bianca*. Could not decipher the plot. Is the hero a villain as well as the hero? And when they rolled open the ceiling at intermission you didn't know where you were, the light for a moment seared your eyes, erased the few last fading images of a man running in circles in a white suit, green trees, red car, all

278

faded to white as the sky stood on top of the buildings like scaffolding, a deeper blue than the Virgin's robe in one of Giotto's frescoes. Later, crossing a bridge over the Tiber, you saw a man dumped from a motorcycle into a hedgerow under the aqueduct where he disappeared, the traffic congealed, and real life began to imitate this aimless but funny, odd, but harrowing film.

*

It is the unplanned you remember most: stumbling on Augustus' tomb one night; a girl carrying a wounded pigeon. No monuments. No masterpieces!

Ravenna: This town where Dante took refuge and bears his tomb, and Blok described as sleeping like an infant in the arms of a drowsy eternity and Antonioni shot *Red Desert*, where factory waste smoke and chemicals mar the blue-green Adriatic, not what lies in the light in the piazzas morning and evening or the still light in the basilicas or through the spokes of omnipresent bicycles, as Venice draws near. . . .

*

What you remember of Antonioni's film: River factory waste lands; the dump smolders, the ground is purple; the whole town, under construction, consists of outskirts; foghorns repeat—distant—ships come nearer—glide through the windows like apparitions. Giuliana saying, "There's something terrible about reality and I don't know what."

Assissi, San Gimingiano: Hilltop towns blend, and the same distances uncurl. Men playing bocci while two roosters crow and haybales pour onto trucks. It gives you pleasure to see someone having fun—relaxing at bocci—while you are travelling: working at it.

After seeing his painting of the Crucifixion in Assisi you feel confirmed in your feeling that Cimabue, the first artist of the Italian Renaissance, may also represent its apogee: Dynamic, expressive shapes, means subdued to an artistic end rather than a story.

The language. The universal ur-language of travelling. Searching for the way to a place, the right bus. For some, who are not adept at map reading, merely finding the Brancacci chapel in Florence with Masaccio's frescoes is an accomplishment. And you remember that frenzy to get there as much as the details of what you see.

Smoke and haze. Sound of chewing in the train compartment. A woman stretches her smelly feet out over the seat in front of her, their stink fills the compartment and her legs block the aisle.

*

But you travel, you spend your tax returns, you splurge, spend everything you have, (willing to return and begin again with nothing) to find yourself, to cut through the surface disturbance. (Vallejo: "From disturbance to disturbance you rise to accompany me alone.")

The secret of travelling is not to travel. Better to go to one place, like a nameless town outside Florence, and venture out from there, returning in the evening. But life and time conspire against the sanity of this.

Preparations? Rooms in advance? Choices. The desire to touch the source. A journey is a passage through this life in which time is literally marked. When your inner life is forced outward. You do not escape your problems, you force them to rise to the surface. You cannot dream of flying away, you have already flown, and *this* is where you have landed. (Hot, comfortless, insufficient funds.)

To travel is to seek correspondences. To find them is to feel affirmed. Travelling, paradoxically, given the accessibility of far off places, isn't far removed from having a *momento mori*, because movement, being a kind of escape, is also a constant reminder of mortality. You, your body, feel time passing—in the very vibration of your vehicle of transport.

*

There would be no World Literature if its heroes had stayed home: *The Odyssey, Don Quixote, Molloy,* the quest in the guise of journey as motive, "le mouvement de chose." And yet it has to do with *movement* as much as anything else. The hunter-gatherer becomes the seeker-wanderer. Journeying, returning.

Isn't the "real" issue at stake in *Henry IV* not the civil war but in King Henry's words their "holy purpose to Jerusalem," a quest rather than an internal struggle?

"Tintern Abbey," "Crossing Brooklyn Ferry," "Sea Surface Full of Clouds," "The Idea of Order at Key West," the Yucatan evoked in the "Comedian as the Letter C," "The Bell Tower," "The Desert Music," *The Cantos* evoking Provence and the paths of the Troubadours, "The Heights of Macchu Picchu," "African Journal," "Schubertiana"... It's clear that the encounter with the otherness of place brings out something that lies dormant within the unconscious that needs this push to emerge. To acquire, not things, but through experience, perspective. . . . Or is it in reality as devastating as Pavese says:

> Traveling is a brutality. It forces you to trust strangers and to lose sight of all that familiar comfort of home and friends. You are constantly off balance. Nothing is yours except the essential things—air, sleep, dreams, the sun, the sky—all things tending toward the eternal or what we imagine of it.

*

You think of Coleridge in his cottage in Nether Stowey, day-dreaming of an elsewhere that would be the antipode of that staid village, where now the caretaker is annoyed to look up from her knitting to answer a question much less let you in the door. And on the path where he and Wordsworth walked as they conceived the *Lyrical Ballads,* rows of empty towers—a nuclear power factory!—zigzags toward the sea. Coleridge pressed against the boundaries of imagination to invent and exhausted those boundaries.

Negative pastoral: you cross Hampstead Heath for the first time after a visit to Keats' house on a sultry afternoon in late July. The grass is brown and dry. The next day you read of the

"Lido Murder," of how a paraplegic was drowned in his wheel-chair that very afternoon somewhere on the heath. Around the time you were there!

And on the path, north of Oxford, through azure wheat fields strewn with Roman stones, on your way to a fabled local pub, you wondered why you had come. . . .

*

Perhaps you broach the question of a restlessness that exceeds the matter of these pages. Your father, for example, never had the desire to go anywhere that wasn't sunny and warm and near the ocean, and is amused by your—or anyone else's—desire to go elsewhere. "Travel is a fetish."

*

The idea of the journey consumes the imagination. And often the place exceeds expectation. How is this possible? Light. The sky over the marketplace in Arles, colors, the sun impossibly bright, and the sea waking. The fountain where you splashed water on your face. The sun through clouds moving like a search-light over the fields from Fiesole. The flowering gorse on the Tuscan hillsides, not quite different enough from forsythia to be as distinctive as it seems—a dimension that eludes you, captures your attention.

You travel, finally, and only that, to experience the aura that dailiness removes from the things that surround you. You feel the changes taking place inside yourself as they occur. To leave means to put an abrupt end to what has been. Realms of possibility open.

To shed your skin. To molt. You feel you have to escape your surroundings, to change your physical space, to accomplish this spiritual act.

To see the sea again. Places are like unread books, like poten-tial lovers. What is it we seek? You, I. Resolution, requital. An erotic quickening.

282

*

The days are framed. People in from out of town catch you up in the whirl of their voyages. Their desire for fresh experience.

The journey disappears in the thought of it. Only the place-names remain: Arezzo, Lucca, Urbino. Places you are still free to imagine, having never been there. And the more your life is hemmed in here, the more your mind is confined to practical uncertainties, travel—this journey you are about to undertake—becomes a time and place free from *worry*.

And it doesn't matter where you go. What matters is the pressure of departure and arrival, of how we live, as Rilke says, "forever taking leave."

*

We ought to live our lives as if we were on a journey, but circumstance, habit, and necessity conspire against us. Travel resembles an illness which suddenly makes our other "real" life stand out in relief. The desire to travel transcends all *places*. And even if it is true that desire always exceeds the object of desire, travel creates a frame: a before, a posited after. And the duration of the time vibrates.

Italy/June 11-July 2 1984

283

PERSPECTIVE

They talk about lying to tell the truth.
Whoever "they" are.
To tell the truth—is painful—
in the face of clocktowers—
invisible—in the black rain—
and my Kodak black and whites
do not replicate those sinuous
mountains that look like mountains,
far off, and the hills dotted with hills,
bent, like haybales—
not to dissolve the question
in the matter of "perspective"
or diminish the fertile beauty
of all that flickering in the vineyards
and olive groves,
slow, heavy,
oozing, pouring,
like honey from a jar:
nothing more useless than impatience here;
or the plotting of charts and courses
beyond the present—tense—:
splitting the atom with the instant's scimitar,
harmlessly, arm in arm,
drinking from fountains,
dunking, bathing in fountains,
and still to tell the truth was—
is—all that mattered.
Lying played no part in it.

FIRST GLANCES

It's close to midnight and we've walked
as many miles as the day has hours,
past the tomb of Augustus rising at dusk,
its cypresses and shadows and crouching cats,
the city more awake than ever
at this late hour, on the make:

and we are getting used to getting lost
as a way of being, as long as we have
squid with lemon and olive oil to revive us,
and the moon, the full moon,
pocked and radiant over
the still furious and surging Tiber,

and hidden in the river weeds
a man fishing from its banks. . . .
You say a man? You see a figure
crouched with a long pole extending;
a bundle of rags; no face, no hands.

Consolation: the straight, yet dignified
statues of poets like Belli, and the moon
in Trastevere where there's more gaiety
than here, near Santa Maria del Popolo
where Nero's tomb keeps watch

as a ragamuffin puts his fingers
through the sockets of the marble skeleton
set in the wall and leers,
and my unseen neighbor down the hall calls out:
"It's alright with just my shutter locked, right?"

only to keep us awake all night
with an operatic orgasm
that echoes in the courtyard—
whose acoustics rise to the occasion
to rival the Baths of Caracalla—

to where a dozen pairs
of closed white shutters stare. . . .

ROME 1

What you must understand
is that it is not Caravaggio's
St. Peter or the Vatican,
nor is it the courtyard in the parking lot
where we eat pollo diavolo and fresh calamari
under the sign of the pitchfork
under the sign "Hostaria La Capannina"
looking at the two-in-the-afternoon
rolled down shutters on the Piazza della Coppella,
where a gray haired man with a grizzled beard
in a tee shirt and army fatigues clutches a can
of "Fanta," and the local cats come over
in homage to possibility, and we are grateful
for the coolness of the shadows on the paving stones
a mere block from where the crowd murderously plunges,
on armored feet! It is not basilicas,
crowds, the whirling of starlings,
not even Velasquez's portrait of Pope Innocent the IV
with its consummate tension,
not the marble galleries or the clay floors of the catacombs
where the Christians used to hide from the Romans,
not the variety of Christs—
the classic emaciate to the bloodless ones,
not Caravaggio's young St. Peter
who mocks your gaze by looking through your eyes,
not masterpieces or competent pictures,
the gracious or the cranky, ease or exhaustion,
not, not denial, nothing, then, other than what is.

ROME 2: RECOVERING FROM MICHELANGELO

For who can decipher the woman
in Adam's bent knee with neck craned upward and strain-
ing. For who can penetrate
the meticulous design, or all the seeming,
as Jonah, emerging from the whale's vaginal mouth,
explodes into relief, and the snake
holding Eve against the tree is
the tree. Light is revelation. For all
aspires to rise, as the saved haul
themselves out of hell. The fall is time.
Which is why Charon waits with such confidence.
Light is what I want to escape from now—
at two in the afternoon.

So many cameras aimed at the separation
of the finger of God and the finger of Adam!
And yet it is equally fine—and this is the key—
to walk the city in the later
afternoons and evenings as it is to squint
at a thousand pictures.
The world-stage surfaces.
You consult the map to get us to
the Via Paradiso through the Via Doloroso.
And where there are no bridges reflections
bear us across. Without you
I would be doubly lost.

LAST MORNING

Streets of Milan, the ultimate hustle bustle, the final mercantile.
Not a leaf in sight—as far as Castello Sforzesco. This street rings
with the turbulence of traffic, the angst of impending departure.
The banks take away . . . and add to the noise and knottedness
of the crowd. Leonardo, Stendahl: both came to live here of their
own free will. But that was before the invention of the Exhaust
Fume. A restless black cat skirmishes back and forth under the
chairs. There is no haven for him in Milan, on this island between
Via San Prospero and Via Dante. Would he rest content on the
Corriere Della Sera if I wedged my copy under a leg of this chair
once I am gone? Is this a just end for Michel Foucault's obituary?
Is it true that we cannot gauge the degree of another's sexual
pleasure? Foucault was obsessed by the repercussions of this. I
read *Madness and Civilization* in the days when I still underlined,
darkening most of its pages. . . . Now the birds, crowded out of
the sky by high fashion, disappear, this Monday morning, just
before noon and, as if the city were a prison yard, two teenage
boys rev up a motor scooter attempting to break out. The absence
of the sun is a hunger of mind pure as the cat's restlessness. Whatever rumbles under the grating will some day be delivered.

MARK RUDMAN

ON THE TRAIN

That spooky girl—a tiger-eyed beauty
Had the white silk skin of her face been uncut,
Instead a red hem was ravenously unripped
On the face she had to go through time with—made me
Wish God's hands could move again to make her not fail
In the flesh, but be bodied forth as all
Innocence is, discovered and surprised by us
Riding under those flames at night, the moon and stars . . .
Not scarred.

*

            At first she seemed a bulky, milky whore—
Hurrying down the sunshot aisle with her guitar.
Why whore? A certain stationariness they have,
Even when walking (the very genius of
Each dumb, deliberate gesture's simply to be
There, somehow seeable before becoming the
Thing it is an emblem of—so much so that
There sometimes seems to be one of them: a building
Front's little pillar swells alive breasted by light,
The black girl with the red dress on is a firebox
Floating on shadow—that lampost with one leaning
On it's only a lampost—*Oh anything, still*
And silent on the city's floor at night, posing
As the original animal of our
Nakedness, desireable and dead.) —And, as she
Slid into the seat opposite facing me, I
Caught a look of crooked hardness escaping the
Side of her eye and what seemed wild rouging.—But who
Ever heard of a whore with a guitar? And there
It lay upon her lap, her hands cradling the toy-
Sized thing like slow hope and comfort . . . waking faint,
Voiceless strings burning gold on their box.
                           She was not
Facing me at all, torso twisted, legs crossed, she

Sat sort of sidesaddle, her face hidden behind a
Great dusty bush of fragile stuff . . . wavering as
If underwater.
                    Twilit landscape roaring past.

We took a curve—
                    (I saw the first car going on
Gleaming rails into forest, following the black,
Sliding river)—she crouched forward a moment, in
A kind of staunch, animal pride—pulling the loose
Summer-green cloth tighter to her.
                                    I wanted to
Touch that bare bright knee with a green vein writing some-
Thing on, no *in* it—next to, *in-between* mine.
                                            Made
The mandatory, silent manipulation
Of limbs, ramming jamming fucking sucking—and that
Momentous leap out of himself any man makes
(In his mind) whenever a woman's un-
Expected loveliness appears.—But, *somehow* . . . still
Had not seen her face. Only smiling-high cheekbone-
Line, nose-tip nub showed past the soft-stiff stuff of hair

Brightening now . . .
                    that the disc of fire burned above dim,
Forgetful blue mountains meeting dark, sleeping pines

Till hurrying cloud-giants covered the sun.
                                        A
Serried fortress keeping all radiance within.

A fat white animal letting its blood of light
Fall through a hole . . .

                    a great glass cane *flashing*

                                            that broke
By disappearing.
                    We passed a river-town that

Has (virtually) no history.—Old and
Mostly deserted, like some worn barnacle stuck
On the rocks.

          —-Cold and wild, too cold and wild to swir
Beautiful too, the river . . . the pines came closer
On the other side.

        So thick sky behind them niched
Bright as small gunsights.
              Some down stripped of their bark.—Long,
Yellow inner bodies . . . the round, revealed faces
Of suns. —Green, evolved heights fallen around.—Skin white-
Cracked, as if melted off from within.

             —–But, what is
It one looks at in life: *Clouds, Trees, The River* . . . ?

                 Our
Bodies are the landscape, and we are lost in them.

So many, empty places nearby.—Then, why *did*
She . . . come so close, stay twisted away from me?
              Asked
Where she was bound-for, and after she answered *Why?*—
Bawled back in obsequious condescencion: "Because,
I want to see your face . . ."

        —"*I have no face.*"
            This last,
An eerie coo, whose guarded pathos and
Appalling fulfillment, construing more than
My pigeon-heart could take, or make into meaning—
Silenced me.
      Let her hide . . . the metal-voiced train sang.
And I fell asleep, looking at others inside.

                RAPHAEL RUDNIK

SAVAGES OF THE BRAZZA RIVER

Far up the Brazza River, in a relatively untouched area of the foothills of the Jayawijaya Mountains, I was accosted by a man wiggling his penis in front of my nose. I had gone to the Brazza at the invitation of the manager of a seismological company searching for oil in order to collect artifacts for a small museum in which I worked in a remote region of Irian Jaya, the western half of the island of New Guinea. The manager had given me complete freedom to travel and I had gone alone in the outboard, which I had loaded with canned goods, tobacco, machetes, and other trade goods. I was hoping to find a people who had had no contact with outsiders, unless you include in the definition of "contact" the killing of four Indonesians.

The aluminum boat was about twelve feet long, noisy enough to frighten the birds and animals, some of which set up their own counterpoint of noise in the squawks of cockatoos, the whooshing wings of hornbills, and the screeching of red and blue parrots. It did not occur to me that the outboard might also frighten away the people I hoped to meet; I had expected instead that their curiosity would keep them close by wherever I was.

Once out of sight of the camp, I felt liberated, as if I were sailing through the sky, swept on by currents directed by Fates that knew what I was looking for. I took off my clothes and traveled naked; whoever might see me then would instantly understand that I was unarmed and vulnerable.

Two hours upstream, beyond a patch of small banana trees, I could make out the figure of a man or boy and maneuvered the boat towards him. He was a youngster no more than sixteen, standing beside a low structure of thin sticks and bark, a pup tent of local materials. He was my first sight of the people of the Brazza and he electrified me with the look on his face and the ornaments in his nose. The look was wild and startled, the irises tiny within the great whites of his eyes, an expression of bewilderment in his eyebrows and half-open mouth. There was arrogance there, too, in the way he stood above me, chest out, bow and arrows in hand. I wondered what prompted him to be so daring as to stand there, alone, so close to me.

Yoshigipi, as his name turned out to be, sprouted decorations from his nose: a short length of incised bamboo through his septum and the long thin wing bones of a flying fox that curved upwards in front of his eyes from his nares. He was naked but for the ornaments on his body, the small fresh green leaf tied over the foreskin of his penis, the waistband of nine loops of rattan, and the necklace of twisted strands of yellow wire, the cap wire used by the seismological company to set off dynamite. A small net bag hung down his back. Below his neck, he was covered with the circular patterns of ringworm, one of the tineas, the skin flaking off everywhere on his body but from his clear face. He smiled when I reached up to offer a plug of tobacco and jumped down into the mud at the edge of the river. He sank to his knees but easily pulled his legs out of the ooze, hesitantly took the tobacco, and put it into his carrying bag. He pointed upstream and said something I did not understand. He took the rattan painter of his dugout canoe, tied it to my boat and climbed inside. He ran his hands over the metal and knocked it with his knuckles, then bent to lick and smell it. At his direction, we went three or four minutes upstream to another clearing, a vast open space where a hundred trees had been felled with stone axes, the stumps still there, the logs still there. The area was deeper than it was wide, reaching back over a thousand feet from the river to the far wall of the forest, where a huge house sat high in trees.

Yoshigipi quickly climbed the bank and ran ahead of me over the branches and logs that were the highway to the house. He turned to look back and saw how clumsily I stepped along the logs my sneakered feet felt no thicker than a tightrope. He walked more slowly then, offering a helping hand when thin logs over which he skimmed cracked under my weight.

The house was well over forty feet above the ground, built on poles with one huge tree trunk in the center. A ladder led the way up at an angle from under the house to the right end where a porch was built so narrow I was inside in one step. Another platform extended at the upstream end, used by the men for urinating during the day and defecating at night. Bending low, we entered through the downstream doorway, used exclusively by the men. The women entered from the back of the house on a long, notched log that angled up from the ground, an easier way up when carrying babies, sago, firewood, and/or other materials and food.

Two women suckling infants screamed at the sight of me, got up and disappeared. Yoshigipi laughed. There was no one else inside the house that I could see. Light came from openings between the irregularly spaced logs of the floor and from between the sections of bark that made the walls. It was so arranged that the houseposts down the center divided the room in half, separating the men from the women. No one crossed that line, either during the day or during the night. Sexual activity took place in the jungle.

Human skulls, blackened with soot, hung from the crosspieces of racks above the fireplaces, while the racks themselves held sago, firewood, skulls of small animals, and the skeletons of snakes and fish.

Yoshigipi sat beside me and kneaded a leaf with the heel of his hand against the inner thigh of his left leg until it was properly softened, then rolled tobacco in it. He lit his cigarette with a piece of wood from the fireplace.

A young man came to the doorway, looked inside, then left. Other men appeared, breathing heavily as if they had been running in their haste to see me. They sat down, touched me, ran their hands delicately over the skin of my arms and chest, examined the palms of my hands and even seemed to count my fingers and toes. If anyone noticed that I was circumsized, he made no obvious comment. The men talked to me as if I understood every word. They all wore decorations in their noses: bone, wooden pins, bamboo, the bones of flying foxes, the head of a rhinocerous horn beetle. Long strands of the twisted fiber of sago palms were tied into their hair and they wore bamboo ear plugs that held the dried moss or shredded fiber used to make fire together with the loops of rattan they wore as armbands. Two of the men wore beaks of hornbills as penis sheathes, the beaks curving downward from their groins, held in place by a string around the testicles. Most of the men, however, wore the small leaf covering the head of the penis. Skin diseases and ulcerated sores blotched and spotted the tough bodies of almost everyone and many had filariasis. A pair of adult albino twins looked sickly with their pigmentless skin covered with large red spots, their red hair and the pale pupils of their eyes.

295

The men touched me, laughed, grunted, rubbed their hands over my perspiring chest and back and wiped the perspiration onto their own chests and faces. One old man sat down and hugged me, rolled me over along the floor, interlocking our legs, pressing our bodies tightly together.

It was not long before an older man came in. He may have been in his late forties. He had an air of authority that immediately led me to understand that he was the headman. His massive and muscular body seemed to give him more strength than the other men. On both sides of his groin were the swollen lumps of the early stages of elephantiasis. There were running sores on his thighs and shins. Scars on his chest and back indicated where arrrows and spears had pierced his skin. His eyebrows were thick, frowning at me above small eyes surrounded by deep creases. His hair and beard were dense, ringleted, and speckled with bits of leaf and food. He wore no covering over his penis, no decoration of any kind. I stood up and he motioned me to sit down again. He stood in front of me, took his penis in both hands, pulled on it until it was half erect and flapped it up and down. He moved closer and flapped it in front of my nose, almost touching it. There was no laughter then; instead, the atmosphere was tense.

I did not know the meaning of this gesture or ritual. An Asmat from downstream might suck the penis as part of certain peacemaking ceremonies or when listening to the secrets of a friend, thereby assuring his silence. A Dani from the mountains might touch or hold the pair of testicles in greeting. No past experience seemed to offer an explanation and I was too startled to react except to stare and smile weakly.

No more than a minute or two passed before the headman, Derepen, pulled me up by the hand and threw his arms around me. He had waited to see my reaction and, apparently satisfied, welcomed me as a friend.

The men yelped and the dogs barked. The moment of tension had passed as if it had never existed. The men were in good humor and laughter circulated around the room. They cooked and brought me food, first sago from Yishigipi, then sago from the others, a small piece from each of them. Large shrimp came my way and taro, various fruits of the forest, and the long thin vegetable that grew like corn, was roasted and

296

shucked like corn but looked more like asparagus and had a slightly bitter taste.

Later, on my sleeping mat, with my thin blanket covering me and Yoshigipi, I stared up at the thousands of roaches clustering on a beam and thought about that moment. What had the gesture meant? Why had my reaction been acceptable? What would have happened had I shown anger or had I opened my mouth and received Derepen's penis? I had visions of myself fellating the men, one after another, a reversal of what had happened in the coastal area when eleven men had held me waist high in their arms, each one in turn sucking the extensions of my body, beginning with my nose, going on to suck my chin, my earlobes, my ten fingers one by one, my nipples, my penis, and then all ten of my toes. It had been a ritual of friendship and adoption into the group. I had accepted it easily, wondering only briefly whether there was any sexual connotation but I had no erection and the men apparently expected none.

My thoughts in this direction went on nightly for weeks. What might have happened had I accepted Derepen's penis into my mouth? Had I sucked it, would Derepen have reached orgasm and I would then be swallowing strength, become an initiate in search of masculinity and power through semen like the Sambia of Papua? Might the gesture have had no such meaning whatsoever? Might Derepen have been revolted by my mouth and a wrong move on my part led into terrifying paths? Might it even have led me into death, perhaps the kind of death I sometimes longed for, being killed by naked savages in wilderness, my flesh eaten, the marrow of my bones sucked out to fill their bellies, giving sustenance to their bodies and thus becoming one of them? Is not part of my search a longing to *become* them.

In Derepen's house, I had only a vague idea of who the people were and what their culture was like. Circumstantial evidence, however, quickly led me to the conclusion that these were the men who had killed the four Indonesians. On a rack along a wall, a pair of boots already covered with soot lay beside firewood and old crumbs of sago; a bag on another rack had a piece of cloth sticking out, almost certainly a shirt; and then two belts and a cap hanging from a peg. The company manager had early on told me the little he knew of the dead Indonesians, two of whose bodies had been found floating downstream. Speculation had it that the other two had been eaten.

"For Christ's sake!" said the manager at dinner my first night in camp. "Those guys in the police, the minute they get their hands on a gun, they have to use it. What were they doing anyway? They left the lines where they were supposed to be guarding the men against attack to go off and chase a pig. The stupid fools shot it so of course they were killed. Did they think the people would just let them kill their animals without trying to protect them or take some kind of revenge? It was obvious the boar wasn't wild from the strings through its ears. And it wasn't as if they were hungry; aside from the fact that they were Muslim and forbidden to eat pig meat. No wonder the people are always mad at us."

It wasn't until several months later that I began to understand the meaning of that flapping penis. Carleton Gajdusek had written on the characteristics of primitive man, comparing some of his behavior with other primates. "The display behavior," he wrote, "of the Gothic variety of squirrel monkey in presenting an erect phallus . . . in the case of two males appears to be primarily an aggressive act because it occurs in exerting and establishing dominance. If the recipient does not remain quiet and submissive during the display, it may be viciously attacked and assaulted." So that weak smile of mine and my hesitation in deciding what to do had been correct behavior.

In this distance of my search and dreams, I see that there had never been a moment that might have helped me into the indecisiveness that was so important at that moment. Experience for me, in fact, has never been cumulative; every moment approached has been unique unto itself, always without connection, without reflection, never related to another time.

Perhaps I always looked for situations that never repeated themselves. The past always disappeared, was never completed in any way. Though it made itself somehow into a whole, it all went by the wayside; it was gone, a series of isolated episodes I preferred to keep in isolation, like dots in a child's drawing that even when properly connected would never make themselves into a finished figure.

Somewhere in *Arabian Sands* Wilfred Thesiger describes his journey across the Empty Quarter of Saudi Arabia as being a time

298

without even momentary comfort. There was sand in the food, sand in his eyes and nose, in his teeth and hair and ears, and everywhere in his clothes. Hot winds blew viciously almost all the time. His back ached agonizingly when riding his camel for any length of time; his ass blistered, his feet burned when he walked. Yet never was there an instant in which he wished himself elsewhere, never a time of pain from which he didn't receive the greatest pleasure.

Where was he going? Where have I been going? If there is an answer, I prefer to remain in ignorance. I go as I must. Sometimes, after the fact, a great pleasure comes my way when the opportunity arises for me to get a glimpse of another's point of view of what I am seeing and doing. It comforts and amuses me to think back again to that first time on the Brazza, a month after visiting the house of Derepen.

I was at the dining table at the camp, chewing on a lamb chop, listening to Stan, one of the helicopter pilots, talking about his girl friend in Waco. He was thin and wirey, of average height, clean-shaven, with short sandy hair and sharp, square features.

Brian came in and rushed over. "Hey, man" he said to me. "I just saw something fantastic! A house being built. Must be over two hundred feet long. Lots of people around. Do you want to go, man? I can drop you there."

"Oh, wow, man!" Stan said. "I want to go, too!"

Of course, I wanted to go, and said so immediately.

Brian was a slightly heavier version of Stan. He walked with a swagger and I always expected him to be carrying a riding crop to slap against his boots in the manner of Douglas Fairbanks, Junior. He looked at Stan for a second and said, "Yeh, man, that's a good idea. He can't go alone, anyway. Someone has to protect him."

So it was settled. "You'll have to jump from the chopper because there ain't no place to set 'er down."

We went off two days later, after the day's work was done. We flew up the Brazza, turned west and crossed the Friendship River. The mountains were just in front of us. We could see a small lake with no houses around it, no canoes, no evidence of fishing paraphernalia. To the west was a vast open space with a longhouse and two smaller ones. "There it is!" yelled Brian.

People were running along the logs, scattering in all directions. Men seemed to be rushing into the house, women and children into the jungle to hide. The wings of the chopper churned up the attap roofs and I feared they would blow away.

The doors of the helicopter had been removed and left at the camp to facilitate jumping out. Below us, the clearing was a jumbled mass of huge tree trunks and stumps, branches and other vegetation. There was no way to land. When we were down to about twenty feet, I threw out the bundle of machetes, axes, tobacco, and other goods with which I hoped to trade. I worried for a moment about the Uher tape recorder, too heavy to throw out, too bulky to jump with since I was already burdened with still camera and Super 8. I left it in the chopper.

I was naked but for sneakers. Stan jumped wearing jeans and boots. The helicopter climbed to about 150 feet. The plan was for me and Stan to jump out while Brian hovered above us until we saw whether or not the people were friendly. If they were hostile, the chopper would come right down and pick us up.

We waited for some of the men to come out of the forest or from the houses, but nothing happened. The only noise or movement was from us or from the chopper. It was obvious that nothing could happen while the helicopter was there. I signaled Brian and he flew off, leaving us alone.

It was not long before the first men, warily, came out of the longhouse. At first, they stood and watched us. I took up one of the machetes and held it out. The men began walking back and forth, screaming, jumping up and down. They ran short distances, shot arrows in our direction, jumped up and down. They tossed clouds of white lime into the air from reed tubes. The men screamed and shouted, whooped and yelled. The atmosphere was suddenly galvanic and exhilarating.

The men ran towards us, then ran back. I waved the machete, offering it to whoever would come and take it. I shouted, "*Ndein! Ndein!*" They came closer, ran back, pointed their arrows and spears at us, shot the arrows and threw the spears above our heads. The hullabaloo was deafening. I shouted again, "*Ndein!* Come on!"

The excitement became frenzied. I raved as loudly as did the men; I was exalted and ebullient as each time they came towards

300

us, they came closer. Soon, I could see the sticks studded with coix seeds jutting from their nostrils.

Suddenly, one of the men rushed up, took the machete from my hand and ran back as if afraid I would demand its return. I smiled and laughed and jumped up and down. They came up to us screaming, whooping in unison, "Whuh! Whuh! Whuh!" a sound so vast and impassioned it drowned out the world. The men were so close around us, the sound surrounded us, reverberated against the walls of the forest, bounced back to increase the din. We stared at one another, we touched and slapped one another.

The great noise, the magnificent chorale, died down and the men were almost speaking and laughing in normal tones. I heard then the squeaky voice to my right. "Tobias! Tobias! Let's get the fuck out of here! They're going to kill us!" Seconds later, the same voice said, "Damn! I've just shit in my pants!"

In the evening, in the immense, unfinished men's house, we sat on pandanus mats, Stan and I, both of us naked. Stan had washed himself and his jeans and felt at ease. We were close to the central fireplace where the men brought us sago and pig meat. I traded for a shield and two drums, always handing out tobacco with the other goods and leaving some on the floor for everyone to smoke. The men talked throughout the night, one of them singing of the day's events and probably telling stories of past glories in war. Stan insisted he had never been so frightened in his life, not even during the war in Vietnam, and he couldn't understand why I had not been terrified too. "They were shooting their fucking arrows at us, weren't they?"

It had been a raucous greeting, no question of that. The welcome may have appeared violent and might even have become so but it could not have been so different from the welcome with which the people downstream used to greet visitors, this same kind of war-like display, arrows shot in ceremonial fashion the prescribed number of times. But I never thought of that at the time. I was too caught up in the thrill of being there to think of anything else.

"Of course, you're right," I told Stan. "They were scared by the helicopter but once that was gone, we were alone without weapons. They knew that the advantage was theirs, even though they did not know what magic we might perform."

Lying on a mat that night, going over the day's events, I thought of our different reactions to the same scene, how I had accepted the incredible uproar as a grand ritual reception, while Stan, with his head full of stories of headhunting and cannibalism could only cringe in fear of decapitation. I tried to visualize Captain Cook's arrival on the coast just west of where we were, perhaps welcomed in this same way. Perhaps his men in the two longboats had misinterpreted the painted faces, the noise, the bows and arrows and spears just as Stan had done, and had fired their rifles.

Before lying down, Stan had sheepishly picked up one of his boots and taken out a small revolver. "Shit, man. I had this ready. I had it in the side of my boot all the time, ready to use. And I would have used it except that I was so scared I forgot about it until I took off the fucking boots!"

We dozed and woke every few minutes to the sound of drumming, singing, talking. Brian returned in the helicopter two days later and the men disappeared again. Brian let down a knotted rope and we climbed up.

At the camp, Stan delighted everyone every day for a month with the story of our expedition. He described in detail his own fear being so intense he had emptied his bowels into his pants. He was proud of having done so; it was proof of the fearsome predicament in which he had found himself. I loved listening to him tell the tale.

TOBIAS SCHNEEBAUM

SOUTH AFRICAN JOURNAL

This is the first part of a journal of a six-week trip to South Africa I took in 1982, with my friend Gerrit. He was returning home after an absence of nine years. I was visiting the country for the first time.

The first thought, for both of us, is that even traveling throughout South Africa we would somehow stand apart from its troubles. It is true that as urban New Yorkers, as white middle-class American and resident American professionals, we often felt outside of the social situations in which we found ourselves. Gerrit made tapes for a radio program that in the end was not broadcast; I made these notes, anecdotes of scenes observed along the journey. As we spent more time in South Africa, we began to participate, sometimes finding to our horror that the only role we could play was that of English-speaking whites. Gerrit speaks Afrikaans, a language shared by urban blacks and Afrikaners, but neither of us spoke any of the many tribal languages, and our customs and expectations were often too sophisticated to permit easy communication in rural areas. Still, because we traveled in a well-equipped camping van and because Gerrit knew the country, we saw places and events seldom encountered by American and European—even white South African—travelers.

South Africa is on the brink of explosive change. Change will bring an end to the apartheid that mars the human dignity of both blacks and whites, but it will also bring suffering. Reviewing these notes I recall mostly the irony and absurdity of the no-turning-back course of the government, the strange twists of reality that make injustice the emperor's invisible clothes.

September 2, Pretoria

Spring was just beginning in Pretoria. In the afternoons huge dark thunderclouds passed awesomely without dropping rain, turning the sky purple to match the lavender jacarandas that line the avenues. In Percy's sloped yard—a bougainvillea and a few crocuses, and stepping stones leading to the door.

He is the father of one of Gerrit's childhood friends and an engraver—retired but not idle. Devotes himself to a medieval craft.

In a studio behind the house, he makes maces for the new homelands. After the government designates an area within South Africa as a tribal homeland-to-be and begins to move white farmers away, a black tribal leader is appointed president, and all of the blacks whose ancestors are deemed to come from that tribe are ordered to "return" there, even those whose grandfathers' grandfathers were born in Soweto and other urban locations. Then the government hires Percy.

For months he fashions the symbols of power for the new sovereign state—wooden staffs six to eight feet long topped with sculpted horns and silver lions rampant, deadly-looking maces with carved ivory bushbuck heads whose real jewels peer into space—incredibly elaborate, elegant, and ugly.

Percy seldom has the opportunity—indeed seemed indifferent to the idea—to consult the tribal leaders for their suggestions as to the iconography of these emblems. He chooses animals native to southern Africa that are suitably fierce and regal. The irony of this pursuit doesn't seem to have occurred to Percy, though he and his wife Enid confessed to having been amused by the pomp of one occasion. At a homeland independence ceremony they attended, where Percy's artworks were to be tendered to the new president, the guests sweltered in the afternoon sun in the new homeland capital. A handful of onlookers, hardly filling the stadium bleachers, worse than a cricket match by several tens of thousands. The television cameras rolled, but the future president never arrived. Rumor had it that an excess of pre-inaugural celebration had made it impossible for him to rise to the occasion.

September 3, Kruger National Park

Lunch at the Tsokwana "tea room"—an open rondawel, a few outbuildings, a dozen green tables and folding chairs, and a charred patch of ground surmounted by a roaring fire—in a secluded grove of trees. About one-half mile away, partially concealed by a bushy ridge, was the compound for the African workers. Five or six of them, in blue overalls, raked underbrush. Another washed dishes, a white cloth French-waiter style around his waist. A woman in a green uniform-dress carried coals in an upraised shovel from the fire to a row of grills, where a few of us tourists, speaking Afrikaans and English, lined up to fry eggs and barbecue chicken.

Sitting crosslegged on the ablution block, Gerrit interviewed the dishwasher, who leaned back stroking his apron with wet palms. The dishwasher said he works six days a week and after a year returns home to his family for a month. This was the same man who strode across the clearing last night, silhouetted against the thick-trunked trees, too large for his context, too vivid in contrast to the dry landscape, still in the pale tones of winter. Yet either from our prejudice or the mysteries of biology, blacks look "right" in Africa, more connected to the place than whites. It is as if we had descended in a spaceship and out of ignorance had lost none of our self-confidence on discovering how truly strange we are.

September 5, Kruger National Park, Satara camp

We saw our first large flies today. I asked Gerrit, "Are these the vicious horseflies you were telling me about?" "No, these are the flies that crawl on babies' faces in *National Geographic*."

We were at a tourist camp, where the people who tend it work on Sundays, where the people who tend it are black. There is a tourist camp for blacks, too, the guidebook says, but we have never seen tourist blacks in the park. "Well," the whites told us, "most of them already live in the country anyway" or "they just don't love nature as much as we do."

At the neighboring rondawel (one bedroom, full bath, and refrigerator) two middle-aged park enthusiasts offered us meat from the ubiquitous grill and too-sweet wine. The woman told stories of her family, in a tangential, leave-nothing-unsaid delivery I have begun to identify with white, English-speaking South African women: her mother-in-law (sister, aunt, daughter) said they would never spot a leopard *there*, but sure enough, they drove and drove, you know, and when they *got* to the water hole, etc., all sung out with a lilting, cooing, teasing, soothing extension of vowels.

They used to live in Rhodesia ("What's it called now?" the man asked) until things got bad in the late 1970s. She was a nursing sister in an operating theater, and people have it wrong about

African whites disliking African blacks. She worked at a black hospital in Rhodesia and another in Malawi. "They were *glad* to have whites there, let me tell you. They used to sell aspirin for one Rand apiece as fertility pills. When we went out to the houses to treat them we couldn't just *leave* the medication. They wouldn't give it to the sick; they sold it, you see. The blacks aren't good to each other; it's *we* who take care of *them*." The we/subject, them/object sentence recurred again and again, a self-calming litany in her speech, which continued to lilt even as her agitation rose.

The woman was the most defensive, possibly defending her mate against the suspicions of Americans, but another, more important matter is in jeopardy. If blacks were not available, white women would have to serve white men. And it also has something to do with etiquette. In Pretoria, when we shopped at the Hyperama, an aptly named acreage of foodstuffs, garden hoses, and bins of shoes, I asked a white woman for help and she instantly turned me over to a black clerk. Apartheid is a social buffer, too, protecting emotional reserve while permitting lavish courtesy by proxy.

The nursing sister got angrier and angrier in a monologue we no longer dared to interrupt. Paul McCartney and Stevie Wonder began to sing on the radio about the white and black keys of the piano living in harmony.

"What do you think of that song?" Gerrit asked.

"What song?"

The smoke drifted from our fire past the Milky Way and Southern Cross, a black sky, and our circle of rondawels, their backs to the bush and the chattering hyenas.

September 7, Shingwedzi camp

In the camp shop, ahead of us in line, a young black, head bowed, argued in Afrikaans with the white, blond cashier, about a broken egg in the carton he had just purchased. Both were smiling, neither yielding. The cashier claimed (so Gerrit translated for me later) that the store had no way of knowing that the egg hadn't been broken by the buyer. Gerrit interrupted in English, posing as an American, and offered to pay for the eggs. The cashier said, "It's just one egg." The black man hunched his shoulders, turned to leave, but Gerrit repeated his offer, and the cashier, still smiling, translated it into Afrikaans for the black man. "Where I come from," Gerrit said, a bit too loudly, "the customer is always right." The customer exchanged his eggs and left without another glance in our direction. We paid for his purchase and ours, then Gerrit went back to the dairy case and retrieved the broken egg—"we paid for it"—putting the ultimate irony on the morning's vignette.

September 8, Shingwedzi camp

In front of the ranger's low stucco house, a blond boy about four years old played with three black dogs in the yard. The gardener kneeling at the flowerbed beside the drive said yes, the *baas* was home. Ranger Bruce appeared behind the screen door of his office—a large healthy-looking man in his late thirties—and quieted his dogs. While we talked he sat behind his desk, piled high with brown passbooks, one for every black worker under his supervision.

As regional warden he operates about fifteen miles from the Mozambique border, mostly preventing poachers from reducing the elephant herds: "They just chop out the ivory, occasionally take a tail, and then push off across the border into Mozambique." The map on the wall behind us was studded with red pins marking the spots where the victims had fallen. "If we find fresh spoor then we follow it up as far as we can." What happens to the poachers he catches? "Let's put it this way. They don't do any more poaching." Still, he has nothing against blacks and is proud that blacks and whites work together in "a much less segregated way" than in the cities. He just hates hypocrisy.

Suddenly the dogs interrupted, scrabbling and barking at the door, with the little boy howling in the background. Bruce leapt from his swivel chair. "Tika! Tika!" he shouted through the door. "You're a black dog!"

September 9, Gazankulu/Venda

Villages stagger up rolling hills of brown grass, soft curls of smoke at dusk lick up out of the centers of dozens of dun-colored round huts with thatched roofs. A smell of burning wood and coal, along with the pungent, acrid odor of cooking mealies, a cross between porridge and a paper mill in intensity. The Tsonga trudged along the shoulders of the road, heads piled with crooked branches gathered for fuel, women in bright-colored tribal cloths breaking the ground with hoes, children with schoolbooks, men on bikes.

Gerrit stopped to take a picture of the cluster of houses on the hillside and the men in a rill at the side of the road mixing mud into bricks. He admired the continuity of color, which makes the houses look as if they had raised themselves from the mud. Seconds after he got out of the van it was surrounded by faces, flooding up from either side of the roadbed, tapping at the windows and squealing "Sweets, sweets." A contrast to children at the southern gate to the park, who flung themselves at cars speeding on the highway at fifty or sixty miles an hour, flashing shoe-blackened wood carvings of crocodiles and impala.

At the border with the homeland of Venda, the sun low—very low, since it was early spring—cast an eerie gray glow as we crossed the Pafuri River. The activities on the two riverbanks were almost a parody of "tribal differences." On the Gazankulu side the hill was spread with drying cloth in blazing reds and oranges and deep turquoise. Women knee-deep in the river scrubbed wet cloth on the rocks. On the Venda shore only men, in groups of twos and threes, stood fishing with sticks and lines in the same waters, just 200 feet away from Gazankulu. When we paused on the Venda side for a last look at Gazankulu in the glow of the sunset, a man approached the car. He has a government job, he told us, but it just isn't enough.

September 9, Venda

On the right side of the highway rows of prefabricated "modern" houses painted pastel greens and blues with scruffy yards and slanting telephone poles: Sibasa, the capital, is a feudal shanty town clustered at the base of the stucco casino hotel, which is guarded by men in uniform with rifles and is frequented by whites wanting the sort of good time that is prohibited by law in South Africa. On the left side is the Venda International Fair, a dirt road passing under a banner to a group of ten or twenty concrete stalls on one end, and a large outdoor stadium on the other. Following the cheers we headed for the stadium, past the army into the crowd, a mixture of new elite in shiny gray suits, tall fat men who unfolded from cream-colored Mercedes-Benzes and strolled languorously toward the bleachers arm in arm. Teenagers in unisex knots. Country people mute and awed. Women in full tribal dress, turquoise flowers on orange and yellow with matching headgear.

The show was a passing-out parade of the new military recruits to the Venda army, but it wasn't much of an event. Even the military men looked bored with the maneuvers. The best moment came during a display of police-dog prowess. A recruit in drag costume over his uniform wheeled a shopping cart onto the stubbled field, a "criminal" lunged for "her" purse, and the police dog sank teeth into the cotton padding around the thief's forearm. The officer arrived, but the dog failed to release his captive on command, which was repeated over and over as the crowd in the bleachers laughed uncontrollably, rocking back on the planks as one unit. The mugger carried the dog dangling from his arm finally, and the rest of the troupe followed sheepishly: the dog had transformed a police state into a vaudeville routine.

Over at the fair a tiny white Toyota spun on a lazy Susan in the middle of a swath of pampered green lawn—a parody of the oasis in the desert. Vendors of washing machines and T-shirts beckoned passersby into their booths. Two Afrikaners, the only whites at the fair besides ourselves and a few South African army officers, lounged at a card table in a dark shack eating sandwiches from crinkled paper. A silent single file of Venda families passed through, gazing unmoved at banks of pineapples and yellow lilies, made an arc around the card table, and drifted out again. According to the Afrikaners, the promotion was designed to inspire Venda farmers to plant luxury crops for "export" to South Africa, but the audience seemed to have missed the point.

Noting Gerrit's fascination with the music being broadcast over loudspeakers on tall poles, a minstrel who introduced himself as Jim offered to perform a spontaneous original song dedicated to us. He wore a kind of pelt headgear low on his forehead, so low that he had to tilt his chin to lead us to the shadow of the

Toyota. A crowd circled around the three of us as Jim began to twang his single-stringed "harp" and croak gruffly, squinting through bleary eyes. The first verse was in Venda, and the crowd laughed whenever he wobbled his pelvis to the beat. When he switched to Afrikaans in verse two Gerrit also laughed. (The song was about a servile black man who begged a white woman for a little "brown" bread; he was too humble to ask for white bread.)

"*Dankie*, Jim." Gerrit handed him a Rand when he finished, and Jim, a cool professional, started to sing again, the same blank expression on his face.

September 10, Louis Trichardt

Gerrit wanted me to know the experience of South African hotel dining, so we undertook a seven-course dinner at the Hotel Louis, bedeviling the black waiter, whose goal was to get us out of the room so he could cross the street to the liquor store by closing time, by ordering every dish on the *prix fixe* menu. In the cavernous dining room with white linen as its only decor, the fleshy, colorless customers chewed impassively, eyes fixed on the TV in a corner fifty feet away. Like mental patients after the evening's distribution of drugs, they stared without comment at Henry Kissinger, on a goodwill mission, who told them in measured tones that Moscow did not have Africa's best interests at heart.

This morning, while I used a public restroom a few doors down from the Hotel Louis at the main intersection of town (population 14,115, the guidebook says), Gerrit got into trouble trying to make photographs of a hand-painted "Whites Only" sign over David's Liquor Store. In his big hat, red socks, hiking shoes, and camera, he looked like the caricature of the American tourist. As he took out his camera and chatted with some of the black workers enjoying their break on the *stoep*, a large gray-haired, mustached man burst out of the screen door and poked a finger in Gerrit's chest:

"Stay away from my boys!"

"What's the matter?" Gerrit asked with pseudo-innocence.

"You're the matter!"

More poking. David—that's who we concluded the attacker must be—turned red-faced, seconds from losing control. A woman shopper passed by, and I flashed her a palliative grin, eager for equilibrium.

"We know what you're up to, you Communists!" she shrieked, then flung her groceries into the car.

Louis Trichardt, northernmost destination of the nineteenth-century trekkers—we were happy to leave its inhabitants and retrace their ancestors' wheel ruts back to the Cape.

September 12-14, Swaziland

The entry to Swaziland up the tortuous pass to Bulembu/Havelock was a nightmare. Gerrit drove as he always does, with determination and speed, taking the precipitous turns as if they were on solid ground and not gravel, ignoring the cliffs plunging a half-mile into the valley. At first I was relieved to be leaving South Africa, on our way to an independent black nation—a kingdom, no less. By the time we halted at the border gate, I had to pitch myself onto the grass, grateful for the momentary respite from danger. Baffled immigration officials allowed us to keep the meat in the van's refrigerator, in spite of the threat of cholera. They took the bananas but passed over the garlic, after rolling it in their fingers for awhile—"White people eat *this*?"

These omens about our stay in Swaziland were accurately dark. The fuel pump blew after Pigg's Peak. No van, no reservations, Saturday going on Sunday, we ended up at the Highland Inn, a whorehouse thinly disguised as a motel—a big hall with piped-in soul music—the disco—seventy rooms with bath, and a parking lot large enough to accommodate a nightful of transients. In the hall a white South African man in a safari suit slipped by me with black prostitute in tow. I was the one out of place; he looked righteously angry, let's get this nasty business over with. She was a cipher with a dark, dusky look.

After three attempts the desk clerk unlocked a room that was unoccupied save for a shaggy hairbrush and slightly used sheets twirled into a heap. We bolted the door behind us and slept in the intervals when no merrymakers bounced among the cars below. Through the blinds in the morning—a street ringed with semitrailer trucks, every driver slumped asleep behind the wheel. We checked out as soon as the desk opened and moved to the Swazi Inn.

While Gerrit worked on the van in the yard, I waited in the lounge under the vaulted ceiling of thatch over poles painted black to seal them from termites, on an orange-flowered over-stuffed chair. For hours I accepted drinks from a nineteen-year-old engineer from England, in Swaziland to supervise a dam project (so he claimed), with the hopes he can accumulate enough cash to purchase a sportscar and enough time to smash it up on a highway in Wales. The waitress who served us wore a hairstyle that began about two inches over her ears, obeying a decree from the royal family that all Swazis must shave their heads to mourn the death of King Sobhuza. Word has it that the army will force compliance.

Over by the TV the waitress's friends, in traditional Swazi dress, had come to visit and to argue with the newscaster, who delivered local news in English without apparently moving his lips, and with the owner's mother—an Englishwoman—who was trying to eject them before their drunkenness attracted any more attention. It was a delicate operation for an elderly white bouncer in a black-run country, and her coaxings and proddings became our afternoon's, then our evening's, entertainment. The young engineer said, "Drink up. The company pays for everything."

Next morning, Monday, the van stood ready in the gravel yard amid old engines, plumbing parts, and an unrolled length of pink fiber glass under a tree. Bees fell onto the fiber glass and onto the dust—*tap, tap, tap*—wings down, feet up. The bees swarmed, Gerrit explained. These were the bees who had lost. When we forgot to avoid the spot, they made a crunching sound underfoot.

When we finally drove away, heading back through Umtata, we observed a mass outdoor head-shaving. It was not the army shearing citizens at the side of the road, but a team of enterprising barbers.

Gerrit had hoped that Swaziland would offer a blueprint for the kind of change needed in South Africa, but its position as a twentieth-century nation seems shaky, its problems mostly unresolved. Beyond the details of enforced observances of mourning, there are the "rules" for establishing Swazi citizenship and rights, which are all too much like apartheid. Non-Swazis, including blacks of other tribes, those of mixed race, and whites, can't get passports and have to tread carefully in business and trade. Killer bees, shaved heads, a beaded king's photograph on a whorehouse wall—these would be the ingredients of an absurd drama, fuel for the sort of stories the nineteenth-century white explorers laughed about at fireside, when they had pause between sickness and mishap to laugh. But there are lives locked in the drama, and though sympathetic we are relieved that our lives are not among them.

LAUREN SHAKELY

THE ISLAND

On one side, a series of marshes.
On the other, the ocean level as a skillet.
Across the bay, the wooden church
suffers under the weight of its weathered circumflex,
beneath which, every Sunday, the natives come to pray,
and every Tuesday, hold town meetings.
And once, when the movie people sent a scout,
—"You want to rent a room?"
—"No. I want to rent the island,"
they threw him out. He ferried back that very day.
The lattice-work on each widow's walk,
like the cable knitted into each fisherman's sweater,
is as individual as a thumbprint.
And the summer bungalows look like pairs of scuffed brown
                                                          oxfords
that hiked to sea from far inland
and stopped short at the harbor.

Mornings, tennis balls
criss-cross the Common like tropical birds;
back and forth they fly, fat, chartreuse, echoing across this aviary
with the lid off.
And occasionally, the tracks of aluminum-boned baby strollers
struggle up the clay cliffs, irregular as molars.
Some dunes are now off-limits, like the Parthenon.
The commissioners would like to bulldoze
the whole community of nudists,
who, by noon, in most weathers,
look like negatives of themselves.
Puckered beercans stud the public beaches, and here and there,
an evicted hermit crab bleaches.

This morning, the lighthouse was up to its ankles in spray.
A Spanish freighter almost sideswiped
the island's cliffs. The sailors were friendly.
They waved tee-shirts from the upper decks
as if hoisting up a patchwork rainbow,
and maneuvered through the channel, blowing kisses.
I watched the ship get smaller and smaller,
(almost colliding with a rust-pocked trawler)
small enough to squeeze through the neck of a bottle,
and then, the horizon swallowed it.

I unfurled my towel, and read, and slept awhile,
(the water was too cold to swim)
and wondered about the glass armada
bobbing along the coast's two hundred mile limit.
At high tide, a bottle detached itself,
and riding the assembly line of waves,
it tumbled up the beach faster, faster,
a lost collie to its master,
and landed six inches from my sunburned feet.
I held the bottle up to light—
a dozen highlights oiled the glass—
and saw a five-masted warship, uncollapsed,
with its antique mizzens still intact.

Crawling like an ant along the hull,
the ship's unlucky stowaway tried to shout
but the plug was stuck in the bottle's throat.
Upon the pages of the sails,
he scrawled his message in letters the bottle magnified
gigantic as a billboard painter's:
Each night, I dream that I walk the plank
of my wife's long hair, but I can't drown.
And now, I've sailed right into your own two hands.
I've survived my island of a shipwreck.
Someday, from your shipwreck of an island,
I will rescue you.

JANE SHORE

Spacing Out

At the close of the sixth volume of *Tristram Shandy*, the narrator offers his reader the plot diagrams of the preceding installments of his *Life and Opinions*:

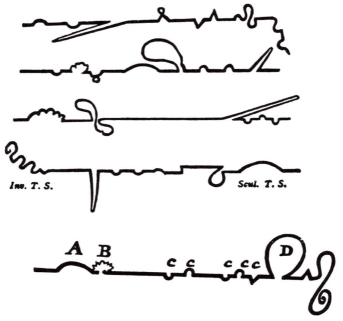

Apologizing for his various digressions and transgressions, Tristram promises henceforth to mend his ways, to go straight. Thus:

which is a line drawn as straight as I could draw it, by a writing-master's ruler, (borrowed for that purpose) turning neither to the right hand or to the left.

This *right line*,——the path-way for Christians to walk in! say divines——

——The emblem of moral rectitude! says *Cicero*——

——The *best line*! say cabbage-planters——is the shortest line, says *Archimedes*, which can be drawn from one given point to another.——

I wish your ladyships would lay this matter to heart in your next birth-day suits!

——What a journey!

Pray can you tell me,——that is, without anger, before I write my chapter upon straight lines——by what mistake——who told them so——or how it has come to pass, that your men of wit and genius have all along confounded this line, with the line of GRAV-ITATION?

Sterne, for one, never confounds his line of writing (or travel) with gravity. He may be the first author to have achieved the state of utter weightlessness. To journey with him along each giddy loop the loop of narrative is to experience an 18th-century version of space sickness. The unbearable lightness of being. Reading as free fall: topsy-turvy events, characters, anecdotes, utensils floating up to meet you in mid-air. Text with no terra firma. Travel without ground.

Out of Line

Or rather, travel (writing) as a question of *line*.

As in: stepping out of line.

As in: feeding someone a line (hook, line, and sinker).

As in: line of life, line of fire, line of work, type, or verse. Learning your lines, reading between the lines; lining up, off, out.

Lineage, a line of descent (ever problematic in Tristram's case), drawn through marriage lines (or certificates) and involving the old randy verb *to line*: to copulate, to cover (as of dogs, wolves, etc.). To trace, furrow, write, fill.

To make a bee-line. Or toss off a one-liner. Un trait d'esprit.

To get a person in a line, "to engage them in a conversation while your confederate is robbing their person or premises, to keep any body in suspense on any subject without coming to a decision" (Farmer & Henley, *Slang and its Analogues*). Hence, to string someone along. Hence, *cut it* (out? off?): conclude.

The *right line?* Always (e)rectilinear. Strait is the gate, and narrow is the way, which leadeth unto life (Matthew 7:15). And make straight paths for your feet, lest that which is lame be turned out of the way (Hebrews 12:13). This is not Sterne's way. Easily distracted from the path, his progress is no pilgrim's. Not a puritan, but a Latitudinarian, broader and more wayward of mind. Not the camel passing through the eye of the needle, but a more oblique, lateral stride. A vocation to vagrancy. Along the inspired lines of Don Quixote. Errantry. Aberrantry.

Stoppages

A preliminary theory of travel/writing. *Tristram Shandy*, vol. 1, chapt. 15 (December, 1759):

> Could a historiographer drive on his history, as a mule-teer drives on his mule,——straight forward;——for instance, from *Rome* all the way to *Loretto*, without ever once turning his head aside either to the right hand or to the left,——he might venture to foretell you to an hour when he should get to his journey's end;——but the thing is, morally speaking, impossible: For, if he is a man of the least spirit, he will have fifty deviations from a straight line to make with this or that party as he goes along, which he can no ways avoid. He will have views and prospects to himself perpetually solliciting his eye, which he can no more help standing still to look at than he can fly: he will moreover have various
>> Accounts to reconcile:
>> Anecdotes to pick up:
>> Inscriptions to make out:
>> Stories to weave in:
>> Traditions to sift:
>> Personages to call upon:
>> Panegyrics to paste up at this door:

Which is to say that the true art of travel/writing lies less in its narrative line of advance than in the various impediments, interruptions, deflections, or "unforeseen stoppages" that solicit the inventory of the pen and/or eye. A musical concept of travel—its rhythm defined by the configuration of rests, intervals, caesurae, ellipses.

Travel: an art of punctuation.

And the traveller: a flâneur, an idler, a deviant, a collector. A bee zigzagging from sight to sight, cross-pollinating language in the process.

Stations——

Stopovers——

Dashes——

The Hobby-Horse

Sterne's "first plan" for *Tristram Shandy* was apparently "to travell his Hero all over Europe and after making his remarks on the different Courts, proceed with making strictures and reflections on the different Governments of Europe and finish the work with an eulogium on the superior constitution of England and at length to return Tristram well informed and a compleat English Gentleman." His novel, in other words, was initially going to be a burlesque of the ethnocentricity of the Grand Tour, a parody of travel as upperclass *rite de passage*, more or less modelled on the travelogue-satires of Rabelais and Swift and the courtesy-books of the Renaissance.

Needless to say, this travelogue never got written—how guide your Hero through the courts of Europe when it takes you some three volumes just to get him born? Jettisoning the conventions of the picaresque adventure story, the *Bildungsroman*, and the quest romance, Sterne instead found himself writing a very different kind of travel text. Rather than dispatch his characters all over the map, he would simply mount them on their respective HOBBY-HORSES and let them ride in whatever direction their talk might take them.

HOBBY-HORSE (q.v. "ruling passion," *idée fixe*, obsession, *dada*). A means of transportation or narrative vehicle. "'Tis the sporting little filly-folly which carries you out for the present hour——a maggot, a butterfly, a picture, a fiddle-stick——or *any thing*, which a man makes a shift to get a stride on, to canter it away from the cares and solicitudes of life——'Tis as useful a beast as is in the whole creation."

A HOBBY-HORSE, then, is a getaway vehicle, an escape route, a way of beating a quick retreat into fiction, fantasy, folly.

319

"When a man gives himself up to the government of a ruling passion,——or in other words, when his HOBBY-HORSE grows head-strong,——farewell cool reason and fair discretion." Witness, for example, my uncle Toby when he gets going on military history or maneuvers, or my father on the subject of names or noses. Off the wall. Out of control. Endless riffs and improvisations on a single tic. The poetry of mania. Sterne (in the wake of Burton's *Anatomy of Melancholy*) discovering the textual tropes of modern neurosis.

And discovering, moreover, a metaphor for travel and for writing, since to journey by HOBBY-HORSE is to relinquish the reins (of reason, of narrative), to allow yourself to get *carried away*, possessed or obsessed by an itinerary that is ultimately not of your own design. Leave the driving to us. Put the prose on automatic pilot. Sterne the first surrealist? At any rate, well before Freud or Lacan, his great Shandean insight: that what passes for the "self" or "I" is not, finally, at the helm; that neither our desire nor discourse lies in our governance; that our words, stories, fantasies, fictions keep running away with us. That we are, absurdly, *driven*—by some Other.

Sterne's HOBBY-HORSE was a brilliant *trouvaille*, and *Tristram Shandy* managed to find a large readership eager to go along for the ride. Over the course of the first four volumes, however, Sterne gradually began losing passengers, as readers increasingly realized they were in for a wild goose chase with no visible destination in sight. Sterne had so effectively mastered the art of digression, he had so elaborately maneuvered his vehicle into a maze of pointless side excursions and scenic culs-de-sac that he had ended up virtually immobilizing his narrative: instead of offering the pleasures of readerly peregrination, his text threatened to turn into a treadmill, a virtuoso display of the fine art of running in place. Sterne's sexual indiscretions and indelicacies could be pardoned, wrote a contemporary reviewer, but his book was becoming vulnerable to that most terrible of all imputations— nothing less then DULLNESS.

Sterne's reaction to the sagging fortunes of *Tristram* is instructive: not only did he try to recoup his readership by reverting to less experimental modes of fabulation (viz., the easy pathos of Le Fever's story in vols. V and VI), but he also attempted to curb his hobby-horsical tendencies in favor of a more traditional species of travelogue—with the result that Tristram, now duly birthed and circumcized after some 500 pages, embarks on a Grand Tour at the outset of vol. VIII.

Abroad

Sterne had himself ventured abroad for the first time in early 1762, shortly after the publication of the fifth and sixth volumes of *Tristram Shandy*. A European celebrity by now, he had spent some six months in Paris, feted in the salons in his role as Chevalier Shandy, before proceeding on to the Midi (Toulouse, Montpellier) where he rusticated for the two following years. Sterne's sojourn in France (as well as his subsequent voyage to Italy in 1765-66) provided him with the material for his most important contributions to the literature of travel—vol. VII of *Tristram Shandy* and, more importantly, his international best-seller, *A Sentimental Journey* (1768), arguably the most influential, most widely-imitated travel book of the entire 18th century.

Sterne's migration southward, biographers point out, was largely determined by medical considerations. A chronic consumptive given increasingly to spitting blood, he was travelling in search of a climate more grateful to his lungs. And in this he resembles a number of 18th-century British exiles and tourists— e.g. Tobias Smollett and Dr. Samuel Sharp, the invalid dyspepsia of whose travel books *A Sentimental Journey* satirizes. But even though Sterne's good-natured Sentimental Traveller, Yorick, is intended as a parodic critique of the convalescent crankiness of such tourists, the euphoria of Sternean travel/writing is itself constantly shadowed by the specter of sickness. The various characters of *Tristram Shandy*—my uncle Toby, my father, Yorick, Tristram himself—are all somehow infirm, halt, maimed, and their respective hobby-horses may either be taken as symptoms of their malady or as its only possible remedy. Sterne, at any rate, is among the first to practice travel/writing as a kind of therapy, as if the mere fact of continual displacement might in itself effect a cure. More specifically, Sterne voyages and spins tales (this is the lesson of Scheherazade) simply in order not to die. If Tristram therefore sets off for the Continent on his "two spider legs," it is primarily to escape from that "son of a whore,"

to outpace that "long-striding scoundrel of a scare-sinner"—
DEATH. The jocularity of Sternean travel barely conceals its
utter panic. Tristram is literally flying for his life.

Quo Vadis

No sooner does Tristram land in France than he proceeds to give
a textbook demonstration of the commonplaces of travel writing:

> "Now before I quit *Calais*," a travel-writer would say,
> "it would not be amiss to give some account of it"——
>
> *Calais, Calatium, Calusium, Calesium.*
> This town, if we may trust its archives, the authority
> of which I see no reason to call into question in this
> place——was *once* no more than a small village belong-
> ing to one of the first Counts *de Guines*; and as it
> boasts at present of no less than fourteen thousand
> inhabitants, exclusive of four hundred and twenty
> distinct families in the *basse ville*, or suburbs——it must
> have grown up by little and little to its present size.
> Though there are four convents, there is but one
> parochial church in the whole town, etc.

The learned etymologizing of place-name, the scientific display
of demographic statistics, the pedantic attention to historical and
geographical detail—all these are the hallmarks of the authorita-
tive style of the guidebook. And if Sterne spends an entire chapter pastiching the description of Calais contained in Pigamiol de la
Force's *Nouveau Voyage de France* (1755), it is in order to
demonstrate that the discourse of travel has become so rigidly
codified and conventionalized that a few strategic lifts from the
local baedeker suffice to *dépayser* the majority of readers: "I
know no more of *Calais* . . . than I do this moment of *Grand
Cairo* . . . and yet by merely knowing what is what, and by drawing this from that in one part of town, and by spelling and putting this and that together in another——I would lay travelling
odds, that I this moment write a chapter upon *Calais* as long as
my arm, and with so distinct and satisfactory a detail of every
item . . . that you would take me for the town clerk of *Calais*
itself."

Sterne calls this purely textual (re)construction of place "dry shod" travel writing, and cites Addison's *Remarks on Several Parts of Italy* (1708) as its prime example. Rather than responding firsthand to the landscapes he visits, Addison first reads about them in the Classics and then sets out "to examine these several Descriptions, as it were, upon the spot, and to compare the natural face of the country with the Landskips that the Poets have given us of it." This mode of travelling or writing dispenses the voyager from ever getting his feet wet, since it comfortably reduces foreignness to a text that has (always) already been read. The logical extension of the dry-shod mentality is Bishop Joseph Hall's *Quo Vadis? A Just Censure of Travel, As It Is Commonly Undertaken by the Gentlemen of our Nation* (1617)—another of Sterne's satirical targets, which earnestly argues that since it is now possible to master (or study) the world in all of its variety without ever quitting England, there is really no point in leaving home.

Unto a Wheel

Vol. VII of *Tristram Shandy* probably holds the speed record among 18th-century travelogues. Landscapes, towns, villages, inns, post stations whiz by at a vertiginous pace. There is simply no time to stop and explain:

> ——No;——I cannot stop a moment to give you the character of the people——their genius——their manners——their customs——their laws——their religion——their government——their manufactures——their commerce——their finances, with all the resources and hidden springs which sustain them——
>
> Still——still I must away——

Sterne's motto for this precipitous clip is the Psalmist's *Make them like unto a wheel.* Gather no moss. A style of travel/writing that is the textual equivalent of the Enlightenment dream of a perpetual motion machine, geared to such a velocity that the French countryside blurs into a streak of unpronouncable names:

> And so making all possible speed, from
> *Ailly au clochers*, I got to *Hixcourt*,
> from *Hixcourt*, I got to *Pequignay*, and
> from *Pequignay*, I got to AMIENS,
> concerning which town I have nothing to inform you.

Sterne, in these pages, invents the high-speed aesthetic of the *glimpse*, a kind of accelerated impression (cf. Tristram zooming through the streets of Paris) that anticipates the mobile camera (in French, *le traveling*) of film.

In other words, Sterne discovers that the art of travel (or narrative) depends primarily on *pace*. The jerky fast-forward tempo of Tristram's canter southward from Calais creates slapstick effects straight out of the chase scenes of silent comedy. But Sterne is equally the master of slow motion—dilating the detail, lingering on ephemera, ironically monumentalizing the trivial. It is to this more leisurely exploration of "nonsensical minutiae" that *A Sentimental Journey* will be devoted. Its narrator Yorick will abandon Tristram's breakneck effort to outrace Death in favor of the obverse strategy: he will instead conquer Time by slackening its speed, by opening up its pores—filling each precious, passing instant with the pulse of his entire existence.

The Sentimental Traveller

The preface to *A Sentimental Journey* (which in typically Shandean fashion falls in the seventh chapter of the book) offers a useful typology of travellers:

> Idle Travellers,
> Inquisitive Travellers,
> Lying Travellers,
> Proud Travellers,
> Vain Travellers,
> Splenetic Travellers.
> Then follow the Travellers of Necessity,
> The delinquent and felenious Traveller,
> The unfortunate and innocent Traveller,
> The simple Traveller,
> And last of all (if you please) The
>
> Sentimental Traveller (meaning thereby myself).

The Sentimental Traveller travels light ("half a dozen shirts and a black pair of silk breeches" in his luggage suffice) and usually alone—though Yorick does eventually find his Sancho Panza in the person of La Fleur. The Sentimental Traveller has no particular destination in mind, nor does he venture abroad in search of "useful knowledge and real improvements." He conceives his journey instead as an "experiment" or "assay upon human nature," having understood (from the reading of Montaigne) that to travel or to write is to *essay*, to render oneself available to whatever "time and chance are perpetually holding out to him as he journeyeth on his way."

The Sentimental Traveller is a descendent of the cosmopolitan anthropology of the Renaissance—inasmuch as he travels to explore the diversity and relativity of customs and discovers in the process what is permanently and essentially human about Man. Sterne's humanistic universalism, however, is tempered by a quirkier (and proto-Romantic) fascination with the local, the eccentric, the characteristic, the individual. Although he retains traces of Everyman, the Sentimental Traveller more closely resembles the 18th-century idea of the "original." Travel thus becomes a means for him to cultivate (and display) his "originality"—a quality which not only defines his difference or idiosyncrasy, but also points to his proximity to Nature, to Origin. Experimental though his journey might be, it is nonetheless driven by the desire to return to the Source: "The thirst of this . . . has led me from my home into France——and from France will lead me through Italy——'tis a quiet journey of the heart in pursuit of NATURE, and those affections which arise out of her, which make us love each other——and the world, better than we do."

The opposite of a Sentimental Traveller is a SMELFUNGUS. Modelled on Tobias Smollett, author of *Travels Through France and Italy* (1766), Smelfungus represents the sour, splenetic British tourist who spends his journey grousing about the natives, exasperated by the food, the service, the hygienic conditions, the expenses. Travel, for Smelfungus, is a stinking swindle; even the vaunted monuments of antiquity fail to come up to snuff:

> The learned SMELFUNGUS travelled from Boulogne
> to Paris——from Paris to Rome——and so on——but he
> set out with the spleen and jaundice, and every object
> he passed by was discoloured or distorted——He wrote
> an account of them, but 'twas nothing but the account
> of his miserable feelings. I met Smelfungus in the
> grand portico of the Pantheon——he was just coming
> out of it——*'Tis nothing but a huge cock pit*, said
> he——

MUNDUNGUS (alias Dr. Samuel Sharp) is another such anti-Senti-
mental Traveller. As his name hints, he exemplifies the pious
puritan for whom the world is merely so much shit underfoot:

> Mundungus, with an immense fortune, made the whole
> tour; going on from Rome to Naples——from Naples
> to Venice——from Venice to Vienna——to Dresden, to
> Berlin, without one generous connection or pleasur-
> able anecdote to tell of; but he had travelled straight
> on, looking neither to his right hand or his left, lest
> Love or Pity should seduce him out of his road.

Yorick, by contrast, voyages precisely in order to be seduced, led
astray. Ever on the lookout for "generous connection," he fan-
tasizes travel as an invitation to promiscuity. The comic point of
A Sentimental Journey is that he of course never quite gets laid.

The Sensorium

Montaigne is perhaps the first writer to give a real sense of the
traveller's body—its exertions, its indigestions, its disorientations,
its exhilarations. Sterne follows Montaigne in his careful attention
to the humors of travel: Yorick's body is virtually a textbook
illustration of the physiology of the Age of Sensibility. Exqui-
sitely tuned to the vibrations of each physical and moral sensation (which emanate, according to Sterne, from the "great
SENSORIUM of the world"), Yorick's body acts as the seismo-
graph of his sensibility, registering the tremor of every motion or
emotion he passes through en route.

   In Shakespeare, Yorick's name and skull epitomize mortality.
In *A Sentimental Journey*, his body—lean, lank, and gaunt like
that of Quixote and Sterne himself—further serves as an eloquent

reminder of Death. Like a figure out of a medieval *memento mori* or a Renaissance anatomy book, he is a skeleton moving through a landscape, a pale rider on a comic ass. But even though his mortal frame is little more than skin and bones, Yorick's temperament is nonetheless described (in the humoral nomenclature of the day) as essentially *sanguine*—cheerful, hopeful, and amorous disposition. He is, in other words, a physical oxymoron: a red-blooded skeleton, an excitable corpse.

"True *Shandeism*," writes Sterne, "opens the heart and lungs . . . forces the blood and other vital fluids of the body to run freely thro' its channels, and makes the wheel of life run long and chearfully round." Sentimental Travelling similarly improves the circulation. Upon arriving in France, Yorick immediately feels a flush of euphoria come over him: "I felt a suffusion of a finer kind upon my cheek . . . I felt every vessel in my frame dilate——the arteries beat all chearily together." It is a measure of Yorick's sanguine susceptibility that nearly every pleasurable sensation in the course of his journey is somehow associated with the circulatory system. Early on in his travels, for example, chance throws him together with an attractive female stranger whose hand he subsequently discovers himself to be holding: "The pulsations of the arteries along my fingers pressing across hers; told her what was passing within me: she looked down——a silence of some moments followed." Later, in Paris, he finds himself alone in a shop with a handsome "Grisset" and, in a gesture whose prurience is barely masked by medical metaphor, proceeds to take the pulse of her wrist, "counting the throbs of it, one by one, with as much true devotion as if I had been watching the critical ebb or flow of her fever."

Sentimental travel, like erotic encounter, titillates the pulse, suffusing the body with a palpitating thrill of risk or tingle of contentment. The most characteristic symptom of this enjoyable flutter of embarrassment or arousal is, in Yorick's case, the *blush*. As in the following little pantomime or *tableau vivant*:

> It was a fine still evening, in the latter end of the month of May——the crimson window-curtains (which were of the same colour of those of the bed) were drawn close——the sun was setting, and reflected through them so warm a tint into the fair *fille de*

> *chambre's* face——I thought she blushed——the idea of
> it made me blush myself——we were quite alone; and
> that super-induced a second blush before the first
> could get off.

The tremulous innuendo of this scene is entirely in keeping with
the sublimated sexuality of the Age of Sensibility. The erotic
irrigation of blood through the body finds its fluid corollary in
the delicious liquefaction of tears—the blush, as it were, giving
way to outright sentimental gush:

> I sat down close by her; and Maria let me wipe [the
> tears] away as they fell with my handkerchief——I
> then steeped it in my own——and then in hers——and
> then in mine——and then I wiped hers again——and as
> I did it, I felt such undescribable emotions within me,
> as I am sure could not be accounted for by any com-
> bination of matter and motion.

"Nature melted within me," comments Yorick—the flow of tears,
like the sudden flush of blood from the heart, transports the
Sentimental Traveller's body into a state of orgasmic dissolution
and ductility. This rapturous fluidity, whose juices are induced by
any "generous outpouring" of emotion (be it pity, benevolence,
or love), is usually evoked in terms of *expenditure*—a concept
that not only underlies the spendthrift erotics of Sternean travel,
but also informs its particular economics.

Sentimental Commerce

The theory of travel propounded in the Preface to *A Sentimental
Journey* revolves around two fundamental models of communication and/or exchange. Sterne first addresses the linguistic context
of travel:

> . . . from the want of language, connections, and
> dependencies, and from the difference in education,
> customs, and habits, we lie under so many impedi-
> ments in communicating our sensations out of our
> own sphere, as often amount to a total impossibility.

328

Having outlined the hindrances to genuine intercourse with the Other (given the semiotic differences among languages, cultures, and individuals, what are the grounds for translation?), Sterne moves into an extended mercantile metaphor:

> It will always follow from hence, that the balance of sentimental commerce is always against the expatriated adventurer: he must buy what he has little occasion for at their own price——his conversation will seldom be taken in exchange for theirs without a large discount——and this, by the by, eternally driving him into the hands of more equitable brokers for such conversation as he can find, it requires no great spirit of divination to guess at his party——

The operative word here is *exchange*, for it defines the business of travel as dialogue or conversation——a traffic in words or signs or sensations whose bottom line cannot be accounted in terms of profit, but only as a delicate balance of give and take.

The majority of episodes in *A Sentimental Journey* turn in one way or another on the (comic or sentimental) complications of such linguistic or economic exchange. Yorick's first task upon arriving in Calais, for example, is to hire a vehicle to take him to Paris, but the negotiations become so sidetracked by "nonsensical contingencies" that it is some fifteen chapters before he concludes his bargain and proceeds on his way. In the course of this protracted transaction, he furthermore manages to enter into rather ambiguous "sentimental commerce" with the mysterious Mme de L*** and, in one of the kitschier scenes of the book, trades snuff-boxes with an old Fransciscan monk whose request for alms he had, out of a prejudice against Papists, initially refused. The exchange of snuff-boxes is Yorick's first great lesson in charity:

> The poor monk blushed as red as scarlet . . . I blushed in my turn . . . He begged we might exchange boxes. ——In saying this, he presented his to me with one hand, as he took mine from me in the other; and having kissed it——with a stream of good nature in his eyes, he put it into his bosom——and took his leave.

Having learned the value of charity from the old monk, Yorick
will henceforth actively apply his philanthropy to the various
beggars and unfortunates he meets en route—though it should be
noted that his eleemosynary benevolence is more motivated by
hedonistic self-satisfaction than by purely altruistic concerns,
since his elans of pity are primarily occasions to experience the
gratifying sublimity of tearful arousal.

The erotic implications of "sentimental commerce" are
amply evident in scene after scene of Yorick's travels. Visiting a
Paris bookstore to buy a set of Shakespeare, he encounters a
young chambermaid whose poverty stimulates his liberality:

> The young girl listened with a submissive attention,
> holding her sattin purse by its ribband in her hand all
> the time——'Tis a very small one, said I, taking hold of
> the bottom of it——she held it towards me——and
> there is very little in it, my dear, said I; but be but as
> good as thou art handsome, and heaven will fill it. I
> had a parcel of crowns in my hand to pay for Shake-
> spear; and as she had let go the purse entirely, I put a
> single one in; and tying up the ribband in a bow-knot,
> returned it to her . . . I never gave a girl a crown in my
> life which gave me half the pleasure.

Some thirty pages later, lest the reader should have missed the
ribald point, the purse again resurfaces, a perfect fetish for sentimental smut, "lined with a little bit a white quilted sattin, and
just big enough to hold the crown."

Yorick's generosity, more often than not, is merely a way of
purchasing gratitude or intimacy—philanthropy verging on prosti-
tution. Indeed, Yorick-Sterne himself complains that his travels
may have made him into something of a whore, turning tricks of
superficial wit in return for dinner invitations to the poshest
salons in Paris:

> And at this price I could have eaten and drank and
> been merry all the days of my life at Paris; but 'twas a
> dishonest *reckoning*——I grew ashamed of it——it was
> the gain of a slave——every sentiment of honour
> revolted against it——the higher I got, the more I was
> forced upon my *beggarly system*——the better the
> *Coterie*——the more children of Art——I languished for

> those of Nature: and one night after a most vile prosti-
> tution of myself to half a dozen different people, I
> grew sick——went to bed——ordered La Fleur to get
> me horses in the morning to set out for Italy.

Yorick's distaste for the economy of French social intercourse—
all form, no content—is expressed, significantly enough, in a
numismatic metaphor. The manners of the French have become
so polished, so conventionalized that they resemble coins whose
original impressions have been effaced in the course of circulation. The English, by contrast, "like ancient medals, kept more
apart, and passing but few peoples hands, preserve the first sharp-
nesses which the fine hand of nature has given them——they are
not so pleasant to feel——but in return, the legend is so visible,
that at the first look you see whose image and superscription they
bear." The superior legibility of the British, in short, lies in their
originality, that is, their naturalness, their resistence to the artifices of cultured exchange.

Sterne's ambivalence toward the niceties of social commerce
is one of the more recognizably pre-Romantic features of *A Sentimental Journey*. If the French come in for his satire, it is because
their "expression professes more than it performs," and because
their trust lies "more in the word, and less in the thing." Yorick,
by contrast, travels in search of a more natural, more original
language, a language in which there would be no gap between
intention and expression, signifier and signified, word and thing.
He discovers this idiom, predictably enough, not in the realm of
verbal exchange, but in the discourse of the body, in the espe-
ranto of gesture, in the international sign language of the blush,
the tear, the glance. This language of silence reaches its sentimental perfection in the eloquent trade of looks between Yorick
and a Parisian shopgirl who has been helping him try on gloves.
His hand tightly sheathed in her glove (sic), the two stand mute,
transfixed, locked in a glance at once lascivious and ludicrous:

> There are certain combined looks of simple subtlety——
> where whim, and sense, and seriousness, and nonsense,
> are so blended, that all the languages of Babel set
> loose together could not express them——they are
> communicated and caught so instantaneously, that
> you can scarce say which party is the infector.

331

Yorick is a superb interpreter of the silent innuendo of glance or gesture, and he justly prides himself on his talents as a translator: "There is not a secret so aiding to the progress of sociality, as to get master of this *short hand*, and be quick in rendering the several turns of looks and limbs, with all their inflections and delineations, into plain words." Transcribing shorthand into long-hand, rendering body into word, Yorick concludes that as a traveller, "I go translating all the way."

Travel in Translation

Whiling away a Sunday in his Paris hotel room, Yorick comes across a scrap of wastepaper on his breakfast tray. Upon inspection, it reveals itself to be a text written in "the old French of Rebelais's time" and "in a Gothic letter." Yorick is so intrigued by its inscrutability that he decides to undertake its translation — "the difficulty of understanding it increased but the desire." The manuscript turns out to contain a typically Shandean shaggy dog story which (in a device lifted straight from Cervantes) is suddenly cut short when the original text breaks off.

This episode (entitled "The Fragment") may be taken as a paradigm of *A Sentimental Journey* as a whole—a mosaic of fragments, a medley of unfinished stories and incomplete translations, all generated by the same hermeneutic desire to unravel the riddle of the Other. Although "The Fragment" provides the most literal instance of Yorick's activity as a translator, he is in fact (as he says) translating all the way, whether it be "by translating French looks and attitudes into plain English," or by providing (often in footnotes) the English equivalents for the many French words and phrases that pepper his narrative.

But whether the translation be intersemiotic (gesture into word) or interlingual (French into English), it inevitably assumes the world as a legible (and exchangeable) script. Travel, for Yorick, is an ongoing exercise in reading, a roving *explication de texte*. Every physiognomy or physique he meets is a page offered to his interpretation: "See Monsieur Le Duc's face first——observe what character is written in it——take notice in what posture he stands to hear you——mark the turns and expressions of his body and limbs——And for the tone——the first sound which comes from his lips will give it you——and from all these together you'll compound an address at once upon the spot."

Like many a traveller (or conqueror), Yorick journeys with a translator at his side: his valet La Fleur not only helps him pen a suitable love letter in French to the mysterious Mme de L***, but acts as his native informant when it comes to understanding some of the more curious of Gallic customs. Translation here functions as the traditional vehicle of ethnographic encounter, enabling the traveller/anthropologist to decipher and master the Other by domesticating its alterity into "plain English." The problem is, however, that Sterne's English is rarely "plain." His fractured syntax and stroboscopic punctuation deliberately confound the reader's powers of verbal and visual assimilation, and this confusion is further compounded by the figural instability of the text. Sterne's addiction to double-entendre makes it virtually impossible to decide whether a given word or episode is to be read literally or metaphorically—the most innocent of objects or events needs only to be slightly transported or troped in order to become utterly obscene. Never quite knowing where, rhetorically or narratively, he stands, the reader is thus forced to go translating all the way—shuttling between the literal and the figurative, suspended between sentiment and smut, hesitating between the snigger and the tear.

Transportation, translation, metaphor—all etymologically imply a form of travel, a process whereby something (or somebody) gets carried over or across. As a translation, *A Sentimental Journey* carries over entire swatches of Cervantes, Rabelais, and Scarron, while at the same time satirically rewriting earlier 18th-century travelogues. But it matters very little in the end whether the ingredients of Yorick's journey are in fact Sterne's original invention or merely the transcriptions of prior (inter)texts. The important thing about travel/writing, after all, is simply to keep things moving, to carry off a translation, to swap a few stories along the way, to enter into exchange.

RICHARD SIEBURTH

A FUSE LINK

Here lie James and Drucilla Gordy;
Zeddock K. Evans, 1812-1863;
Hezekiah Shockley, Arabella Shockley,

and an acre of bad writing.
"Till Thy Name Shall Every Grief Remove
With Life. With Memory. And With Love."

That is to say: Pray, so I may be forgotten.
O God, Horatio, what wounded names
(words standing thus misplaced) shall live behind us!

*

Parked outside the station,
can it be? Yes, it is.
We'll kiss and make up,
pretend it hever happened.

The mechanic has something to show me
in the palm of his right hand.
"This is what did it."
I stare, and he explains. "A fuse link."

A flat little piece of metal
scarcely bigger than an earring.
A fuse link. Of course, that would explain everything.

*

Goodbye to the bronze Napoleon,
the cemetery on the hill,
and smoke at the heart of a valley.

It's good to be travelling again
though I'm in a single land
behind an old Studebaker,

with children looking out the rear,
making faces, sticking out their tongues,

for so many miles
I am practically one of the family.

LOUIS SIMPSON

FANTASY MAPS: SOME ORIGINS

Travel? No, I have never gone anywhere, I have everything I want and need here in Peoria. This is not so. I did spend a (wasted) year in Champaign/Urbana, I was once threatened, by parents and school authorities, with Joliet (for "anomic" behavior). But I did contract my obsession with maps when I was a child and I find these imaginary journeys more satisfying than actual ones. How can I be sure if I have never traveled? Because I can't imagine anything more satisfying or mysterious to me than the places I have invented. *Contract an obsession?* I fear I phrase matters imprecisely. I am a man of images, not of words.

There are advantages to growing up in the Midwest that no one speaks of, to say nothing of staying there.

Origins? I used to go to meet my father at his office after school. I couldn't share a ride with any of the other kids because we lived in a trailer park fifteen miles out of town, in a place that had no name. School was over at 3. We hung out in the playground until 4. His office was a few blocks from the school and I would draw maps while I waited. I will confess that I felt some irritation with my father for making me wait. He was rarely less than an hour late. At first I complained but it did no good. In fact, the look he gave me was downright fearful. He did, on the other hand, supply me with all of the drawing pads and soft pencils I wanted. That means, if I calculate correctly, I have never scrutinized these matters before, and forgive me if I am overly scrupulous with details, that I was there from 4 to 6 every day five days a week, that's ten hours a week, 1/4 of the average man's work week! No wonder these maps multiplied and my room was strewn with them. I filled my wallet with maps until it bulged grotesquely. I invented whole populations. Envisaged droughts. Made a boom town spring up on a Monday afternoon. Surrounded it with circuitous trails on a Tuesday. Installed railroad tracks on a Wednesday. Greening suburbs on a Thursday. Set it on fire on a Friday. . . . These places could age hundreds of years within the course of my week. I only drew maps while waiting and never worked on weekends. Weekends I would put the week's maps up on the walls and color them in with crayons.

And although I'm freelance I now work only from 9 to 5 and never on weekends.

On weekends I dream.

I did have a kind of conversion experience that made me think I might do this for a living as an adult. One afternoon, in the summer after I finished my first and last year of college, after a long day amusing myself in the map section of the picture collection in the public library, one map remained underneath my briefcase, like an afterthought. The "Carta Pisana," "the oldest surviving portolan chart," a surface of crisscrossing hieroglyphic territories of borderlines and lines of demarcation, water and earth so blurred and intermingled I could not tell a mountain from a fissure in a ravine. The known world was reduced to the size of a fist. It could have been the map of a continent or an arrondissement, a street, or series of lines signifying roads or waterways. A floating mass, land or water. This "real" map gave me a sense of possibilities. . . . Of vocation.

Regrets? Who knows, I might have learned from experience. Even if real cities and countries like San Francisco, New York, Paris, Calcutta, Belgium, and Canada were inferior in every way to my imagined ones, I might have learned something from being there that I did not derive from looking at maps (though if the slide shows I have attended over the years are any indication of what's out there I doubt it). Who knows, maybe I went to the wrong ones. I remember falling asleep during a long movie about India that friends insisted I see.

I may never "travel" but I am not a hermit or antisocial being. I have many friends and participate in many "normal" social events. I am not married but have remained close "friends" with my girlfriend (now my next door neighbor, our bedroom windows are separated only by maple trees) since 5th grade. We retain separate houses and see each other for dinner every night. Marriage is like travelling: why do it if you can have all of the advantages without the entanglements.

The demand for fantasy maps varies not from year to year but from decade to decade. Right now (otherwise why your inquiry?) the demand is high, higher in fact than it has ever been. And I hear the travel industry is booming too. Which shows that for most people there is no contradiction. I have had letters from people who commissioned maps saying that it "saved our trip," pulled them out of labyrinths "too real to be imagined."

I draw fantasy maps because they are useless. And because useless, pure. You can travel one of my maps without an overdose of diesel fuel. And since every one is different know that you are going somewhere no one has ever gone before. And yes, to return to your question, I have thought that there might be something sexual in the subtle alternations of the exaggerated mountains and ravines, hills and lakes, roads and ditches that form the basis of my landscapes. But then I can't think of anything that isn't.

DOUGLAS GORDON SLOANE

TRANSLATIONS FROM THE AMERICAN

I

Variety Show

The seasons are changing,
we cannot help it
the leaves cascade onto artificial lawns
and in our parks square as television sets,
spring, autumn, summer flicker in full color,
and wedding, christening, disease goes by,
the restless images of changing channels
on nights which offer no important news
and no network has a good thing on.

II

Lullaby

Sleep little daughter, sleep while you can,
before your breasts come, and the monthly blood,
while you still lie beneath the general night,
not that darkness condensed into man.

III

Conundrum

The trouble is there's no word for a man
to whom I've sworn nothing, so can't betray;
nameless, you're neither finite nor immortal;
Are you my mistress, then?
Or shall I coldly call you a male interstice?
You or this word. One is unattainable,
and I'll have to choose, as it's language
in the end sustaining what we do,
no hero earns his destiny without his vow.

I'll never find a verb, infertile, but incendiary,
a way of addressing you without endearments,
conjunction to express how utterly —ardently—
I don't love you.

IV

In An Office

One, two, three;
the champion clock is striking me,
brawny with hours, pins me to the ground,
the clock I punch hits back, the bully.
My skin yellows like a legal pad,
lines ruled evenly across my face,
and the lawyer years write opinions
there of my expensive, unresolved case.

V

A la Mode

Lady, no one is sufficient master yet
of heart's sad craftsmanship, to forget
your opalescent skin, your drifts of brilliant hair—
we suffer you less in losing than in vigil,
watching you living the same way you began
in your silken time, your white height pliant as a shawl.
But now this raised embroidery of ferns unravels
and the glimmering unbalanced fringe shows tears
and too many years of wrapping any shoulders,
anatomied by any insistent airs,
undone by any fingering hands.

VI

Child's Play

A child windmilling madly on a bike,
shrilling the soprano-bass motif
of ambulance, the rhythm of emergency,
lurch to the pavement, digitalis,
syringes, bandages, disaster.
Speed—speed is naive—
he pedals faster.

VII

Love Song

I fall from the hundredth story
                    into love.
Fifty, forty, fifteen floors
                    above,
My kisses plummet towards your eyes,
                    dive
to your shoulders, shatter on your chest.
                    Love
slips deep through your cracked lips;
Fragments which can never be removed.

PATRICIA STORACE

from LETTER TO AN IMMIGRANT

It is a long way to God.

Andrei Yevgenievich,
                    I am here
to send you some welcome
to America, and what I have to tell you
fills the window:

this arc of pale Massachusetts sky,
the sand-bitten soil of my place,
a scattering of apple-trees—:
not these, exactly, but what gathers them,

the mapped longing
of a single self, one
of many Americas,
composed.

. . . . and past the several barns, the one
lean squirrel (*byelka*: they are grey here)
in the wooden orchard,
figuring a new nest before winter.

It's almost ready,
the scrappy abstract loft he's worked
of birch wattle, flim, heaped leaves.
We will see if it will hold him.

*

In the old maps, with Europe at the center,
America is what white
destination, pure
latitude, where public monsters

thrash the meticulate little ships
that are so brave,
sailing out singly toward the empty
selvedge. Here where the whales lolled

over acres of paper
hugely innocent
Andrei we are:
at large here quietly

in Pontiacs and Plymouths
while the far hills drop off like waves
along the broken
white center line.

                                    *

You should know America
was not so much discovered
as invented, drafted

novelty on surmise
on novelty: an earnest unsendable letter.
In America, Andrei, you will move

often: soon
it will even seem natural, the highway
gathering to a green point,

folding the map that folds
back on itself,
our palimpsest.

You'll learn to hear the Indian,
the steady loamy vowelling,
in the names that survive;

and in those that follow, superimposed,
a history of the future: Providence.
Philadelphia. Corpus Christi. Los Angeles.

*

In this America, space
builds towards time.
concretely: we say
Washington is *nine hours* from Boston,

California *six days* from here.
Most everyone you meet will have a brother
in the West, parents who have gone
south to retire, to invest

in real-estate, to die
tanned. A family means
a web of timing:
we seldom correspond.

And therefore an American
is a spider,
as modest Whitman says:
noiseless, patient.

what bouys him is
space, wide
intersection, the random ringing
shiver of news through the wires.

*

In America, Andrei, one afternoon
at the bell: a warm anonymous
woman, her smile a harness.
How welcome she will seem
to a man who works at home! bending
bending slender shoulders through the frame
she will step in,
you will assemble,

as is your right. Your ease and your hope
confound you: you have come
so far for this! She will explain:
she is a Witness, a kind of Prophet,
a Saint. has come to offer you a program
of salvation. will you accept her
illustrated literature
with no obligation? you pose some neutral, some

half-personal question; she will oblige —:
comes from Zion, or Navoo, or
Salt Lake. does enjoy her
missionary pilgrimage. meets such
interesting people. . . .and holding her coat closed
across her throat she will back off,
nodding, you will stop
to pay for her pamphlet, to wish her the very best

luck. By the river of churning traffic,
a man in shirtsleeves, you will surprise
yourself: so this is
loneliness here. so clean. so democratic.

*

In this postcard of Boston,
geometry and vista
in the red brick
pistons on the river.

The Enlightenment ignited this machine,
its internal combustion, churning its inner
and outer clouds: for Americans confuse
eloquent work, devoutly, with manual prayer.

Partly what you cannot see is the city
asleep, in the filmy weekday night
above the warehouse and the regular streets
of wrath and wages and offices

where futures are speculation:
and where the city dreams
it sees, in public compensation,
the old movies that play all night.

How can you learn what they mean, those icons?
As if we had never had to learn
their fundamental grammar
they happen out of time all night.

Harold Lloyd is dangling off a clock-face,
Marilyn Monroe laughs
in her gusty skirts, a man walks into the perfect
Western sunfall and nobody smiles

like Judy Garland in *A Star is Born* and therefore
any moment in America somewhere James Mason is walking
into the lunging irregular sea
in despair and out of work.

STEPHEN TAPSCOTT

TRAVELLER

I cross a world to ratify a good
Tasted before, and now to be renewed
In the company of friends. A stranger's wine
Who would not delight in, who decline?
But friends, a source and station of affection,
Pledge, not only place, but resurrection
Of past days into present; future press
Already to the threshold's openness
Under the vine-leaves, not yet to be known,
For time is time and cannot be forgone.
But wine is wine and who would dare annul
The hope that hovers where the glass is full
To greet the traveller, present and to come,
Who finds his world is spacious and a home.

AT CHIMAYÓ

The sanctuary was begun in the New Mexico of 1813 by one Don Bernardo Abeyta. It is a low-lying church of cracked adobe adjoining the chapel of the Santo Niño Perdido, the Lost Child. In capital letters, pinned to the door, hangs a warning:

NO FOOD
DRINK OR
PETS INSIDE
THE CHURCH

This, as we discover, is a place of notices, messages and names. Particularly names: the givers of ex-votos have inscribed theirs; those who believe it was this place brought about a cure for themselves or their relations, have written signed letters to say so and these are duly exhibited within; the saints are labelled for us — among them, the less familiar San Galletano and San Martín de Porres. Christ is not simply Christ, but Nuestro Señor de Esquipulas.

As we go in through the vestibule the custodian is saying to a travelling salesman that, yes, she will take two dozen. We do not know whether she is speaking of the ex-voto images that are for sale, or the layettes for expectant mothers, blessed on behalf of the Santo Niño. Not only is this place associated with the Santo Niño but with healing, and beside the altar of the Niño there is a hole in the floor from which the miraculous earth is scooped up as a medicament.

We push open the door into the church. It bears another notice, complete with Spanish accent and intonation:

DONT LIVE THIS DOOR. OPEN.
PLEASE

A cloying smell of melting wax from the candles inside. The great vigas overhead and the rough, sturdy walls compact the silence. There is a gaiety about the images: a sculpted Christ wears bright mocassins, a painted Saint Michael dances on the dragon he has overcome.

The chapel of the Niño also has its notice:

HELPUS
KEEP A
CLEAN SCENE

—for many pilgrims come here and perhaps the excluded food, drink and pets somehow find their way inside. After all, what could be more rational, if one has a sick pet, than to bring it in to the source of healing? There are pilgrims here now. They file intently past the bright-red carving of San Rafael holding his fish, into the pósito—the room where the healing earth lies, and where a crucified Christ hangs from his cross wearing a baby-dress of turquoise-coloured rayon decorated with nylon lace and plastic roses. Innocence of taste possesses its own fecundity to which these crowded walls bear witness, covered, as they are, with letters of thanks, photographs, crutches, Leonardo's *Last Supper* in several reproductions, a Raphael Madonna, pictures of Christ from paint-by-numbers sets, an airforce uniform (a sergeant's), keys, a penned description of the sanctuary, beginning, 'In a valley protected by wild berrytrees', a poem—'The twinkle of a stary stary night'—by G. Mendoza of Las Cruces, a framed portrait of the black-faced Guadalupe Virgin which also contains those of the donors in passport-size snapshots. In the midst of all this sits the effigy of the Santo Niño de Atocha in his wooden stall, cloaked in green and white, his cherubic but sallow face shaded by a cockaded hat of seventeenth-century cut. There is something dandyish about his attire, but the rope of turquoise beads he wears round his neck has been broken. Someone has cobbled it together with a plastic-coated hairpin. It serves to display a tiny white cross with a minute Christ on it.

In this fecund chaos, the messages on the walls carry a sole discordant note, a confession of waste. It is written by a prisoner, still in gaol, who admonishes himself with a cross composed out of two words:

G
MOM
D

The others leave crutches, thanks for cures, or the pictures they have painted. He is the one sinner to confess his faults, and the thought of them jars his prose into unpredictable clusters of rhyme: 'I've wasted my life and its cost me my family and frinds. . . . No longer with a home not even a place to roam and this cell has become my domain. I know that its blame for bringing shame to my name and now I must part with my time.' 'Bringing shame to my name. . . .': among all these Mendozas, Gonzalezes, Medinas, Antonios, Serafíns, Geias, he alone guards his anonymity. In this place of names, he is the only one to realize that to use his name would be a sort of blasphemy and that, here, he must forfeit it.

Driving back through the dusk I find it is his unsigned letter keeps returning to mind, outdoing the presence of those garish saints. And I wonder from what source a feudal word like 'domain' came to him in his cell where, King of Lackland, he is monarch of all he surveys. Perhaps, turning it over on his tongue, he tastes anew each time the lost liberty of these vistas, this unfenceable kingdom of desert and mountains.

INTERPRETATIONS

Distinctive, those
concretions known
in Oklahoma as 'rose
rocks'—an allusion
to their red-brown sand-
colour and
similarity to a rose
in full bloom. Petals?
Clusters of barite
crystals are what they are—
the rose-shape made
by the growth of barium
as a divergent cluster
of blade on blade.
The rosettes fed
on an ancient red
sandstone—the host
rock whose colour
they acquired as they
lost their own:
quartz sand-grains
bonded together to become
$BaSO_4$
and await the rigours and the rains
of two million and more
years to petrify then expose
the rose rock or barite rose
in positive relief.
To the Indian eye
those years brought forth
such blood-bonded
and bunched tears as show
a grief of dispossession
no rocks or rock rose
forming could foreknow.

THIS

This is the Great
American Desert—
you can state it
differently if you so wish,
for what is scenery
if not preconception?
This, then, is—
to begin again—
the Great Plains;
ecosystem, system
of echoes, this
is the Flower Speech
the poet did not write,
each voice distinct
along the refuges
of tree-lined creeks—
arrowfeather, bluestem
nimblewood, black
samson, snow-
on-the-mountain
and beebalm witnessing
what stretched once all the way
—Minnesota to Texas—, a
wilderness now betrayed
by flowers to confess
it was the Prairies then.

CHARLES TOMLINSON

STREAMS

Whenever wirelit rain
leaves its trickling meshes
on rocks back of the brain
I keep hearing a Wales
so windswept it refreshes.
Slag-hills with white runnels
and drizzle-prodded sheep,
pastures brighter with news,
Wales, all of its green length
runs with my mother's voice in
its widowed, heartfelt strength,
by bright ale and firelight
that sang in Taliesin.

Streams flash like buckles,
rooted handshakes of wrists
with corduroy voices, consonants
bedded in rock, in the mists
of a mossed-over language.
I saw all her paradise in
our deal-board Methodists'
vision of lamb-flecked passes,
the cloud-lit country of Vaughan,
its Lewises and Thomases,
and coal-black abolitionists
once the heather-haired princess
bowed with her milky stallion
into the leafy verses
that close in Taliesin.

But I saw Wales's capital sin,
I saw Rhondda afflicted with
mineral silence, and a seine
trawl empty Aberystwyth;
my tongue probed its carious
mine-pits, sick of the singing,
its faith was another curse
and screw the curraghs!
Wales was shut tight as Sundays,
glazed pubs screwed like a ship's
portholes in sargasso silence,
and its stubborn, bilingual signs.

Rain rises up from the page,
I saw the colonial submission
of grass, in the cloth gaps
bared at the evening Mission
as drizzle moves its harps
over stone-fields, and the rage in
our friendships increasing
in voices that made a religion
like hills in the wet sun
of poetry, and the damp ruin
of their lonely language.

                DEREK WALCOTT

MANTOVA

Mantegna on all the walls,
The Mincio puddled outside the gates,
                    clouds tatooed on its blue chest,
Mantova floats in the pigeon-light of late afternoon
Twenty-two years ago.
Rain shoots its white cuffs across the scene.

I remember a dream I had once in Mantova,
Everyone in it in full dress,
                    refrectory hall,
Goblets and white linen.
At the near end of the table, heaped on a bronze salver
Like quail, all wishbone and delicate leg,
The roast children were served up.
                    "You must try the thighs,"
My host said, his gloves still on.
                    "You must try the thighs."

Half the sky full of rain, and half not,
Reeds under water pressure to stay still,
The river oncoming but not flashed,
Everything upside down,
                    the sky at rest underfoot.
Words, but who can remember?

What words does the sky know, or the clouds know?

On the wall of the summer house,
                    where Giulio Romano left him
The lion sips at the river bank, and the trees provide.

                    CHARLES WRIGHT

YEHUDA AMICHAI's many books of poetry include *Amen* and *Love Poems*.

MICHELANGELO ANTONIONI, the director of such films as *L'avventura, Blow-Up* and *The Passenger*, is among the greatest living filmmakers.

WILLIAM ARROWSMITH's translation of Antonioni's *That Bowling Alley on the Tiber* will appear this fall with Oxford University Press.

CHRISTIANNE BALK's first book of poems, *Bindweed*, received this year's Walt Whitman Award.

RUSSELL BANKS is the author of the novel *Continental Drift* and other books of fiction. "The Gully" is from his forthcoming book, *Success Stories*.

SVEN BIRKERTS is working on a book of essays on poetry and poetics called *Hamann's Bone*.

BOHDAN BOYCHUK is the author of six books of poetry in Ukranian and is the editor of *Sucanist*. Other translations of his poetry appear in recent issues of *Translation* and *Grand Street*.

WILLIAM BRONK's recent books include *Life Supports*, his collected poems, which received the American Book Award, and *Vectors and Smoothable Curves*.

MICHEL BUTOR, in such books as *Degrees*, has written extensively on travel, in addition to his many novels and essays.

ALBERT CAMUS wrote a number of marvelous lyrical essays as well as his better known works.

ALFRED CORN's latest book is *Notes from a Child of Paradise*.

CARL DENNIS' latest book is *The Near World*.

STEPHEN DIXON's books include *Fall and Rise* (a novel) and *Time to Go* (short stories).

EDWARD FALCO's prose poems have appeared in several journals.

JONATHAN GALASSI's poetry has appeared in *The New Republic* and *Poetry Nation*. He has translated Eugenio Montale's *Otherwise* and his selected prose and edited an issue of *Pequod* devoted to Montale's work.

DAN GERBER is publishing a book of poems and a book of stories with Winn/Dutton this fall.

DANA GIOIA works in corporate acquisitions and travels too much on business.

JUDITH GLEASON is a novelist and anthropologist. She is the author of *Santeria, Bronx, Agotime*, and *A Recitation of Ifa, Oracle of the Yoruba*.

DAVID GUSS' recent books of translations include *Watunna: An Orinocan Creation Cycle* and *The Selected Poems of Vicente Huidobro*.

MARILYN HACKER's latest book is *Assumptions*.

RACHEL HADAS' recent books are *Slow Transparency* (poems) and *Form, Cycle, Infinity*, a study of Seferis and Frost.

SAM HAMILL is the author of *Night Traveling* (poems from the Chinese) and *Animae*.

MICHAEL HELLER's latest books are *Knowledge* (poetry) and *Conviction's Net of Branches*, the first book on the Objectivists.

ZBIGNIEW HERBERT's two latest books to be published in English are *The Barbarian in the Garden* (essays) and *Report from a Besieged City* (poems).

EDWARD HOAGLAND is the author of *Notes from the Century Before* and *The Courage of Turtles*.

DANIEL HOFFMAN is the author of *Brotherly Love*.

VICENTE HUIDOBRO introduced European experimental writing into Chilean literature.

ROBERT KELLY is the author of *Cities, Coils*, and many other books of poetry.

PAUL LAKE has published poems in *The New Republic* and *The American Scholar*.

JAN HELLER LEVI's long poem "Baltimore" appeared in the *Beloit Poetry Journal*.

PHYLLIS LEVIN has work in *The Paris Review* and *Shenandoah*.

JACK MARSHALL's most recent book, *Arriving on the Playing Fields of Paradise*, received the Bay Area Book Reviewers Award.

J. D. McCLATCHY is the author of *Scenes from Another Life*. A second book of poems is due out this fall.

HILDA MORLEY's two last books are *What Are Winds & What Are Waters* and *To Hold in My Hand*.

STANLEY MOSS' books include *Skull of Adam*.

ANN NEELON lives in Amherst, Massachusetts.

HOWARD NORMAN's books include *Where the Chill Came From*. He is at work on a novel, *The Northern Lights*, from which the story in *Pequod* is excerpted.

GEOFFREY O'BRIEN writes a terrific column on poetry for *The Village Voice*.

GREGORY ORR's latest books include *We Must Make a Kingdom Of It* and *Stanley Kunitz: An Introduction to the Poetry*.

LINDA ORR is the author of *Jules Michelet: Nature, History, and Language*, and a book of poems *A Certain X*.

BORIS PASTERNAK's poem is from the book *My Sister—Life* which was translated by Mark Rudman (with Bohdan Boychuk) and recently received the Max Hayward Translation Award.

JOHN PECK is the author of *Shagbark* and *The Broken Blockhouse Wall*.

MARIE PONSOT is the author of *Admit Impediment*.

MARK RUDMAN is the author of *In the Neighboring Cell*. Two chapbooks, *The Ruin Revived* and *The Mystery in the Garden*, are forthcoming.

RAPHAEL RUDNIK's latest book is *Frank 207*. He works as a scout for European publishers.

TOBIAS SCHNEEBAUM's most recent project is *Asmat Images*, a catalogue of artifacts in the Asmat Museum of Culture and Progress, Irian Jaya, Indonesia.

LAUREN SHAKELY, a frequent contributor to *Pequod*, received the Walt Whitman Award for her first book of poems, *Guilty Bystander*.

JANE SHORE is the author of *Eye Level*.

RICHARD SIEBURTH has translated Holderlin's *Hymns and Fragments* and Walter Benjamin's *Moscow Diaries*.

LOUIS SIMPSON's recent books are *Selected Poems* and *The Best Hour of the Night*.

DOUGLAS GORDON SLOANE earns his living as a freelance maker of fantasy maps and has never left the state in which he was born.

PATRICIA STORACE's poems have appeared in *The Agni Review*, *The New York Review of Books* and *The Paris Review*.

STEPHEN TAPSCOTT is the 1985 Rockefeller Writer-in-Residence at the Poetry Center, YMHA.

CHARLES TOMLINSON's latest book of poems is *Notes from New York*. He is the editor of the *Oxford Book of Poetry in Translation*.

DEREK WALCOTT is the author of *The Fortunate Traveller* and *Midsummer*.

CHARLES WRIGHT has dealt obsessively with travel in such books as *China Trace* and *The Other Side of the River*.